SPINNING THE GLOBE

SPINNING THE GLOBE

by

Noel Purdon

DUFFY & SNELLGROVE

SYDNEY

Published by Duffy & Snellgrove in 1998
PO Box 177 Potts Point NSW 2011 Australia
dands@magna.com.au

Distributed by Tower Books (02) 9975 5566

© Noel Purdon 1998

Cover design by Alex Snellgrove
Maps by Sally Beech
Typeset by Cooper Graphics

Printed by Griffin Press Pty Ltd

ISBN 1875989 35 8

CONTENTS

To Shane, who lifted, who laughed, who loved.

PROLOGUE

For my fourth birthday my parents promised a wonderful present: the Marvel, a thing that would enable me to see the whole world. 'The whole world?' For days I repeated it. 'With all the places and people?' When the Marvel came it was in a large box. I already knew what it would be like. It would fit around my head and I would be able to look at Indians and Chinese and ladies dressed in blue like the ones painted by Vermeer in my parents' books. Probably I would also be able to see the Milky Way. They couldn't understand when I opened the Marvel, looked at it for one stupefied moment and threw it across the room. It was a globe of the world. For some time it spun in the corner. My grandmother consoled me by taking me to see *Pinocchio* and *The Beast with Five Fingers* at the cinema, which was more the sort of device I had in mind.

After a few days I forgot their perfidy and became reconciled to the globe, at first spinning it as fast as possible to see if it would break, and then matching up the names with the pictures in the books and tracing the rivers in blue crayon: Mississippi, Congo, Amazon. With atlases, telescopes, microscopes, and movie projectors added by successive birthdays I found to my delight that the moon too was a globe, because my father showed me its craters. And a thousand Robinson Crusoes, Moby Dicks and *Tempests* later, I came back to the globe and spun it again. It said Florence. I boarded a boat which took six weeks to go through the China Seas and the

Indian Ocean, and disembarked at Naples. From now on I would see everything that was dark and light; calm, secret, wild, wicked, magical; everywhere that flowed, froze, erupted or hid half-buried in sand. And not just see, but be part of. What was strange would become familiar; what was beautiful breathe on me as well; and even what was frightening become something I could acknowledge, like Prospero's Caliban, as my own.

Graham Greene remarks that all writers must have a sliver of ice in their hearts. I would add that all travellers must have a sliver of steel. Without these two splinters, the one cold and the other adamantly hard, you would never set out in the first place, and certainly never keep on recording when the trail switches its letters and becomes a trial. Travellers, like soldiers and women in childbirth, are not masochists. They undergo pain in order to make life. The ice cools them at boiling-point. The core of steel preserves determination, as the camel's hump prudently stores water.

Wars and politics have certainly deterred me. I would not cheerily set off for Iraq tomorrow. But I rejoice that I slipped into such places as Iran, Afghanistan, Colombia, Burma, Bosnia, Rwanda, Cambodia, and even, though it was the toughest, Zaire. There are times when my skin is so thin that I feel permeated by everything around, and wonder whether I am an individual or an organizer running a series of colonies, like a starfish. Each place, from Samarkand to Savannah, transforms me into itself. From Haiti I still keep a magical egg from a voodoo ceremony. Its shell guarantees detachment.

Of islands there are thousands whose shores send out their scents, and of all the beautiful water-cities – Venice, Stockholm, St Petersburg, San Francisco and Amsterdam – Sydney is the best. But rivers are eternally alluring. They provide simultaneously the sensation of stillness and infinity. Like the cinema, they match my thirst for movement and continuity. Ideas grow beside them like the first shoots of grain along the Tigris and Euphrates. As we all are born of man and woman, one bank may be a granite cliff, the other a grassy meadow. The river finds its own way in between. The globe is round; rivers curve. They hate regulators who would make them straight. They demand their own course to navigate. That's why I'll write of rivers, because they invoke people and places of every variety, even deserts, which are their determined opposites. Split into a fractal delta, they flow, violently, innocently but inexorably, until they reach their destiny the sea. You can skim their surface, or trouble their waters and disturb their beds. Then they show their depths.

It's no accident that each of these rivers is lined with the fecundity of animal and floral culture, the masterpieces of human art. The stage is set. The globe is spinning; the rivers ready to run. Here's the Nile, river of origins and playfulness, and of the dead. The mighty Niger will even irrigate the desert. The Cam spreads its vision of civilization; the Danube is astonishing, as wild and proud as its rivals, the Mekong and Irrawaddy, unwilling rivers of war. The Congo rushes to engorge the others, and coils around them like a python. They are curling and beginning to flow onto the page. There was the time the temples of Pagan came up like heaven on the Irrawaddy, and the delirious lack of time when I fell with malaria among sheikhs and Samaritans in Central Africa. And there was the time the Khmer Rouge crawled from the ruins of Angkor Wat, and the New Moon from the pylons of Amun at Karnak. And then there was the time of sand at Timbuktu. And once …

CONGO

CONGO I
Under the Volcano

The Hotel des Chutes was held together only by the vegetation enclosing and engorging it. In 1990 I arrived there flying close over rainforest so impenetrable that no life lower than trees could be seen beyond its green; green of flowering broccoli, green of jade and jealousy, light green of lettuce, green of springtime hope, glittering green of malachite, green of reflected water, black green that covered all. My fellow passenger from Goma, a banker who politely addressed our driver at Kisangani airport as *Citoyen*, took one look at the decaying liana-wound pile with its broken louvres invaded by bush, and asked to be driven to the 'best' hotel, the Palace. But I was bewitched. The three-storey villa stood just below the falls from which the Congo becomes navigable 1,000 kilometres to Kinshasa, before the Matadi cataracts again curl and tumble it, and open its waters to the sea.

A single electric bulb without a shade announced the lodging's interior. Green again. Green and yellow like the forest, yellow enough to show the vines entangling the old balconies, strangling the pillars; and green with the beauty of painted leaves or mould. The rooms themselves peeled from their surfaces, green and yellow wallpaper, moist green carpets, jardinières from which the plants had long ago escaped and curled round the furniture. The bedroom was high and enormous, even more like a colonial ballroom than other port-hotels I'd been in. 'Every traveller's dream,' murmured an ancient voice, and died to a whisper. 'Or nightmare.'

The leprous bathroom had aged its bronze taps to the colour of things dragged up from water, and the water itself had left green lines of slime trailing down the tiles to the plants it nourished. I soaked my feet in the lime-tinted trickle and fell gratefully on the damp mattress. In the midnight silence the falls purred like a leopard.

Conrad called this place the heart of darkness. But for me next morning it all began in brilliant light. From the balcony, blistering visibly in the sun and flaking at the lightest touch, I could see the weir, and hear the rainforest buzzing, humming. I could also see directly below me the dock area muddy with shipworkers, and the three-decked *Colonel Ebeya* at its mooring in the midst of half a dozen other boats. From the steps on the distant shore, pirogues, dugouts still as rough as the trees which shaped them, skimmed like water insects, ferrying across people and goods. Eager to ensure that my booking had been received, I walked quickly down the steps to a large wrought-iron shed. There were already hundreds of people milling with grim determination in their eyes and voices. Nearing the docks, I realised that those six other boats were attached to the *Ebeya* as barges, organic units of multiple heights and dimensions, which would fold and unfold as they crawled down the Congo like a caterpillar towards Kinshasa. The *Ebeya's* engines were already churning, gathering steam for the scheduled departure tomorrow. Even though the Congo is navigable for sections of its 3,000 kilometres length from Ubundu to Lake Upemba near the Zambian border, no boats were running. There was trouble round the most southern city of Lubumbashi and the nearby province of Shaba. Trains had stopped. Missions and markets were being deserted. Southerners were making their way by whatever means to Kisangani. The river was the only highway to the capital. It looked as if it might be a crowded trip.

I found that I couldn't get near the ticket office. The quarrelling crowd jammed the doorway. I stood on an oil barrel and saw another hundred or so people inside. Their common surge was towards a caged recess at the far end. A counter-movement of successful passengers writhed their path back, to emerge brandishing hand-written tickets. Khaki-uniformed police shouted at everyone indiscriminately, including those trying to get out.

Still, I had written to the steamship company months before and even sent a telegram from Rwanda. 'I already have a reservation' I yelled, and kept on yelling till I shook myself free of the police, the protesters at the door, and smiled apologetically as I pushed my way through the mass. A few blond heads stood out among the black. They were arguing as furiously as everyone else. I pushed them out of the way too, and presented a smiling face to the ticketeers.

'I have a reservation,' I said confidently, and spelled out my name. The official screamed in my face 'No reservations', and when I insisted that he check the names, screamed even louder 'No names'. So I screamed back, 'Look, I wrote to Onatra a month ago, and I have a first class cabin, and I will complain to the company.' He laughed in my face. 'No first class. No second class. Only third class.' I hesitated, which in that atmosphere was dangerous, because two people immediately snapped up third class tickets.

'Are there beds in third class?'

'No beds,' he spat, 'deck class.'

I couldn't afford to wait. I'd come to the middle of Africa to do this. There wouldn't be another boat for at least a fortnight, maybe a month. Should I back out now? I'd never be within an inch of coming down the Congo again. I got a third class ticket and wriggled my way outside.

Just in time. The guichets in the ticket cage were being slammed, and the people in the shed dragged out. I joined the white girl I'd nearly trampled and apologetically helped her on with her rucksack. Her name was Kitty; she too had a third

3

class ticket. She said we were lucky. I supposed so, though I worried whether I'd be able to stand it. Our conversation was cut by the increasing din and the sound of lashes. The police whaled into the remaining crowd with whips and batons. Men and women howled and were knocked over. More people fell on top and were lashed until they managed to crawl away, blood glistening from heads and shoulders.

In Nairobi I had seen a group of anti-presidential demonstrators clubbed and beaten, and as I ran with everyone else nearby into the shelter of the university, the police shot five of them. Surely that kind of state brutality only happened in South Africa, where it was practised by wicked colonialists? My vision of African life had been shaken. I had come to sub-Saharan Africa with a mission, and I wanted greatly to love the place. I went through a stage of blaming myself, a voyeur who indulged his wish to see lions, hippos, elephant, gazelles, gorillas, and the makers of a new voyeurism, cinema.

For six months I had planned this trip. I would collect material on African cinema, meet its creators, see the reality. I had letters of introduction. I had read Soyinka, Achabe, Fanon, Cissé, Ayi Kwei Armah, V.S. Naipaul. Africa was the cradle of humanity. The rifts and rivers of the first humans were its nurses. I had seen the footprints in Olduvai Gorge, been to a conference at Victoria Falls, gone on safari in the Serengeti. The soldiers were an unwelcome reminder of what I already knew: that outside the cocoon of safaris, first-class hotels and enclaves of privilege, human life precariously and constantly was led along the cliff of death.

My first encounter with the Zairian military had been at Goma. The sleazy one-street border town, with its brothels and bars and brawls that tumbled into the dusty street, was ruled by tattooed youths on motor-bikes. When the Yamahas of the police appeared they vanished with a spurt of black smoke. Goma sits incongruously beside an emerald-blue lake. Only the reeds and the craggy hill at the top of the street separate intolerable heat from inviting cool. From the road winding up to the volcano of Nyiragongo, Lake Kivu looks like paradise. The clerk who cashed my traveller's cheques told me there was a fine hotel way up the slope. In December wealthy people came across the borders from Rwanda and Uganda. In July it was almost deserted. It had a pool, French wine, fresh fish.

I toiled upwards, the volcano's lower forest providing shade, gaining appetite during the three-hour walk. The hotel was indeed luxurious. It seemed empty. I entered a cupola-topped marble hall and was greeted by an agitated waiter. They were closed, he said, but before his salver-bearing hands shut the inner door I saw a roomful of uniformed men, some in the act of turning for a curious glimpse. A private function, he explained. 'Ah *Dieu,*' I sighed, 'I've walked up here since nine this morning specifically to have lunch.' He hesitated and was replaced by the manager. I did my best to look both pathetic and affluent. The waiter returned. If *Monsieur* would not be *dérangé* by eating outside near the pool, perhaps something plain, a fish, some salad – 'and some wine' said the traveller – then that could certainly be seen to. I dined beneath an umbrella, gazing down on the intensely blue lake and eating its fish slowly and with pleasure. The waiter became friendlier as he shared my enjoyment. While I was mopping up the lime sauce, a young soldier in jungle uniform, beret and mirror sunglasses approached. He knew he looked intimidating, and was probably surprised when I smiled and offered him a glass of wine and a chair.

'What are you doing out here?' he asked in French, more with genuine curiosity than interrogation. I explained that I had arrived from Kigali by truck, and was en route to Kisangani.

'But how did you get here?'

'I walked.'

'Why?'

I shrugged. 'I wanted to see the lake, and I don't have a car.'

'Do you have a passport and a visa?'

I showed him. He shook his head in something approaching amazement.

'You're not frightened?'

No. Why should I be? Fresh with bundles of makuta currency from my cheques, I was in good health, the food and wine were excellent, and the scenery was breathtaking. He shook his head slowly from side to side, and laughed. He introduced himself proudly as Lieutenant Bokombi Borginda. He was at a reception for new members of the President's personal bodyguard, and everyone was wondering who I was. Because I was respectably dressed in a panama and light linen suit, they thought someone might have invited me. Others suspected I was a spy. I laughed in turn. 'The only spying I'm doing is on your beautiful lake.'

'But don't you understand? That's the President's palace over there. It's strictly forbidden.'

'I know. But we're miles away.'

'Yes, and this is a private military meeting at the hotel.'

I poured him more wine. 'I'm sorry for ... for intruding. But it's so beautiful.' He removed his shades to show fine gentle eyes, looked at my passport again, and handed it back. He had decided that my first name was what appears on the passport as the second.

'So you like Zaire, Francis? And the Zairian people?'

I did. He shook hands, walked back to the French doors, and returned a few minutes later. Obviously he had talked with his superiors. Their faces peered from the arched windows.

'How are you going to get back to your hotel?'

'On foot.'

'I'll give you a ride on my motorcycle.'

Gladly I accepted. As we mounted the bike and he kicked off, he shouted, 'You like Zairian lakes, Francis?' Did I ever. 'I will drive up the mountain track, Francis. Maybe we will see gorillas.' As we leapt and skidded higher, he waved his left arm. 'There are many lakes in Zaire. Over that mountain is another one, and then another one. You can't see the top, but it is covered in snow. Kasenye is my home. Very beautiful.' I nodded enthusiastically. We entered a patch of relatively smooth bitumen and he increased speed as we tilted round cliff-hanging bends. 'Many beautiful rivers, Francis. A great river starts there.'

'I know,' I yelled. 'The Congo.'

'No. Over there,' he gestured. 'The Nile.'

Of course. North of the volcanoes was the source of the Nile. Ptolemy had called this region the Mountains of the Moon. Lieutenant Borginda gave me a two-hour trip through the foothills of these planetary ancestors and then headed for the township. We'd talked in shouts the whole time; he knew I wanted to get to Kisangani and had been told there were no flights. He pulled up directly outside a ramshackle office with a boardwalk, and greeted the fat woman who sat fanning herself in front of a map of Africa showing aerial freight routes. Within ten minutes I had a ticket on the two-prop plane due to depart at four; and within another fifteen he made the lethargic customs inspector write me out a proper currency and filming permit. I thanked Bokombi warmly. 'Now, Francis, you will take a good impression of my country back to your country.' He roared off, youthfully, blithely waving, the first person for whom I had felt real affection since leaving my film-maker friends in Kenya.

As an encounter with a man dedicated to war it had been surprising, assuring. I packed, paid for the extra night in exchange for the proprietor promising to drive me to the airport, and sat in the back garden reading. Despite my trust and confidence, some hidden fear was waiting to surface. At a slight swishing sound I turned, and nearly jumped out of my skin. Three boys were staring at me. They were holding machetes. When I continued to stare back, they looked down and began slashing the long grass. Nonetheless, I had an aftershock of fright, and left the garden to wait in the lobby. Whatever power, money, will or charm I had, I recognized that I had also been lucky.

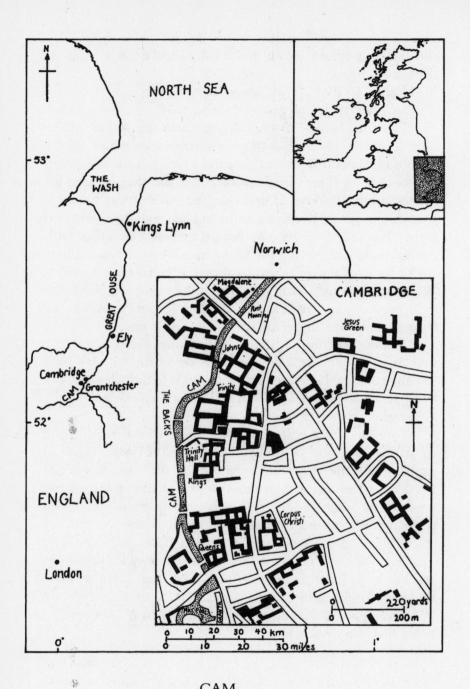

CAM

CAM I
The Punters

This is a gentle river, but in its setting as commanding as the Congo. Neither great in length nor size, it flows sweetly under willows, and flourishes with bridges of wood and stone and iron. Its ripples resound with laughter, flutes and the steady plash of poles as punts glide past meadows of lupins and glowing colleges of stone. In the most brightly cushioned of these punts, poled by a handsome boy with hair the colour of the buildings, sit a woman wearing a brocaded vest, a young man in shorts basking in the sun, and Pier Paolo Pasolini.

Voices from the colleges of Cambridge ring out the past and mingle with the bells of Saint Benet's and Great Saint Mary's. As Coleridge from his rooms in Jesus reminds the man in his Australian stubbies, this sacred river, with all its sunny spots of greenery, is a miracle of rare device. The litter of the May Week balls and plays has been cleared, the last fragments of The Who's smashed guitars have disappeared with the marquees and dawn Bollinger; 'Kubla Khan' is chanted on the fenland winds and we will arrive in Xanadu tomorrow.

Pasolini is enchanted. Tense from his recent court-trials and the prosecution surrounding his film *The Decameron,* he thinks he has reached that ideal educated society where men and

9

women of sensibility describe their lives and tell each other the stories of the globe, tales that Boccaccio culled from Egypt and Persia, magical stories exchanged in the hills above Florence to ward off the fear of European annihilation, the plague.

'Ah, we're in Venice,' Pasolini murmurs when we pass beneath the Bridge of Sighs which arches the courtyard of Saint John's.

The Cam, at the confluence of the Granta and its source in Bedfordshire, offers a civilization equal to Boccaccio's Tuscany before draining into the marshes of the Fens. There Ely Cathedral's island in the waters of the Ouse points to the North Sea and the wool-port of King's Lynn. The medieval wharves have washed away. Chaucer's Trumpington Mill is no longer invaded by bawdy Cambridge undergraduates. But Grantchester, thanks to Rupert Brooke's silliest poem, is open still for tea. And there, four kilometres along the Cam's most idyllic stretch, is where we're headed.

In their several ways the others on this little journey are also dreaming of Xanadu, but an explosive one. It's the '60s. A year of Eden, three years of the garden of earthly delights, and after 1968, two years of the Surreal. Like Columbia and the Sorbonne, Cambridge has been shaken by revolt. Riots and demonstrations have reminded the university that its students are following a greater tradition than the one dogmatised by F.R. Leavis. Across Jesus meadow, Coleridge is still not appeased. He wants a perfect society or nothing. From Trinity Byron too is calling for revolution, sexual liberty, Childe Harold's travels to the most exotic places on earth. He will have the Orient, harems, perhaps Sennacherib. 'I have been more ravished myself than anybody since the Trojan War,' he drawls, and those who catch the impudent echo smile as if they have just seen a kingfisher flash. Even if the travels reveal a great deal of wretchedness and cruelty, or the traveller becomes disgusted and bored, the journey must continue.

As we pass beneath the wooden Mathematical Bridge of Queen's, a voice more confident of reason reassures the European caught perpetually between civilization and bar-

barism. Erasmus plays with our fears of revolutions in time and space and speaks ironically in praise of folly. The woman is trailing her hand in the water. Her ancestor Lord Edward Fitzgerald, captured by the English as a rebel, bled to death in prison while his young wife went mad with grief. The Lady Rosemary is the eldest daughter of the Marquess of Kildare, and she has renounced the court to befriend Chris and Mick Jagger. Marc Bolan has just written 'Lady Ro'.

Drawn by a local cartographer, this river would encourage you to believe that you were at the centre of the world. The journey from Cambridge to Westminster, Threadneedle Street or the Royal Shakespeare Company, with its invitations to mansions and palaces and galleries, seems short. But this too had been one of the dark places of the earth: sacrifices to Gog and Magog; at the ford Romans hacking Celts; Wat Tyler's peasants in full massacre in the square. Ro knows that as we near Grantchester we will glide over the reeds where her lover Spike drowned himself last year. He was found in three feet of water. Like Virginia Woolf, he put a stone in his pocket and his fists were clenched. Otherwise his young body was perfectly healthy. The coroner's inquest and his parents' grief were appalling.

The blond boy Nick Gill is wearing a pair of cut-off jeans. They show off his muscular calves – Nick needs no padding when he acts in Restoration comedy. His face and body are fair, framed by hair curling round his shoulders. His voice is trained and resonant, an English actor's voice that could address the great Globe itself. He punts, as he sails, with expertise.

The third man is me. After the arts of Florence, I spun the globe and went up to Corpus Christi, the college of my hero Christopher Marlowe. Now Fellow in English at Trinity Hall, I do May Week productions influenced by painting and mythology instead of revising my thesis. These open-air extravaganzas terrify the Masters but delight the London papers; *The Massacre at Paris* with hanging bodies and galloping horses, *Bartholomew Fair* as a carnival. I have just played

Tiresias naked in *Oedipus the King* and Launce in *Two Gentlemen of Verona,* amusing everyone except Clive James by impersonating Clive's accent, because Clive has learned to impersonate it better himself.

Loved revellers and travellers Kate and Caroline have just gone down from New Hall. Good friend Germaine Greer calls me her little brother when she is being affectionate and 'Nohole' when we're having a fight, as we did recently when she had her cat gelded and I dismantled her banister post by post. All the members of this little clan, with the exception of Clive and Germaine, might be drug-fiends of DeQuincean depravity. Ether can be bought over the counter at Boot's. LSD is manufactured at night in the chem labs; hashish and opium arrive daily from the London docks. I love the Renaissance, am immersed in its sciences, narratives and paintings, but my infatuations are for the minds and bodies of other people, and my passion is cinema. Raymond Williams, Stephen Crofts and I have founded a quarterly. We will make film part of the English Tripos. For these reasons, my interests converge on Pasolini.

With Nick in the winter of 1969 I had seen Pasolini's *Teorema* and *Edipo Re*. From the summaries, it seemed that *Teorema* was a sort of satyr play, a French farce in which a young man arrives in a wealthy household and beds the lot: daughter, son, mother, father, even the maid. We saw *Edipo* first and came out stunned. Sophocles' tragedy had been turned into a Freudian detective story plunging its Oedipal baby from Fascist Italy into a nameless society of the past. We walked through the raining city to *Teorema*. When we came out, afternoon was dying into evening. It seemed that the rest of the audience, straggling down the street in silent ones and twos, must feel as we did. *Teorema* had shaken us. Far from being a comedy, it demonstrated the effects of a world in which God has offered his love and withdrawn it, a world of frozen capitalism and superstitious workers, catatonic and despairing youth, adults dying of prohibited desire. We were devastated, but exhilarated that someone else was feeling as we did about the disturbed society around and within us, and saying it with so much visual beauty and light. In Italy I knew of Pasolini from *Mamma Roma,* mainly because of Anna Magnani's performance. Within a week I researched as much as I could about the director, told everybody I was going to write to him, and wrote. To my great joy, I received a reply suggesting a meeting. This was followed by a phone call to the college. I was surprised at the dryness and thirst of his voice. The times were altered, but he would let me know. Finally, on 24 June 1970 came the long awaited telegram:

'I'll be in London for two days 25/26 Poetry International Festival 70 Queen Elizabeth Hall. See You. Pasolini.'

I phoned him that night at his house in Via Eufrate. We would meet in London. I shooed everyone off: no interviews, no photographs, no introductions, not even to any of the editorial board of our magazine. Simply a relaxed couple of days where Pasolini and I talked.

At the festival reception he was quite tiny, surrounded by Italian embassy officials who were relieved to see me. 'Ah, you're the gentleman he's meeting.' He had begged off other functions to meet LOEL. 'What is the derivation of Loel?' he asked, having misread my signature. Did he want to stay at the reception or go somewhere and talk? He said gratefully that he'd like to go. I suggested Soho, where I knew a good Italian restaurant. He murmured that he would like that. Since I didn't drive, I had arranged with Ro to take Pasolini by car wherever he wanted. I introduced them and we were soon at the Amalfi. Here came my first surprise. Pasolini wanted nothing to do with Italian food, and wouldn't be persuaded. He chose a steak with chips, which he ate in the same time it took me to demolish a lasagna, a saltimbocca, and a flask of Orvieto.

From the very first, there was something so serious, so 'obedient', that both Ro and I were seized with a desire to make him happy. There was something apprehensive in his manner. He quietly unscrewed a little bottle and took several pills, apologizing for the fact that he had an ulcer. It's a miracle I've never developed one, since my behaviour in such situations took the form of getting quickly drunk, being boisterously over-familiar, and explaining to people the ontology of the universe. When I noticed that he was replying to my few 'Pierpaolos' with a meek and resolute 'Professore', I had the sobering reminder that I should try being a little more European. I didn't know what to call him. 'Maestro' sounded gushy, 'Professore' copycat and technically wrong, because he wasn't a teacher. I settled on 'Dottore'. It gradually became clear that even when he was talking about quite close friends, except for his lover Ninetto Davoli, he used surnames.

I was anti-American, and, by that stage, extremely anti-English. Surprisingly he was not. While granting arguments about American domination, he found New York fascinating, cosmopolitan like Naples, 'Pharaonic'. Architecturally and culturally it had a quality of funereal grandeur to which he wished to return, to feel the dead capitalists hidden in the depths of their pyramid-skyscrapers while a million workers toiled. And he could not understand my diatribes against the English. He loved London. Soho was wonderful. The English were the most tolerant nation in the world. He envied my living in Cambridge, surrounded by medieval peace and beautiful students. I said the English were repressed and hypocritical, that I loved the baroque sensuality and freedom of Rome.

He stared. He told me Rome was a disaster, that all his closest friends were raving mad. There had been problems with Ninetto and military service. He was terrified of what military service did to young men in Italy. In fact, he often hated Italy so much that he wanted to give up talking Italian. He would go and live somewhere in Africa, where he could speak French, or even learn an African language. All this astonished me, since I was a fervent Italophile, and part of my desire to meet him came from my admiration for his use of traditional Italian painting and poetry.

'I love Italian,' I offered. 'For me it's a language of freedom. Bits of my dreams are often in Italian, the sensual bits.'

14

I favoured him with some impressions of a heavy Tuscan accent and recounted that I had taught English in a village on the Arno. My students spoke vividly and taught me in turn the *parolacce*, the swearwords.

'Italian is – or was – a beautiful language,' he finally agreed. 'It's a pity that it's spoken by Italians.'

I walked him back to his hotel. We arranged to pick him up next morning at eight. His eyes as I left were solemn and searching. In retrospect, what a chastely proper little intellectual I was. No doubt he would have enjoyed cruising Soho. When I look now at the postmarks on his letters and telegrams, I notice they are stamped 'Termini'. That's Rome's central station, miles from his house. He had no reason to be there except that it fronts the Piazza del Cinquecento, the city's most notorious beat.

Next day he was waiting in the lobby. In the car, his neck was on a constant swivel for labourers, passing motorists, farmboys. My own erotic fires were burning low. I said sourly how unattractive the English were, with their faces like horses. He replied that on the contrary, even the technicians at the airport shone with English beauty in their overalls, with that especially typical russet-coloured hair. I said that was Irish.

The punt was waiting, bobbing gently in a row of others beneath the irregular red walls of Magdalene. Ro had the hamper full of Fortnum and Mason delights packed under the seat. One glance at Nick was enough to tell me that he was tripping along in a state of fugue, and not the kind controlled by Bach. When I glared at him he stuck out his teeth like Bugs Bunny. Pasolini studied the willows, the passing punts and the over-beamish boy.

'Is Nick mad?'

'Only if Hamlet was.'

'He's a beautiful boy, in the English way. Is he from an old family?'

The Cam is a docile river. Like all others it has its seasons and its moods: icy in winter, melancholy in autumn, a pleasure dome in spring. From my leaded windows, which give the best view of the Backs imaginable, I have watched it in all its clothes of flower and snow. Now I am watching Pasolini, as he turns his head this way and that to admire a beautiful building or a body. He has taken off his dark glasses.

'Ma questa e una meraviglia.' Yes, it is a marvel, despite my fanaticism about the university. Maybe even the Marvel itself.

'Have you ever been in a punt before?' I use the English word because I can't think of an Italian equivalent except 'gondola', and that would sound daft. As if catching the connection he murmurs, 'I've ridden in gondolas, of course. But this is just as opulent. And I've been in the barche piatte on the Po. And in pirogues in Africa.'

'I didn't know you'd been to Africa'

'That's where I shot most of *Oedipus*. Last night, remember, you told me how you and Nick had been to Ourzazate? And you set off to walk across the Sahara? That made me smile as I fell asleep, thinking of you marching through the desert.'

Dear God, what else had I blathered?

'No. I meant Africa underneath the Sahara.'

'Oh yes. When I was looking for locations for the Oresteia. In Uganda. The animism's still there. You can see it in the trees and the water.'

I trail my fingers in the Cam's cool liquor and say, 'One day I'll go there too.'

CONGO II
Hearts of Darkness

I walked with Kitty through Kisangani's crumbling streets, some areas made sweet by jasmine and boulevards of bougainvillea, some pitted and dusty as we reached the market. She was staying in a hippy rathole called the Olympia. She had a foam mattress in her sack but wanted another for barter. While I moaned about the prospect of eight days without privacy or shelter she enthused over the market. 'Oh, look at the pygmies.' She grabbed my arm. 'Aren't they great?' The Ituri pygmies appeared not to care whether they were immense or minuscule. They moved through the crowd with their staffs and head-bundles, selling and selecting. They ignored me and I tried not to stare. Kitty performed an elaborate dumbshow with them and invited me to meet later at the Olympia.

Like many Third World markets, that of Kisangani contained the gamuts of nature and man-made objects. Rows of manioc, rice, spinach, herbs and fruit were set beside hanging black cubes that I realised with disgust were bits of pork or beef covered with envelopes of flies. The envelope opened for the vendor's hand and disclosed raw red and yellow gristle. There were horns, whole or ground, elephants' hooves, live river and forest fowl, gorillas' paws. Opposite sprawled car

17

frames, screws, tools, pumps, outboard motors, cauldrons, cables, rope of every thickness. A long awning at the end held a religious supermarket staffed by nuns and children in school uniform stitched 'Orphelins de Saint Vincent'. Madonnas glowed fresh from their last appearances at Lourdes or Fatima; the Sacred Heart obligingly demonstrated where that organ was; boxes of rosaries and crucifixes rattled as devout hands probed their contents. One section was a bookshop. Besides pamphlets of the more edible saints' lives, it contained accounts of missions. I ruffled through, and found a book called *La Zaire Catholique par fleuve.* Its opening pages offered the information that missions along the river often reserved steamer cabins, which were charitably shared, as St Vincent de Paul would have wished.

Reserved cabins! My heart sprang. My brain raced through absurd scenarios that only the desperate concoct. The cheapest items on display were some comic books of the New Testament in Swahili. I took them plus the *Catholic Zaire* over to the merchant I picked as the chief nun, since she was officiously tidying up trays after the depredation of irreverent fingers. My face assumed an expression of Franciscan piety and my voice would have melted the nails of Martin Luther. I explained that I was an Australian Catholic far from home and had noticed that her order of Vincentian charity had missions along the river.

'Also here, of course,' she said warily. Would it be possible to obtain a cabin on the *Ebeya*, for any section of the route, through the good graces of the mission? She looked at me with incredulity. How? The face from Assisi explained gently that it said so in this book. I showed her the passage. She flicked to the title page. 'That's out of date. Look when it was printed!'

'Ma soeur, vous êtes mon dernier espoir,' I said.

'Non, Monsieur, c'est Dieu qui est votre dernier espoir,' she reproved.

Old bitch. I bought the comic anyway, and trudged down the market rows displaying track suits, running shoes, and fabrics. There were stalls of thin mattresses; nearby were sleeping sheets and mosquito nets. They were cheap. Once rolled up, even with the tightest string, they were also unwieldy. I had a pillow case in which I stuffed dirty laundry. That would do for a head rest.

I turned down the red alley to the Olympia. A pantheon of gods and goddesses, including Kitty, had pitched their tents in the grounds and were drinking Primus beer at a long counter. When I told Kitty of my attempts with the nun, she shrieked with laughter. 'They hate all that sort of thing. They think we're total parasites and the children of Satan.' She introduced me to the curly-haired boy beside her. 'Bim's just got off the *Ebeya*.'

'Oh yeah! What's it like?'

'It's like Conrad,' he said, 'except Conrad didn't get busted.'

Bim had forked out $200 and had to report to the immigration station tomorrow, but he seemed calm and healthy.

'They're insane. The one who really runs it is a guy called Kissinger. He's the *commissaire du bord,* which means the chief extortionist. He'll get you anything if you pay him.'

'What I want is a cabin. But they reckon it's full.'

'I had a cabin,' said Bim. I sat up. 'See that guy over there. He works with Kissinger. He came with us from Kinshasa. He's the one who fixes it.' Bim jerked his head in the direction of a dark but less than black-skinned man stuffing manioc into his face with his fingers. He was dressed in a singlet and combat pants.

'Invite him over,' I hissed.

'He's a shit.'

'Was he the one who got you the cabin?'

'Yup. He's also the one who got me busted. He smoked all my stash and then turned into a gorilla.'

'I don't care if he's King Kong. Invite him over. I'll buy everyone a drink.'

Morality abandoned, I meet Jiai. Jiai liked his beer, and had a second and third one. When I brought up the topic of a cabin, he burped, 'For her too?' Kitty quickly shook her head. Jiai rolled his heavy body out of the chair and beckoned me to follow. I left my portable home with Kitty. For the next half hour, as we walked down to the river, I endured his comments about Kitty with ingratiating sniggers. Not that Jiai wasn't a moralist. *Ce Salaud de Bim* was a criminal, bad for the Bantu People. He was really going to cop it up the arse. Like all Americans. Even though Jiai's own name was American. Gee-Eye, did I get it? Jiai could fix anything. He certainly couldn't fix his fly, which he kept open to pull out his cock every ten minutes or so and spray down the dust. 'Zairian beer no good,' he burped. He then suggested we get some more from the Hotel des Chutes, and pumped me about my profession and financial status.

When we got to the boat it was evening. Jiai carried on as if we were finalising the invasion of Tripoli, and told me to wait on the river bank, and be inconspicuous, which was difficult. Set among hundreds of labouring blacks, one solitary and idle white body tends to glow in the dark. Finally Jiai appeared at a small door in the stern, and let me up a companionway. Monsieur Kissinger's cabin was marked with a plate. In response to a knock which Jiai accompanied by winking to show it was a secret, the great man himself appeared.

Kissinger was a jolly, robust figure of my own age, with the alert eyes of an antelope and the grinning lips of an unashamed sensualist. What an honour it was to meet me, a university teacher, *un professeur*. How unexpected the gift of beer. How fortunate that there was just one cabin left. First class. *Hélas,* how unfortunate that it had two berths, and I would have to pay for the second as well. I calculated quickly. $510. That was better than dying of sunstroke. So it was air-conditioned? His eyebrows rose. What could I be thinking? That was de luxe, and there were only three such cabins, reserved for the doctor, the captain, and his poor self. It did have a fan. I accepted. Still suspicious, I asked if I could sleep in it tonight. Kissinger and Jiai looked at each other. 'My bag is just up at the Chutes.' Kissinger beamed. Of course; why, I could even pay now and he would write out a ticket. That was a problem; I would need extra cash and only had traveller's cheques.

20

American dollars? Not a problem. Kissinger was an accredited exchange agent. He pulled out a calculator. $600 exactly. I protested. But no, Professeur must have the wrong exchange rate. And that included the extra night and all meals. The cheques were in my money belt. I was annoyed at having to pull up my shirt and show it, as well as at the extortionate cost. But the ticket was written; Jiai slapped me on the back and told me I was his brother. I got my torch from the hotel, and we stumbled back to the Olympia, where I gave Kitty the bedding, for which she insisted on paying me, and bought Jiai a crate of beer, which was a mistake, because he insisted on carrying a bag of it back to the hotel, where the manager in turn insisted I pay for that night; whereupon Jiai bought more beer, accompanied me to my cabin, passed out on the other bunk and snored.

I slept fitfully. There was constant movement around the boat. The fan didn't work. Jiai's snores were like those of an amplified pig. I worried about my bag being stolen, so I chained it to the bed. The diesel engines gathered power. When I woke properly, Jiai was still in porcine heaven. Passengers were boarding, and the jovial person of Kissinger appeared at the door accompanied by a tall white man in pressed khaki slacks, white shirt and tie. Without ceremony, Kissinger kicked Jiai awake, and exchanged a dramatic dialogue in Swahili which soon had him rubbing his eyes. He gave out a volley of good morning farts and belches, and buzzed out of the cabin and down the gangway like a deflated bee.

'Professeur Noël, I present Docteur Jeppe, who is a hydro-electric genius from Denmark, worth twenty Belgians, isn't that right? And whose father I have the honour to know as the godfather of my own child, isn't that right, *Ingénieur?*'

The Dane acknowledged all these facts with courtesy, then brought his suitcase into the cabin. Kissinger leaned out and clapped his hands until men appeared with clean sheets, pillows and towels and a large fan. 'There, everything *propre.*'

Now the deck swarmed with other passengers. A burly gendarme talked out of the side of his mouth with Kissinger as the cabins filled with more people than could fit them, and was introduced. He entered with an ironic smile, examined the large fan and my portable one, lazily opened the drawer of our table, pulled back the curtains of the wardrobe, grinned and left. 'He's just making sure that Jiai has left the ship. An absolute criminal, a Tutsi not even from Zaire,' explained Kissinger. 'Whereas Commissaire Biharzi! *Un homme respectable.*'

As soon as they left to continue their routine along the deck, I quizzed Jeppe. 'You realise he charged me for your berth as well? How much did he charge you?'

Jeppe smiled politely: 'I really don't know. My father arranged it. They've known each other a long time. In any case, I'm getting off at Basoko. It's a difficult track up to Tamanrasset, but Pa knows it. I won't disturb you, I promise.'

Nor did he. Equable, considerate, he was perfectly acclimatised, and his father's work was held in awe.

At noon, with the last trucks and cranes pulled away, and a shuddering wrench as we gripped the barges, we unglued ourselves from the dock and set off from Kisangani. A dolorous bass hoot echoed from the shore. At first we made good progress. The surge from the two sets of falls sent the *Ebeya* spinning past the last roads and houses, and when the bell rang for dinner it could just be heard above the roar of the engine. Jeppe and I were introduced to a table of expensively dressed and already tipsy Zairian men and women. The soup brimmed with vegetables, and unidentified shreds of fresh green that tasted like spinach. There was chilled Bordeaux and beer, beef and rice, and a lemon pudding. After coffee and brandy we wandered the decks chatting, watching the banks grow ever more distant as the river expanded and the stars of the entire galaxy appeared.

After the taste of air-conditioning in the first class salon, the cabin was intolerably hot. The new fan didn't work. Jeppe advised leaving the door open, as our neighbours did. Kissinger appeared to help finish the Bordeaux I had bought for dinner. He cooed over a baby already wet with his kisses. More children played on the deck. Everybody talked at screaming point to be heard above the engines. Even that didn't drown out the sound of the thousands of insects hitting the bulbs with the whirr of propellers and thuds like possums caught in a headlight's glare.

The noise of machinery and people was increased by the racket coming from the barges. Clangs, bangs, shouts, laughter were the signs of the cities that lit up around us, electricity hissing, open fires streaming in the breeze. I moulded wax plugs deep in my ears, took two malaria pills, stripped to boxer shorts, set the portable fan an inch from my face, covered my eyes with a padded mask, and slept.

I awoke to the engines throbbing even through the ear plugs. Children were framed at the open cabin door by a rose sky. Jeppe was already dressed. He told me Commissaire Biharzi had dropped by an hour ago 'to check our luggage was OK'.

'He looked at you sleeping and said, *"Ah, quel gaillard!"* It's not a bad expression, you know it?'

'Like goliard?'

'What's that?'

'A medieval troubadour. A travelling scholar. A West African griot?'

'No, it means … well, anything from someone who is very gallant to … a man on the town.'

'A what?'

'Someone who is a *chien gaillard*, you understand?'

'A gay dog? Is that what he thought?'

'No, it's a form of praise. When he saw how smartly you had prepared.'

'I'm overwhelmed with joy.' I said sarcastically. 'Anyway, I don't like him. *Il est gâté.*'

We breakfasted in silence. I left before finishing, to explore the ship. Three times around the decks, I thought, and then to the barges. The barges were the suburbs of the *Colonel Ebeya*, each one with its own demography, each a step down from the other: the *Bangala*, the *Lokokele*, the *Myanza*, the *Mangbetu*, the *Wema* and the *Mongo*, the last a menagerie of crims, dope, prisoners, and a few Europeans among hundreds of Zairians on the roof.

It took all afternoon simply to tour the *Ebeya*. Kissinger bustled me up to the bridge and introduced me to the captain, whose name was Trudeau. Why all the officers of the boat were named after famous politicians was puzzling. After meeting De Gaulle and Nixon in the engine room I concluded they must be noms de guerre, adopted either out of play or because they had something to hide. The head barman was also called Noel. Kissinger's son/nephew/catamite was Sammy, and permanently toted around one of Kissinger's latest progeny named Nehru. We encountered the nervous banker from Goma. His Kisangani meeting had been unfruitful; he was travelling second class but preserved his self-respect by coming up to the main boat. He had given up addressing people as *Citoyen* and *Citoyenne* after the manner of the capital, and I could see why. He was greeted with mockery, as if the whole business of naming had some secret joke concealed within. As indeed it did. In 1971 Mobuto, Zaire's President, had initiated a programme of Revolution-speak. Everyone would address each other as 'Citizen' and 'Citizeness'. Some conformist toadies still did; others struck out via bush and radio towards the tower of Babel. Knowing how to address someone was further complicated by the fact that some Africans, like Chinese and Japanese, put family names first; even more delicate was the habit of prefixing a stranger's given name with an honorific and therefore making it perfectly respectful. The system was in constant flux. People were calling each other the equivalent of 'Smith', 'Mrs Toad', 'Bob', 'Teacher Jane', 'Elephant-head', 'Premier Howard' and 'Bubbles' with enviable abandon. I gave up, and simply asked people directly what they wanted to be called.

One of my table companions was a small neat man with a black moustache who called himself Monsieur Dubrois. Like most of the male passengers in first class, he was a high-ranking member of the police and its associated branches in the army. He wore well-cut European clothes, and watched me with an alert smile.

Dubrois explained that the President's attempt to adopt the manners of the Directorate while Africanizing personal and place names had not succeeded. The country had too many languages and tribal factions for this to be embedded, as it were, in the base of the Congo. The educated found the use of the terms of the French Revolution itself petit-bourgeois, an etiquette for clerks and *comerçants,* and the peasant farmers and other workers were already thoroughly African. Catholic and francophone they might well appear, but beneath they were animists.

I joined the other first class passengers leaning on the rails. Most of my conversations with the Zairians were conducted hanging over these rails, forward beside the stairs that led to the wheelhouse, or aft in the enclosed space that opened into the first class saloon. Even then, the indescribable roar of the ship's engines made it necessary to shout, but at least it guaranteed that no-one except the person standing next to you could hear what you were saying. By Bumba it became evident that the *police fluviale* were the monitors of every entrance and exit into the saloon, and watched who talked too long. Silently, gradually, those who befriended me from the barges, Joseph, Madame 'Luhasa, and the others, were denied access. The prohibition was in force especially when we docked and the salon was locked altogether. Then most passengers crowded aft to watch the canoes hurtle out with their loads, and studied the onlookers sheltering under umbrellas or clutching bicycles on the wharf.

Everyone on the *Ebeya* spoke French, except the engineers. On the barges it was Babel. Students and townspeople were fluent in French, but the others spoke Luba, Tutsi, Kongo and Mongo. Besides using Lingala and Swahili as linguae francae they chatted and argued in a hundred dialects. Kissinger had a stock of American phrases that ended with, 'Right on, man'. Bryan, an Australian I met, taught him to say 'Beaudy mate', and, I am pleased to remember, a variety of invitations so obscene that I hope he had the chance to use them in the event he was ever at the mercy of the U.N.

Joseph was a student of literature at Kinshasa University. It was he who first showed me the news of the massacre at Lubumbashi. Students and faculty of the university had been hacked to death by government troops as they slept. I showed it to Kitty and Jeppe.

'Mobuto is a psychotic,' Joseph yelled in my ear. 'No writer or intellectual in the world ever dares speak up without the support of the military.'

'Oh, I think there was one, at least.' And I began to tell Kitty and Professeuse 'Luhasa of my encounter with a teller of the tales of the world, as remarkable as Conrad's Marlowe, but real.

CAM II
Canterbury Tales

Pier-Paolo Pasolini was quite simply the bravest and most intelligent man I've met, which is perhaps why I spent a great deal of time arguing with him. In manner he was quiet and polite. On the various occasions I saw him, he sailed to every part of the emotional compass: in one direction towards the anxious, in another to the tender, and in his last journey towards the melancholic. Above all he had a kind of grace. The translator of his novels, William Weaver, told me that as a young man Pasolini was aggressive and ambitious. But in London and Cambridge what struck me was his shyness. In Bristol and Oxford, when we met again, he was more confident, but also grim. He wore tinted dark glasses almost constantly; he dressed neatly, somewhat sportively, but without ostentation. His body was slim and fit, his cheeks gaunt, his eyes brilliant and demanding. As we splashed laughing down the river he showed none whatsoever of the conventional small talk perfected by his sociable and voluble compatriots. Nor did he have much capacity for irony, or what the English and French think of as wit. He was direct, and, if he had nothing important to say, silent. He reminded me – and there's even a smell I associate with it, a smell of his freshly washed shirts and severe, country soap – of a calm, intellectual priest, a smell of austerity and celibacy, of someone helping a pupil with a Latin exercise. In contrast I, in my curiosity to know what he was thinking, had a tendency to blurt things out without considering them, and even to lecture him. Nick gladdened him instead, giving him the physical contact he needed by teaching him to punt.

There is not only a skill to punting but an art, which the adept knows and relishes. The pole is grasped with hands of steel, wedged backwards into the riverbed and leant against like a lever. This can have the result, if the pole gets stuck in the mud, of leaving you clinging to it in mid-air while the boat glides gracefully on, and you catapult into the water. But once you get over the peril of stilt-perching, it's a stunning performance. Punters of all ages and experience, in doctors' gowns and pleated skirts, vie in swiftly shifting their mitts to the top of the pole and effortlessly allowing the slippery stick to slide through the cupped hands ready for the next push. No wonder boys with a good Public School background do it with ease. Nick had such a supple wrist that we shot past everyone else like a rowing four, and Ro asked him to slow down because a jetstream was being directed onto the hamper. Ro spoke softly, without seeming to open her lips or needing to agitate her throat beyond an occasional purr, a habit of speech far beyond Received English or Oxbridge: the unmistakable accent of the Royal Family.

In summer the mowers never cut the gardens of the Backs. Fields grow tall with wisteria and wildflowers. With typical English expertise in botany, Ro and Nick lazily identified every single weed. Lupins towered, those flowers of Ophelia that liberal shepherds give a grosser name. One boy nearby was playing Vivaldi on a mandolin, and another bouzouki music. Pasolini had with him some poems and asked whether we could go over the English translations. I began to read them, particularly admiring one full of images of light, colour, humility in the face of art.

'Yes, I think that's one of the most beautiful poems I've ever written.'

It sounded like boasting, yet he said it with naive directness. It was a poem about a workman looking for the first time at the frescoes of Piero della Francesca. I translated: the glow of Arezzo's hills, the emperor dreaming in his asiatic semi-shade.

'Ah, that sounds good ...'

The ecstatic light and colour around us might well have been conjured by Piero himself. Pasolini's head was on castors. He turned with a composed expression and sank a little into the cushions. By now we had left the colleges and the town millpond and were gliding through pasture. We might have been on a Persian carpet flying along the gardens of Naishapur. Punters in Tunisian wraps and Greek tunics slid beside us.

'What do they do in winter?' he asked. 'Do they disappear completely?' He studied their billowing robes, which were strictly Early Ashram. 'Or do they migrate like birds to the Orient?'

When we reached Grantchester, I dived immediately into Byron's pool. Fastidiously packed within the Fortnum hamper, separated into compartments by crisp white napkins, the food was uncovered. Out came the ingredients for an *insalata verde* with miniature flasks of olive oil and balsam vinegar, a moist ham, jars of caviar, red and black, and others of unsalted Norman butter. There were fresh green pears and melon, a plate of dripping brie, orange double Gloucester, pitted Roquefort, sturdy white cheddar and a bottle of Bordeaux chilled in the cooler. I had also liberated two bottles of Château Latour, Keats's favourite wine, from their prison in the college cellars.

As we picnicked I made a few efforts to talk sexual politics, but Pasolini was tight-lipped. After he had been criticising Italy again, I said 'Homosexuality's legal in Italy, isn't it?' 'Yes. That doesn't make any difference,' he replied tautly. After lunch, we walked off along the Backs. I showed him the Fellow's Garden at Trinity Hall which Henry James had called the most perfect small garden in England, and which I had ploughed up with my production of *Bartholomew Fair*. Then we visited Corpus library, where I wanted to show him the maps of Ortelius, touched by Marlowe's hands and mine. Marlowe followed these maps, including their mistakes, when he was writing *Tamburlaine*. My predecessor's supposed portrait hung in the Hall.

'Can you read the motto? I've just traced it back to its Italian emblems,' I said.

'Quod me nutruit me destruit,' Pasolini spelled out. 'What nourishes me destroys me. How hungry he must have been for exactly what was killing him.'

He told me the story of Hunger. To console him for the worries over the unbacked and unmade *Accattone,* Fellini took him out to dinner. Fellini's choice of a cheery restaurant was the locale in which he had shot the most neurotic scenes in *La Dolce Vita*. Pasolini reacted with a severe attack of indigestion, and lay awake that night entertaining paranoid fantasies about the cook. In a way, his story had been the same ever since. Someone is hungry, and the way in which his hunger is satisfied makes him sick.

When we stopped at King's, the Chapel had tourists as usual, so I took him to the unlocked Hall. And here, for some reason, we were happy. I have a distinct image of him at that moment smiling on the other side of a table. He made me laugh; he was playful. We joked about the pomp of the Hall. I sang, and stood on a table. He imagined the Hall full of students. We expressed solidarity with Tudor architecture and Gramsci rather than Lenin and socialist realism. I asked if he wanted to meet anyone. Cinephiles and journalists were lurking near their telephones in case he did. He was happy as he was.

He reiterated his love for the English, and said that he would one day like to shoot a film here, perhaps dealing with a major English poet. Shakespeare? That would be impossible, and anyway the idea didn't attract him. What about Marlowe, one of the boldest writers between the pagan world and the present day? Again he said no. He wanted to do something from the 'early English renaissance'. From the same period as the chapel. It took me some time to realise that he meant

Chaucer, since that wasn't how I thought of Chaucer at all, and the chapel was fifteenth century. In this way, we passed mutually uncomprehending hours strolling and talking about student life in Cambridge. I told him that a great deal of my dislike of the place had to do with the conditions under which I could love Nick.

Nick was not the first man I had fallen in love with. Most of my experiences in Sydney and Florence were heterosexual, and so flagrant that after catching me in bed with women on several occasions, my mother abandoned Catholic morality and became preoccupied with fantasies of adoption and abortions. Nick had appeared like a replica of Lord Alfred Douglas, but manly, handsome, an actor and poet. When he set about seduction, I was more than willing. We collided like racing cars and I wanted to shout our love to the world, and not engage in the traditional Cambridge hypocrisy which encouraged its practice everywhere but in the open. Do anything you like after the sherry, but don't frighten the porters. Pasolini listened sympathetically, and volunteered nothing.

Our discussion was now of the courses I taught or attended. I told him about my difficulties with Dante, that I had even studied the *Purgatorio* intensively for a year in Florence, but that generally he left me cold. 'I find more in Petrarch. Perhaps you think that a curious opinion.' He furrowed his eyebrows. What was it like to be a teacher? We debated. I teased him by calling him Socrates, and saying 'Yes, Socrates' or 'No, Socrates' to each of his questions. He countered, 'Ah, no, here, it's you who's the teacher, *professore.*' I replied that I needed good teachers, that the only teachers I really respected were Anne Barton and Muriel Bradbrook, who had studied with, and loved, Malcolm Lowry. That was scarcely surprising, he said, the intelligence of women was savagely held in check and would savagely explode.

'That's just what I mean,' I burst out. 'Can't you see how monastic Cambridge still is?'

'These young students aren't monastic, though, are they?'

We turned our eyes upwards and talked about architecture,

31

its ability to make you feel good or depress you. He returned to the value of the colleges as locations for a film. Did it disrupt university life too much? I said the College bursars were always pleased at extra income, that I had seen three films being shot in Cambridge and that many of the students were keen to be extras. Images of him become jump-cuts: standing under the tall glass of King's Chapel, racing each other in Clare Gardens across the river, groaning over the little humpbacked bridge where I had knocked Prince Charles off his bike, and returning by the little side gate to my rooms. I had sandwiches sent up, and read him my own poems. We prepared to leave for London while there was still light.

As we settled into the train and it started to glide out over the flat fields round Cambridge, Pasolini pressed his face to the window like a child.

'Are you tired?'

'On the contrary, I feel alive. Sometimes I feel very alienated from things. But in a train, with the window frame like this,' he traced a rectangle with his hands against the outline of the train window, 'I feel absolutely calm as I look out at the world, because it seems to be passing as it does in the cinema. It's framed, comprehensible. In a train you see the origin of the tracking shot.'

He said he thought of the day on the river as a kind of thawing, and offered me his trust. Over the next year we corresponded about his plays, which he gave me permission to translate and produce. There were phone conversations and telegrams about the articles and lectures I now gave on him as part of the Tripos. After many exchanges and queries about Freud and Eisenstein I received a surprising letter:

Dear Purdon,

I've always meant to thank you for the very fine article that you published in *Cinema*. I do it now very belatedly, but I hope just the same you'll forgive me. I'm always caught up in all sorts of work, and so I let a lot of things slide, even important ones.

I'm about to leave for Rumania, where I'll write the screenplay for my next film, *Canterbury Tales,* taken from Chaucer, remember? After that, I'll naturally do the location research in England, because I'll be shooting it there. More or less, my immediate journey to England will take place in early July.

I've been wanting to ask you if you were prepared to help me, whether in checking out places and characters, and in the long run verifying the translation of the text I'm using – or in yet other things which might come out of my English trip.

I ask you seriously, if the proposal interests you, to write here to Rome, to my house, giving me a place where you can be reached in your own movements, so that as soon as I've arrived in England I can get in contact with you.

I greet you cordially and I thank you.

Pier Paolo Pasolini

I wrote back immediately telling him that I'd be in Bristol in mid-July and Oxford in August. We talked excitedly on the phone. He wanted Oxford and Cambridge as main locations and had heard Somerset was good. English river-towns were the best.

On 16 July he drove up from Heathrow. He made obsessive phone calls along the way, from Wiltshire, Stonehenge and Bath, telling me where he was, and exactly what he was looking at. I was amused to hear him every half hour or so; on the last call I said, 'There's no need to phone all the time.' He replied that he was worried that he would be late.

Both Nick and I had grown beards since we'd last seen him. He was frankly uncomplimentary. He reached out and tugged them. 'Why are you all growing beards in England? So many young men ruining their appearance. And Nick too! Why do you want to look like old men?' I couldn't possibly say that I was hoping he would cast me as Chaucer, a sort of scholarly, but obviously amiable man of the type he had admired on the Cam. Or maybe I could be the Franklin. But here was one immediate problem. He wasn't impressed by the Franklin's Tale; and he had already written the screenplay. I tried to persuade him. It was the best tale in the collection. He replied that it was too late, that he saw Chaucer as an essentially comic writer. When he kept carrying on about Chaucer's comedy, I pointed out that perhaps he understood Chaucer about as much as I did Dante. How did he see Chaucer? He replied that he would play Chaucer himself. This was a shock. Besides the egotism, he was far too skinny.

We had prepared salami, prosciutto crudo, frascati, olives, ricotta. As before in London, where he had chosen steak, he wanted no Italian food, and only accepted the frascati after much persuasion, when I said that I had specially bought it. But he would take Nick and me to dinner that night. Where did we want to eat? We chose the most oriental venue we could think of, the Mahal.

The waiters wore the clothes of the Raj, and light came from bronze lanterns onto cushioned recesses. At 7.30 on this hot night he was flanked by two English production assistants. He took us by the elbows and positioned us on either side.

'Now, tonight I feed you,' he said emphatically. 'What's the best they have? Order anything you want.'

'I hope you like Indian food,' I demurred.

'I like Indian food very much, don't worry about that.'

'They make an excellent tandoori, but it's very hot, and it takes a while.'

'Order a lot of hot lime pickles and Bhendi Bhaji,' said Nick.

'Does Nick know about Indian cooking? Let him order then!'

Nick's tastes in Indian food resembled those of a fire-eater; I wondered how Pasolini's ulcer would respond to a diet of Madras curries and incandescent peppers.

But he was chatting with Nick in his rare English, telling him that he loved India, and asking whether Nick had been there as well. Depending on his mood, Nick was capable of giving the impression that he had recently spent a stretch there as Viceroy. There was an atmosphere of fun and excitement. We ordered a feast of food and wine.

We began talking about his pre-production plans, then shifted to a discussion of other Italian film-makers. I had been writing about Bertolucci, and was eager to hear what the director of *Before the Revolution* was doing. He was disappointed in Bertolucci. He said merely that he himself felt stronger than before, and that he needed strength and resolution as he prepared to shoot the *Tales*. No one else spoke Italian, though Nick and one of the P.A.s could understand some of what was being said. It became a repetition of Cambridge. I was expansive, argumentative: a great oaf. I translated for the others. 'Pasolini says ...' Pasolini watched with a calm smile. I repeated Sartre's famous joke about waiters.

'You realise that these waiters are not really waiters? They're Indians playing at being waiters.'

'No, I hadn't realised that,' he said owlishly.

He expressed further curious opinions, ones that in translating I suppressed. He was anti-divorce, anti-abortion, anti-student, and anti-working class to the extent that he claimed that it no longer existed. Yet he presented himself as a genuine radical, and I believe he was. As he continued, he became vehement. Gentleness left him, and he launched into a long and bitter lament about Italy. He claimed that everything that he loved had been taken away from him. I saw here a glimpse of what Weaver told me about the younger man he'd known. Pasolini's actual words, which struck me vividly because he repeated them so often, were: 'Mi hanno tolto il sottoproletariano ... mi hanno tolto il terzo mondo ...' There was a kind of infantile resentment all the more startling for being expressed with such innocence. He felt personally deprived. 'They took them away.'

He hated Rome. He had to get out of it. He was worried about the rise of neo-Fascism. The possibility of a coup was a daily one. The details of his persecution are astonishing in terms of the process by which a man and his work were hounded to death. Besides attacks on him in the press, posters, television, and psychiatrists' reports, he had five times to endure organised physical assaults. These were accompanied by anonymous letters, death threats and, in broad daylight in the Piazza d'Espagna, a bashing by a group of youths wearing swastikas and armed with chains. One has the impression that had he survived Pelosi and his associates' butchery, he would have been charged for that too: inciting innocent young criminals to violence.

The complaints against Pasolini were ludicrous. He used Mozart to accompany sexual scenes. (As if Mozart had nothing to do with sexuality ...) His films would cause cerebral thrombosis. They showed people farting. They would turn people against 'the Church, the Italian bourgeoisie, capitalism, and the angels and saints'. In response to his argument in *The Decameron* that sex was not a sin, hundreds of sinners up and down Italy denounced the film to their magistrates, because the church told them it *was* a sin. So they did it and confessed it and then did it again. Anyone who tried to break such an efficient chain of unreason could be treated in only one way: unreasonably.

From being placatory and defensive, he became bitter. As an instinctive communalist, his first attempt at alliance was with the Communist Party. As a homosexual who was expelled from that false equality for 'decadence' he had the choice of seeking solidarity with the liberal bourgeoisie to the right of the party, the extra-parliamentary groups to the extreme left, or remaining completely alone. He tried all solutions. All had failed. He was worried that he, like most Italian intellectuals, was on a death-list.

'In Germany and France also, there is an imminent possibility of a return to Fascism,' he argued. England was the only country in Europe where Fascism was impossible, because there was an ingrained opposition and tolerance in the bourgeoisie. *'In the bourgeoisie?'* I protested. Yes, England's bourgeoisie were the safeguard of Europe. He was particularly hard on hippies and longhaired *cappelloni*. They were simply liberal nihilists. All they were interested in was drugs. You could hear their intellectual emptiness in their language, or read the language of their clothes. He had lost faith in the young, he said. I was twenty-nine, the others at the table even younger. Nick had shoulder-length hair as well as his beard; one of the P.A.s a droopy hippy moustache. I had to make some defence.

Wasn't it the young in England who were trying to create some opposition to the exploitation of the Third World, to pollution? Would not students always be the bravest to insist on change, because they were both the scientists and artists of the future and the dissidents of today? I told him about the Bath Arts Workshop's fight against a motorway destroying the city. He replied that, yes, this was important, that Bath was an especially beautiful town. When I translated this, one of the P.A.s burst out, 'Well, I'm glad he likes some bloody thing!'

'Has he been giving you a hard time?' I asked the P.A. The boy half closed his eyes.

'It's not that he gives you a hard time. He's just not enthusiastic about anything.'

I told Pasolini that everybody thought he was too hard and cruel. The levity failed.

'Perhaps I am hard and cruel,' he said grimly. 'Everything around me has become hard and cruel.'

He went to the lavatory. Nick and I had smoked two joints before coming out to dinner. 'Maybe we should get him stoned,' Nick suggested.

'I wish you luck,' said the P.A. wryly.

'Maybe he just wants a fuck,' said the other.

'He'd say so,' said Nick with the authority of experience.

The cannabis was manifesting two of its notorious effects, euphoria and what is known as the 'munchies'.

When Pasolini returned, I recited the General Prologue of the *Tales* in extravagant Middle English. His good humour came back, and he offered Nick the rest of his tandoori. Nick graciously accepted, having already devoured everything except the tablecloth.

37

If I were in Rome, he said, he would do what he could to provide prints of the films I hadn't seen. Even he didn't have prints. There were aspects of the film-making process over which he had no control whatsoever. 'Like now,' I suggested.

'Not like now. I have done some unusual things with the script. It's being typed up, and it's what I want.'

I pressed him about the personality of the pilgrims. How would he develop them as characters? He replied emphatically that he saw Chaucer as the only story-teller, and that I should wait until I saw the script next week.

When we left on our separate ways, his face was lit by neon in the back of the car retreating down the hill. I was acutely aware that he saw us walking behind him with our arms around each other, emblems of contact.

I had not expected him to turn up at Oxford without ringing. By now I felt casual. Whatever the promises of his letter, he had never offered me a proper contract. I made coffee. Doves throbbed outside the window.

'So, you leave Cambridge, which you tell me you hate, and you come to Oxford. What are you doing?'

'Summer course. I need the money for holidays.'

'Where's Nick? And Lady Rosemary?'

'In Cornwall. Do you want to walk in the garden? There's a nice seat in the wall, and an astrolabe.'

'Are you a fellow of this college too?'

'No. I'm a summer school lecturer.'

'Beautiful college.'

I led him out over the water-meadows.

'What's this river?'

'The Isis.'

'Did you get the script? What do you think?'

The truth was, that, in a slough of nonchalance, I hadn't even read the whole script till yesterday. I had skimmed through, seen that there was no Franklin's Tale, read the beginning in a sour frame of mind and thought it was corny. Away from Nick, heterosexuality had again unleashed itself. I resumed my relationship with Diana, another teacher on the course. I wanted a spectrum of sexuality, not a division. When I came across his sequence of the sodomites in the Friar's Tale, it sent me running to Chaucer in the college library to see if I had missed something. No. He had made the whole thing up. It seemed bizarre, as if everything was going to be roly-poly Chaplinesque except for these burning and betraying homosexuals. Beneath the forced comedy, I found the selection of tales bleak and moralistic.

'It's very interesting,' I began, not wanting to lie. 'But ... but the sodomites are like something out of Dante rather than Chaucer.' He nodded, patient, enquiring. 'I mean it seems a very negative portrait.'

'What is negative?' He watched me attentively.

'Everything. The imagery ... the language.'

'You mean the language of the translation? You could help work on it!'

'I don't know whether it's the translation or your original script.'

'There's something wrong with the dialogue? That will change as I shoot –'

'No. It's not just the dialogue. The mood and the language seem ... artificial.'

'Ah, no, it can hardly be artificial. It's written exactly in the language of Chaucer, a popular idiom.'

'The language of Chaucer isn't a popular idiom. It's cultivated, mobile.'

'Yes, yes. You misunderstand me. I realise Chaucer himself was a bourgeois, but the language of the tales ...'

'He wasn't a bourgeois. He was a courtier.'

'I don't think you understand the sense in which I mean bourgeois.' I didn't and wouldn't. 'My intention is to follow the line of Chaucer as a comic writer.'

'What you've written isn't comic,' I blurted out. 'It's paranoiac and guilty.'

He was silent. Embarrassed, I continued.

'I don't see how you can make a film of *The Canterbury Tales* without the cycle on love.'

'On the contrary, there will be a discussion of marriage throughout.'

'I mean love. Take The Franklin's Tale,' I insisted. A knight adores his wife, and when he goes to war she's inconsolable. A young squire in turn is dying of love for her. From pity she promises that if he clears the treacherous sea-rocks around their castle, she will sleep with him. He offers a scholar the entire globe if that can be done. This man, also moved by pity, by magic accomplishes it. The knight returns, and when his wife tells him the story, nobly agrees that she may keep her promise. But when she presents herself to the squire, he is so touched that he releases her. Now he is fatally in debt to the scholar. The scholar, hearing how they have all behaved, releases the young squire.

'Don't you see? That's real love, breaking the chains of possession, people one by one letting each other go.'

'The Franklin's Tale is unrealistic. It doesn't seem part of Chaucer's world. It's medieval, fantastic.'

'It is not.'

And for the first time, I understood that to an Italian for whom Boccaccio and Petrarch had already created a Golden Age, Chaucer might well seem the epitome of a Renaissance writer; and that my love for The Franklin had more to do with my own needs than Pasolini's. His severity, perhaps his despair, was increasing. Yes, I thought, like Dante he would have kept Paolo and Francesca in Hell, from whose whirlwind Chaucer would have released them.

I went off on a tangent about the English being difficult people to understand, that perhaps only their close neighbours the French and the Irish knew what they were really like. And even if Italian cities were already republics on the edge of the *rinascimento* in 1400, England wasn't. He listened gravely. He would think about my feelings but the script was as it stood. And he was about to go out and check locations. Could I come? Later. I had to teach Shakespeare in the afternoon, and then take the students to Stratford to see *A Winter's Tale*.

'Well, Chaucer already contains Shakespeare, doesn't he?'

I was speechless. He thanked me for the coffee, which he hadn't drunk.

'I don't mean that I don't like the script.'

'No. Perhaps you're right. But the dream is one *I* have.'

On location in Bath a month later, technicians were crowding around him seeking direction for the next set-up. He looked lost among them. I tried to encourage him; he shared his reverie of the great cycles of adventure tales.

'Sometimes when I'm making a film I wish I were making a different one. I've loved the *Arabian Nights* since I was a child, but I've never got near them.'

'"What *I* really want is to ride in triumph through Persepolis."'

It sounded weird in Italian; of course he didn't catch the allusion.

'*Come?*'

'Persepolis. It stands for all the places I want to go. The line's from Marlowe. *Tamburlaine.*'

Awkwardly I said goodbye. He was distracted by setting up the take. We used the conventional Italian phrase to wish luck while warding off danger.

'*In bocca al lupo*, eh?'

'In bocca al lupo.' In the mouth of the wolf.

Two years after the *Tales,* both Pasolini and I did get to Persepolis. I was spending a week in Isfahan on my way back to Australia. He had just shot *1001 Nights* in the courtyard of the Great Mosque. I sent a postcard and urged him, if he liked deserts, to come and make a film in Australia, the continent of the absence of rivers, the biggest desert of them all. A year later, in a sunny suburb of Adelaide, where I had risen early to get the milk and paper, I woke Nick and said: 'Pasolini is dead. He was murdered.'

In a rush of indescribable shock, we both burst out laughing.

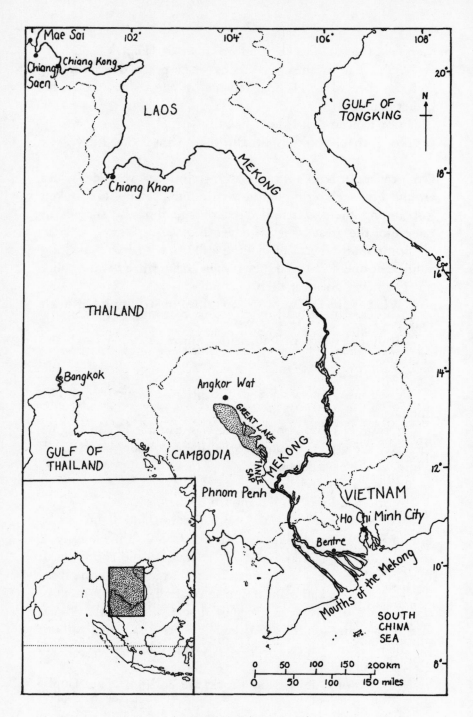

MEKONG

MEKONG I

Near to Vietnam

At the same time I met Pasolini, a group of French intellectuals made a film of political protest called *Far From Vietnam*. They were indeed far. So was I. Years later I talked with one of them in Venice. Alain Resnais was sincere about his film, but now distanced and discreet. Throughout the Seventies I saw books, plays, films, countless representations of an endless river of war. Now I'm not so far: it's 1989 and I'm flying over the nine Dragon Mouths of the Mekong. I'm here.

I almost hadn't made it on the flight to Ho Chi Minh at all, for the simple but crucial reason that the guide from Falcon Adventure Travel didn't turn up. Instead, while loudspeakers announced last calls, a courier I had chatted to in their Bangkok office skittered through the departure lounge and headed straight for me.

'I'm awfully sorry about all this,' said the company representative breathlessly, 'but our guide Madame Pactol must be sick, and we need a French-speaking group-leader to get through. Also there's a bit of a problem with one of the passport stamps. So if you could just do this now ... we'll fix it up later.'

'But I'm not French.'

'Your name sounds so. And there are some people from

Latin countries. And the rest speak English. Please. There are itineraries in each passport. Here's the group visa. You'll really have to hurry. Remember, hand-luggage only.'

'Can't you deal with this?'

'I'm just a courier. I can't take you all through. I'll fax you at the Majestic Hotel in Ho'ville. There'll be other guides to take over. I do apologise.' She delivered sixteen passports into my hands, and disappeared.

'Falcon Adventure Travel?' I called out stupidly. Fifteen pacing, watchful people approached. I explained what had happened, dealt out the passports like playing cards. Thai officials waved us through. The rest of the group still didn't understand who I was or what the holy lotus was going on. And yes indeed, there was a problem with one of the visas. Berthe, a Dutch woman travelling on an Indonesian passport, had somehow managed to get a stamp for Vietnam only, perhaps because she had refused to provide her vaccination certificate. This dusty blonde was behaving like Leni Riefenstahl, with an immediate zeal for the people she thought of as her 'primitives', and colonial contempt for everyone else. She had a sharp tongue and the argument was turning nasty.

'You must travel on group visa. Who has this visa? Who is the group leader?' asked an officer testily.

The others paused only a second. Then they decided.

'He is,' they chorused, pointed at me, and walked briskly to the plane.

This unique tour had been advertised the world over: the temples of Angkor Wat; a trip on the Mekong; post-war Vietnam; Cambodia, a bare five years after the Khmer Rouge had been officially deposed by the U.N. The area was still, we discovered, in civil war. The Vietnamese had established a puppet government and were about to withdraw. Perhaps only the Buddha knew when such a journey would again be possible. So sixteen intrepid people made their way to the Bangkok office of Falcon Travel from every corner of the globe. We surrendered our passports for the mandatory group visas controlled by Hanoi, and filled out forms in which we listed countries already travelled and languages spoken. I outdid myself in boastfulness.

The plane's shadow falls over the glittering Mekong until it disappears into the clouds, wriggling through Vietnam and Cambodia, digging borders between Laos and Thailand, proclaiming its final mystery by running through China from a source 4,000 kilometres away in Tibet. As we descend, the shadow stitches the patchwork of green squares, striped alternatively across and down with lines of young rice. What a lot of blue circles there are scattered among them – twenty, a hundred, a thousand. Then I wake up. They're not reservoirs. They're the bomb craters of the Vietnamese war, just a few of the twenty-five million.

When the last bottle of chablis has been collected, and the curtains open into the first class nose of Air France, he is sitting three seats in front, a familiar face in profile. We are held back at the top of the steps. The reception unrolls as smoothly as the carpet, just as you see it on the news: the row of dignitaries, the flowers and the smiles. The Vietnamese Foreign Minister steps up; handshakes, buzz of newspeople. Then the black Russian limousine glides off with Gareth Evans and his wife in air-conditioned comfort. An Australian aide tells me we take in 2,000 more Vietnamese refugees per year. The response is enthusiastic. Evans is respected as a careful diplomat; Australia must mediate.

This takes place some years before I watch him sipping champagne while he signs disgraceful documents about East Timor. Or, for that matter, before I realize that the unchecked arrival of thousands of so-called refugees has resulted in the import of vicious gang-war to Sydney.

But watching Evans' limo disappear, my regard is full of hope.

That night, settled in the Majestic, another diplomatic plot is being hatched. A fax from the Chief Falcon has arrived. Madame Pactol won't be coming, cunning Madame Pactol. Now we are a small group, risky and independent. Ten of the older ones have retired to bed. Tomorrow we fly the short distance to Phnom Penh. So what do we want?

Angkor Wat is what we want, the largest and most magnificent religious building in the world, and we want more of it than the itinerary allows. The gang includes five archaeology fanatics: a sculptor, Dominique, and her suave husband Quiquer; Cornelius, a journalist who has been to Vietnam six times but never to Cambodia; an upper-class English couple, the Honourables Roger and Sarah, friends of Prince Andrew and trained since birth in getting their own way. Our Vietnamese guide, Tung, is scheduling the itinerary with me.

'Just agree with everything he says. We'll do exactly what we want later,' says Sarah serenely. We want Eden. We want the giant faces our archaeology books display smiling down in Second Empire engravings, illuminated by lightning flashes in the middle of the jungle. Angkor is the navel of the world. French existentialists, English psychoanalysts, American beats come to be for one moment at the centre of the earth.

We get up at 6.00 am to do the same, to be on the Mekong, to see the wonder before someone explodes it. Because of the jutting curve of the shore, and the summer backflow of its tributary the Tonle Sap, the Mekong at Phnom Penh almost cuts into the hotel. Already I am feeling the tension of having to mediate about luggaage and plans for the boat, especially since Tung and his supervisors betray an uncontrollable apprehension about how things must be done. I have been made responsible for listing everyone's possessions on innumerable forms. It's like a case of mistaken identity, *The Inspector General* or *The Man who Knew Too Much*. I'm suddenly responsible for a group of complete strangers in a country which I have never visited and where I have every reason to need protection rather than offer it myself. I've been given the Wrong Suitcase, the one with the Secret Plans, and the Cambodians and the Vietnamese are going to stick like limpets until they get it.

We are to visit an orphanage. We have prepared pathetic packages of gifts and medicines. Tung says, 'After you leave, they'll take them all away.' Who will? The same people who are smilingly leading us around, the baby-faced Cambodians.

A girl who can be no more than sixteen leads us through the courts and pavilions of the Royal Palace, elaborately restored, a sparkling repository for Fabergé eggs and emerald crowns. Is this a preparation for the equally Fabergé-headed Sihanouk to be restored to his setting? The palace guide is a dreamy young dancer, with gentle manners and assured knowledge. I imagine her performing at a court ballet. I walk with her at the head of the group, frankly admiring her graceful fingers.

'When foreign visitors praise my hands, I sometimes wish that they would like my speech instead. Or maybe invite me to their own country. I have a severe music teacher of the old order. Every time I make a mistake he slaps these fingers. They are hurt, not beautiful.'

A large sign says: IT IS FORBIDDEN TO BRING IN CAMERAS WITHOUT PAYING. Berthe's husband is brandishing a camcorder like a missile. The guards chase them. Next thing I hear is Berthe screaming: 'Get your filthy hands off me.' I do my best to pacify. In revenge Berthe lingers over every last image of conjugal monarchy and detestable nineteenth century taste. My assignation of rooms the night before still rankles. She finds her accommodation inadequate, and she knows whom to blame. When we are reverently led to the King's domestic chamber bed, she says: 'They could have always put Our Leader up here.'

'And I'm sure they could have found a kennel for you,' I snap.

Her husband catches the insult with a flush. Will he sock me in the jaw? By now, through the painful process of installing them in rooms, I am getting to know my companions. Dominique comes rapidly to my side and says in French. 'Pay no attention. She is a very disturbed woman.'

In the background I can hear Berthe growling to the others 'Who does that shit of an Australian think he is? Him and his little Commie friends? Look at him crawl.'

I'm fed up. I'm in an impossible position, since I have paid to be a traveller, and have ended up as a chargé d'affaires. In trying to help this woman, I have incurred her hatred. She insists on a taxi back to the hotel. I tell her to find one herself, thank the young girl and take the rest outside to await our bus. Lounging in the shade, I feel fury working against everyone. Quiquer and Dominique, for example, are French. Why couldn't they be responsible for the group? The courier must have taken the most superficial look at the list. Their surname is Roscoff, which may sound Indo-Nothing, but is in fact Breton, an ancient name. Their French, of course, is perfect. Sarah's and Roger's is also good. So why me? Because I listed other Romance languages on the Falcon form? Hubris! The Latins in the group are neither Spanish nor Italian. They're Brazilian and unmarried. Berthe thinks they're immoral. She has also been extremely aggressive with the elderly Hungarian Lásló. We learn from Sarah that Berthe spent her childhood as a Japanese prisoner of war and now lives in Saudi Arabia.

'How on earth does she survive there?' asks one of the Americans, who works as a dentist in Riyahd. 'She treats all non-Europeans with contempt.'

The National Museum is filthy, exposed to the elements, shrilling with bats and swallows, like a post-Bauhaus installation full of sinuous sculpture transcending Donatello. What philistine decided the priority of redecorating a tawdry palace, and allowing the most precious art of the pre-Renaissance to be ruined? Dominique runs her hands over a curving torso.

'C'est un opprobre.'

Yes, it is a disgrace. No doubt, Dominique, they should be in the Louvre. And if Dominique feels that way, I say, why don't she and Quiquer deal with everything, the anxious officials, the reservations, the unhinged Berthe?

'You have every right to be angry. Please not with us. After Quiquer met you at the Falcon office, he told me he'd encountered one of the most charming men in his life. Neither of us can offer to be the group representative because we can't afford to be prominent in any way at all.' She softly calls Quiquer, away from the guard who sits on a rickety chair by the door, and explains my anger. They study each other's faces for a full minute; then Quiquer turns the same look on me.

'I am going to trust you. Listen. We are both carrying far more money than we have declared on the forms. Far more. It represents gifts to hospitals, and to people who are trying to do something about art like this. We are also making a report on the restoration of Angkor. If our hand-luggage had been more carefully checked, or our persons searched, we would have been detained.'

Dominique takes over. 'We have been writing for more than a year to anaesthetists, surgeons, art-conservers, printers, engineers. None of the things they need can come through the Vietnamese, who are only interested in a last-minute show. And they certainly can't come through the official aid organizations to the Cambodians.

'So we have millions of francs worth of antibiotics, of surgical instruments, of mine-detectors, any item that we have been specifically asked for and that was small enough to bring in.

'We're not political subversives, if that's what you're thinking. We simply fear that without this kind of help Cambodia will effectively cease to exist.'

I stare at them with a mixture of amazement and the inklings of relief. So *they* are the ones with the Secret Suitcase.

'We have met the Prince privately. He is a cretin. His best friends are some of the worst people imaginable. The rest are no better. His sons intrigue against him. The other candidates are all ex-Khmer. Every day helpless people are being made more helpless. Blown up. Abducted. God knows what will happen to this country. We are told that it won't really change. It will go on for ten, maybe twenty years. Every fifteen minutes someone is killed by a mine. They keep on laying them at night. The temples were booby-trapped. It's frightening.

'You are not involved in any of this. We'll seek our friends ourselves. And all the time, we can't tell you how grateful we are that you're the one out front. Believe us.'

I do. I admire them, as I admire all those brave enough to put themselves on the line.

CONGO III
The Ebeya

Before setting sail, people are fond of christening boats as women, even to the extent of bribing them with champagne to get in the water. But neither the blindest nor the most sentimental of voyagers could doubt for a second that the *Colonel Ebeya* was male. Masculine in its undisguised roughness and desire to penetrate the river, in its imminent danger, from the sound of the engines, of suffering an aneurism. It would die long before the river, who would survive as an indifferent widow. It had forced, bullied, suffered appalling damage. As the womanly river embraced life and death with equanimity, the *Ebeya* puffed, laboured, chugged, fought, inflated itself with cargo and riches, ignored illness and pain to the last point of consciousness. One day it would die like other men, worn out, rusted, scuttled if it was lucky, with a service of civil regret; perhaps an evasion during sleep; more probably as it rounded a bend for a final encounter, murdered.

At the stage of life I met him, this dirty old man had taken quite a battering. His gunwhales were dented where he had rammed other colonels. Half his railings were ripped off; he appeared to have started at one stage to devour his children the barges, whose gashes in their sterns matched the ragged steel teeth in his bow. But the *Ebeya* must once have been a handsome young vessel. Its three decks were crowned at the bow by a fourth which held the bridge and the captain's quarters. The lowest barely confined the engine and paraphenalia of cables and machinery. The other two were enclosed at bow and stern by a white carapace of iron. Stuck like lung-fish to its left-hand side were the smaller barges, a mass of open spaces separated by columns, and so crammed with people in carriages like freight-trains that many chose to camp on the flat roofs.

Shackled even further out on the river were the larger, double-decked second- and third-class barges, the *Lokokele* and the *Bangala*; these, in turn, pushed before them the broken hulls of the *Wema* and the *Mongo*, whose rusty iron prows opened briefly before being topped by decks where the steel had torn at both sides. They were overhung by curved thin roofs, which together with the columns and balconies gave them the appearance of floating tenements. This impression was reinforced by lines of washing of every shape and spectrum from white sheets to red baby clothes, and by the packs of people joined together and squeezing past each other like files of ants. Ladders, catwalks, gangplanks and companionways connected every last part of the structure, constantly in motion with the traffic of people, goats and pigs and squawking bundles of chickens, baskets of fruit and wild birds swinging upside down from their bound claws.

It seemed impossible that this village the size of central Kisangani would move, let alone hold together. The downstream current was strong, the speed surprising. As I descended into the barges, the human mass was overwhelming. Second class had corridors, like the *Ebeya* itself, but these ran bewilderingly through the bowels of the *Lokolele* and the *Myanza* before opening into larger chambers and closing in again to walkways on the outer railings. I caught glimpses of steel bunks in tiers of two and three, prison-like dormitories of wooden beds piled to the bulkheads. You would then enter caverns the size of ballrooms, with makeshift bars, tables and chairs, barrels and vast cargoes of square palm-matting bound with twine.

Every centimetre of floor and bulkhead was stowed with sacks, cushions, bags of onions, plastic garbage cans, jute flag-covered boxes, rolled-up foam mattresses bound to the pipes. Tins, wicker fish traps and petrol cans swung from the ceiling. What looked like lacrosse rackets pressed together the flesh of drying game. Babies slept in twisted cribs, their parents sheltering them with their legs from the feet of passers-by. Men read newspapers and played cards. Women squatted on small circular stools and chatted while they peeled tubers into enamel cauldrons. There was a thick smell of hemp, both as twine and cannabis, mixed with diesel oil, kerosene, and charred bread. Mud and vegetation, mashed together, stirred up new scents from the river, as fresh as lawn clippings after rain.

The impression was of a giant termite nest, seething with workers circulating round the still points of babies and sleepers, apparently chaotic but regulated by some principle that gave everyone a place, even if they had to nudge or let fly a sting of argument to maintain it. Along the outside decks open to the river and occasionally washed by it, as the *Ebeya* rounded a bend and the whole block tilted, shop-keepers had set up stalls. A strip of flowered cotton, a plank on trestles, and goods strung on rails behind, defined the elements of this seemingly infinite market. Shoelaces, fish-hooks, buttons, canned food, amulets, rosary beads, beer and soft drinks, T-shirts, cassettes, soap and Doc Martens were on offer. The traders made no attempt to promote their wares. They awaited customers with confidence, read comic books or stared out at the water or the parental *Ebeya*.

The cooks were a more active fraternity. On oil-lamps and circlets of small stones they kindled fires, drew water from the river by trailing rope buckets, and sliced up ingredients for their pots. Some of the ingredients were still alive. After being yelled at for stepping on snakes and a cage of small finches, I decided to head for the roof. It took a long time to find the right connections of gangways and ladders. Even here the space was marked out like allotments, with tents and sleeping bags and a sort of soccer pitch on which a team of teenage boys were miraculously keeping the ball from flying into the river.

From this height, the forest looked much denser, but the expanse of water was so broad that I watched its curves with exhilaration. A small group of whites was doing the same. At their head was Kitty, dancing.

'Isn't this incredible?' she shouted.

A red-haired boy beside her introduced himself as Fergus. An elegant couple emerged from their bubble tent. I discovered with pleasure that they were Italian. A girl sitting next to the air vent on the prow was Israeli; she looked tough. Two quiet young Belgian men completed the band.

After filming the sunset, I followed Kitty. She knew a quick way down. You jumped from the roof of the *Myanza* onto the *Lokokele* or the *Wema*. Kitty thought the *Lokokele* was safer. Even so, I kept both hands free to land in a crouch. Some of the nearby resting Zairians grumbled at us for disturbing them as we thudded down one after another. *'Mazungu!'* Bloody whites.

As evening approached, one of the large central staterooms was blaring out the infectious music of central Africa. I still love it. How can anyone hear it without wanting to dance? Kitty knocked on an inner cabin which opened into a ramshackle duplex and was enthusiastically greeted. The cabin was a cave of sacks of ice and boxes of beer. The half dozen Primuses we bought were cheap and deliciously cold. We clambered our way – 'Pardon, m'sier, 'don, m'dme. Oops, je suis désolé.' 'MAZUNGU!' – until we arrived at a cabin which proclaimed itself 'Australian Embassy' in felt-pen.

Bryan was from Melbourne and was quite mad. His calling card showing a biplane which styled him as International Barfly Unlimited. He strode the barges and the boat, gave cheek to the Commmissaire, smoked almost the entire stock of ganja in the hold, cheered everyone up, revelled, danced. In the space of the next few hours we met all the other foreigners on the convoy. Simonetta and Daniele Damiano were environmentalists based in Ethiopia. They were joining another group of scientists in Tanzania. They thought this would be a chance to see what was happening along one of the great rivers of the world. Simonetta was Roman, and Daniele from Verona. They had a collection of light Arab clothing that Armani could have designed, a water purifier, and a tent that could be settled anywhere. The third and lowest barge was a test for tent pitching, but theirs stood, and they emerged from it looking like angels from a fresco by Pisanello.

Yukio was an elegantly strong Japanese adventurer with the assurance of pull-out American dollars, ignoring the thousands of curious Africans who watched him write his diary in characters while he stared into the jungle. The Israeli girl Leah, perhaps because she unwisely wore camouflage pants, was harassed and tormented by the adolescent boys on the barge, but Yukio walked through them like a robot. The rest of us christened him R2D2. Hendrijk and Hans were Belgian nurses who had worked for five years at the hospital upriver in Kindu. They were being expelled with hatred, like all Belgians, and they knew it. It had taken them a fortnight to get up to Ubundu, only to find that there was no train. They walked to Kisangani. They had to be out of Zaire by 31 July or else. It was now 13 July. They knew some of the Zairian officials by reputation. They frequently took me aside and warned me not to be so loud. There was also a group of four Canadian teachers; they got off, exhausted, at the next port.

Fergus was Scots. He had both guts and style. He appeared at dinner in a kilt. When the tittering had finished and the taunting began, he acquitted himself in excellent French by a discussion of the introduction of trousers to a colonised Africa which had every reason to hold them in abhorrence. The tightness around the balls which prevented the free flow of air so necessary to scrotal potency, the absurd increase of heat and inhibition of freedom of movement. Fergus had come down after completing Classics at Cambridge, and was taking two years off to travel before entering the Inns of Court. All these people were to become terribly important to me over the next eighteen days. In such circumstances intimacy grows like a protective tree. I came to know their abilities to bear the unbearable, their pooled possessions, their books, the bibles of travellers: *A Hundred Years of Solitude; Du Coté de Chez Swann*: some geological texts and *Il Decamerone* for the Damianos, Le Carré, my own copy of *The Interpretation of Dreams,* lugged everywhere more frequently than Freud had revised it; and for Fergus, *Heart of Darkness.*

Monsieur had by now completely replaced *Citoyen.* The formal address was followed by first names. A system seemed to have been established, still confused by the French use of *tu* for intimates, children, inferiors, and moments of affection. The tutoiement made it impossible to tell whether you were being emotionally embraced or insulted. The police insisted on their *vous* and *commissaire,* but the secret police were more ambiguous. *Professeur* became formal, Monsieur *Noël* intimate. The civilian passengers, who were in any case mostly wives and children of the Police Speciale, had already decided I was 'Father Christmas' because of my beard, medicine chest and brightly labelled canned food. *'Jour, Père Noël, ça vas?'* they cheered as I wandered down the second deck. 'I am making you a mask.' On one dawn promenade *le Commissaire* greeted me with a nasty smile.

'I see Christmas is coming early this year.'

At night the music got wilder and the beer was cool. We soon had a lot of Zairian friends. While I was in full discourse on the roof of the *Lokokele,* French peppered with manageable Swahili words such as *Simba* and *Jumbo,* and helping a group of Zairian *jeuneshommes* solve the world's problems, they pointed out to me that the *Ebeya* was slowly backing away into the distance. What? With all my things and dinner on it? I raced down and was about to take a leap onto the edge of the stern, but was mercifully prevented just as the cables were pulled away. Jeppe told me later that Trudeau was seeking a safer passage into Isangi, because on the trip up the *Ebeya* had grounded near this spot for five days.

Ah bon. I could see the funnels drifting away among the silhouetted trees. *Au revoir, mon colonel.* The *Lokokele* served dinner to its second class passengers. Bryan generously queued up, shared his stew and offered me a joint. If the barges had caves of ice, they also harboured an entire holdful of ganja. Many passengers and crew were smoking quite nonchalantly. Some, from their red eyes, also constantly. I hadn't smoked dope for years, and couldn't then; especially when there were brawls breaking out. One of the stall-holders accused a boy of theft. Amid a lot of cuffing and screaming, he was chained to a pipe. I was glad when the *Ebeya* returned. It was now pouring with rain. The wet thief chattered.

Manoeuvering between Isangi and Basoko was a task of great complexity for Captain Trudeau. I joined him on the bridge and lent him my night binoculars. The banks had shifted because of the rain. We took a smaller but deeper tributary which rejoined the main river after about five kilometres. On Wednesday, seeking the best passage, we sometimes got so close to the shore that overhanging branches made a clean sweep of passengers on the *Bangala* and transferred them and their chattels onto the *Mangbetu*. A few lacrosse piles of reeking baby antelopes and monkeys were consigned to the depths.

Unexpectedly the tree canopy would clear, and from the banks one, two, three, a dozen pirogues dart out. Simple dugouts, some as big as the forty-foot trees they had recently been, they had astonishing speed and accuracy. Frantically paddled by six or seven men, steered by another holding a pole at the stern, they zoomed at the boat, the man kneeling on the prow straining all his muscles to hurl the coiled liana rope onto one of the barges.

These men were hunters, their villages no more than a few round huts in reeds by the shore. The pirogues were laden with living and recently killed prey, heaped, inert or struggling, piled over their own desperately knotted bodies as they dug at the water to reach the ship. If Trudeau was certain of his navigation – or, as I discovered, if Kissinger was greedy for particular booty – he would generally slow down. The men, arms, legs and backs corded with exertion, would be hauled aboard with wails of triumph, and trade commence. Along the lengths of the river, these men and occasionally women with gigantic gourds, would watch for the smoke and listen for the horn of the riverboat. Like pirates, they prepared themselves for the attack.

Sometimes, even at the last moment, they missed, failed to connect with the rope, were dashed against the walls of the ship, capsized, floundering, their animals tumbling into the river, raising arms, and voicing unheard shouts as we glided on. Today was such a time. Trudeau was preoccupied with his channels. The pirogues more often than not crashed into the sides of the *Ebeya* and overturned. A few hardy and determined people swam, grabbed at the boat and were hoisted aboard. At the next village, with people who were often their deadly enemies repeating the ritual, they were discharged back into the pirogues.

Slowly the *Ebeya* stuffed itself with crocodiles, enormous fish, monkeys of every variety, deer as big as horses. Trudeau, his brow furrowed, pushed on. Kitty was a frequent visitor to the bridge. Squealing, whirling golden hair, she distracted Trudeau, who indulged her because of her attractive spirit. When I joined them with Polaroid sunglasses that could detect the colours and shades of the water, he abandoned himself to our dubious assistance. Kitty's French was English schoolgirl accented, but grammatically perfect. Trudeau was slow and deliberate. Unlike Kissinger, he conveyed an impression of decency, and genuine affection. Kitty and I made him laugh. He relaxed. He used the Polaroids and the night binoculars with gratitude. He humoured us and allowed us on the bridge whereas Biharzi and the purser were clearly resentful. He was the first to notice that Kitty's ebullience was actually the result of fever. She twirled round the wheelhouse. When she fell, the midshipmen helped her to her feet and she continued raving about her love for Africa. When she collapsed in a sweat, Trudeau was the first to feel the pulse in her temples, and suggest she go to bed.

'It's just the flu,' she pouted, and outlined her plans of buying a canoe and going down the tributaries to Zambia. Trudeau was now so intent on the depths and colour of the water, which I too could see through my glasses, blue, green, yellow, black deceiving shelves, that I left him to it. A short while later we anchored in the middle of the river, cutting the engine. In the silence, ravens cawed from the forest, and something else made a miaouling sound as if it wanted to come out to the boat. Night fell quickly. The Cross and the Scorpion strung the sky.

Madame Celeste was one of the few middle-class civilians. She had been to Kisangani to visit her sister and mother, and was returning to Kinshasa. She was a pleasant woman with a girlish giggle and the only one besides Fergus, myself and Monsieur Dubrois who ordered wine at dinner. In the Kisangani markets she had brought a Minolta camera which she couldn't load or operate properly, and which for all I knew was made out of a recycled clock. From watching me film she was convinced I was a photographic genius. Everyone teased her with bawdy jokes because she was travelling without her husband. She took it all with more giggling, and was also kind and shy.

Like me she hung over the rails to get shots of the pirogues, and within a few clicks would murmur, 'O Dieu! C'est pas juste.' As the mechanism jammed again she would soundlessly present the camera to me, flustered but confident.

'It's your fault for taking all those pictures of Monsieur Kissinger having a shower,' I said. Her turban and breasts shook as she pealed with laughter and wagged her finger.

'O M'sr Noël, vous êtes méchant.'

Madame Hortense, whose figure was even more ample and expensively dressed, and whose preferred beverage was rum and cola, was more of a problem. She stalked me at twilight and became nightly more amorous. 'I love you,' she boomed, leaning over the ship's rail like some enormous Bette Davis. We would stare off into the distant shore, lit by a rising moon. Now, *Voyageuse!* was her motto. One night she invited me to come and make love on the roof. Fortunately, despite her insistence and pleas for just one kiss, I declined. The next day I met her husband and four children. He was a plain-clothes policeman.

'You told me you weren't married.'

She blew out her lips. 'Tulla Tulla.' Which means roughly, 'Frankly, my dear Mazungo, who gives a damn?'

He did. The next day she had a black eye. In fact, as I got to know the people in the other cabins on my morning strolls round the decks, when most would be sitting leaning against their doors, I noticed that many of the women had cuts and bruises. Their kids would be playing chalked board-games with coffee beans. The women rolled banana leaves, or washed caterpillar grubs in wicker baskets.

A young woman on the top deck who always greeted me today swished her head briefly and then hid it in her basket of caterpillars. On black skin purple looks almost like cobalt, and I thought at first it was cosmetic. But I could see that her lips were split open and her ear had fresh blood on the lobe.

'Toinette! What happened? Who did this?' She looked up and whispered, *'Lui.'*

I knelt down. 'Who?'

She shook her head.

'You should go to the doctor.' There were flies buzzing round the ear. 'That must hurt.'

She started to rock backwards and forwards and then burst into sobs, which she sucked back as she pushed out each phrase. 'My head hurts so much,' she repeated, while the children kept playing, brushing away the grubs that escaped onto their gameboard.

My medicine kit was stocked with painkillers, bandages, iodine, tweezers, clamps, and drugs of every description: benadryl, immodium puritabs, antibiotics. I came back with it, gave her two Panadeine, gently washed the ear with iodine and stuck on a band-aid. For the bruises I left her some cotton-wool and a precious ice-cube.

'Who did this?' I asked again.

'Him,' she sobbed. 'Kissinger.'

I stormed back to the cabin.

'An accident?' asked Jeppe.

'Kissenger has bashed Toinette! You know, the woman

above us. I'm going to tell the shit what I think of him.'

'I wouldn't,' said Jeppe. 'She's his wife. One of his four wives to be exact. Don't get mixed up in it, you don't understand Zairian society. Really. I assure you. The other wives are just as likely to hate you for it. And so is she. And if anything goes wrong with what you've done to her, they'll accuse you of sorcery. Really, take my word for it.'

I did. The wounds healed quickly, her headache vanished, and instead of being cast as a sorcerer I acquired an instant medical degree. People came with cuts, which were common for bare feet on uneven iron decks, and for pains in every imaginable portion of the human body. At first I protested. There was a ship's doctor, but he refused to emerge from his air-conditioned cabin even for meals. I banged several times on his steel door with a patient in tow; there was never a response. Jeppe as usual had the answer. 'He's an alcoholic. A real alcoholic. He has a clinic on the end of the *Wema* and he does what he can down there. But forget it.'

I asked the Belgian boys. They were, after all, nurses. They confirmed Jeppe's advice. 'Besides, the Zairians hate Belgians. They just want us out. If we touched them, they'd throw an epileptic fit.'

'In Zaire, what you're seeing is nothing,' Jeppe added. 'The doctor wouldn't even bother with it. Be careful. Once word gets round they'll use you like a treasury. Half of it's psychosomatic. They'd be better off having a puff of ganja. On the barges they sell every drug you can imagine. And syringes. They'll use up all your medicine. Give them vitamin pills, if you've got any.'

To my shame, I did. I hope vitamin C did no harm, and I was sparing with the bandages if their wearers were going to keep them wet. Otherwise, I had plenty of iodine, and despite Biharzi's malevolent glare I enjoyed the affection that greeted me round the ship, and the bandages displayed like gifts. In return, two of Toinette's daughters plaited and shaved my beard as relaxedly as they sat and formed each others' hair into delicate and intricate geometry. It took hours and was like a massage. 'Ah, Monsieur Noël's found some slavegirls,' commented the commissaire.

Jeppe disembarked by pirogue at the tiny port of Basoko. His father was waiting for him at the dock in a jeep. Kissinger went down to say formal *adieux* and staggered back with a portable television. The rest of our cargo was less processed. Logs, squashed mongoose in wicker rackets, like dreadful mummies that might be uncovered from the bowels of the Ashmolean, blue monkeys as large as mastiffs, freshly dead, carried by their tails with blood dripping from their mouths. Maggots like Toinettes' crawled on the deck round sleeping mats.

Basoko was an unprepossessing town. No one showing ostentatious signs of wealth had embarked. Bryan turned the water-hose on us, which didn't please the Zairians. Fergus appeared with some bananas and a live baby chimpanzee. We gooed over it and took it and the bananas up to my cabin. Kissinger was onto us like a blowfly. '*Ah messieurs et mesdames les européens se jouissent de la nature.* But ... no animals in the cabins.' After a brief riposte by Kitty about the number and variety of wild-life all over the ship, Kissinger held up a fat admonitory finger, 'In the first class cabins.' Kissinger was right about the animals. They had lice, ticks, fleas and could have given us rabies. But his real purpose was to fill the other bunk in Cabin 8 with as much expedition and extortion as possible.

Fergus disappeared with him, leaving Kitty to try the bananas on the chimp. Feeling its little fingers clutching our own, we mashed the bananas and soaked some bread. It smacked at the results as carefully as a baby. It turned its big eyes from one of us to the other. Fergus filled the doorway. 'Congratulate me. I'm a citizen first class. Mind you, the bastard made me pay the full fare from Kisangani.' My good mood broke. I had hoped Kitty might have taken the cabin, and Fergus, despite his wit, was intrusive. But we had a bottle of iced beer to celebrate, since Basoko had the only purified ice machine between here and Bumba. For a small fortune Kitty purchased the chimp from the man who had followed Fergus aboard. She put it tenderly down the front of her dress and took it back to the barge. Fergus lolled. '*Oh Saint-Esprit,*' he sighed. 'A pillow. Tell me, don't you find your fellow Australian a trifle naif?'

'About what?'

'About the chimp, for example. *Les noirs* will keep on killing chimpanzees and bringing us their babies till the jungle is empty and we get to Kinshasa. Kitty will play mother and we'll all turn into Mr Kurtz. Remember Conrad.' He fished the book from the sporran of his kilt. 'Here's a good passage for you:

"'The wilderness had patted him on the head, and behold, it was like a ball – an ivory ball; it had caressed him, and – lo! – he had withered; it had taken him, loved him, embraced him, got into his veins, consumed his flesh, and sealed his soul to its own by the inconceivable ceremonies of some devilish initiation.'"

I swung round. Everything he said filled me with a shadow of superstitious dread. It was like mentioning Macbeth in a green room.

'Listen, Fergus. You bought the chimp onto the ship. You know Kitty's soft-hearted. Furthermore she's not Australian. And if you're going to share a cabin with me you can shove your copy of *Heart of Darkness* exactly where it belongs, up your Stygian English arse.'

'I'm Scottish,' sulked Fergus 'Anyway it's my cabin too. And I douche frequently.'

A confetti shower of moths floated and drifted over the boat, apparently endless and innumerable. The rain forest was a hundred feet tall right down to the river's edge. Palm fronds peeped from the covering cloth of vines. Giant podocarpus trees soared above the canopy and hung their great heads. Islands dotted the river, some a size to host Lilliputian villages of straw, some with sandbanks trailing for miles before they burgeoned with green. The water surface was here crinkled, there as glassy as a mirror.

Captain Trudeau stayed at his wheel, carefully navigating

the sandbanks, steering between clumps of floating lilies and hyacinths. Each night as the sun went down before us on the river's horizon, as it would on a sea, he was especially vigilant. Some of those clumps were drifting faster than we; some could themselves be anchored to a shallow bottom. Now and then the rainforest canopy fell back; a stretch of beach appeared with neatly cropped grass and shrubs behind that could almost have been a golf course. The moths continued their magical float. If you went on deck, blue and brown butterflies landed on your nose or forehead, glued to the sweat. They were everywhere, flickering against the boughs as if considerate deities had covered the rainforest with tarpaulin.

No such deity was operating in the cabins. Half the bed of the Congo seemed to come up every time anyone had a shower, and after the nightly troops of filthy *Mazungu* used it, our neighbours complained. The bath was blocked. The toilet wouldn't flush. They muttered. That's the trouble with having whites living opposite you. It's all right if they're only a couple. But when they invite their friends, living standards hit the rocks.

On Friday I was up before breakfast. There was a commotion on the *Mangbetu*. A floating town was dealing out summary justice to a thief with stones and a machete. He was screaming and knocking over people's things, which made them hit him more. The machete frightened me, and I stayed well back, remembering the outskirts of Goma, and the boys walking towards me, starting to slice at the grass. The thief, pursued by his attackers, ran onto the *Ebeya*. The spectators were jostled. We followed. He stumbled up to Trudeau's wheelhouse for sanctuary, but was ejected. Bloody and trying to protect his head and his genitals, he howled:

'Ah, Jesu! Jesu!'

'What did he do?' asked Fergus.

'He stole a duck,' said Kitty.

'What? Without oranges?'

We laughed involuntarily.

'You're not in the Savoy now, Fergus.'

MEKONG II
Angkor Wat

From the roof of the Hotel Monorom, one of the temporary safe places during the Khmer Rouge evacuation, you can imagine this city silent and empty except for those final few who thought themselves preserved from death. Even now, on its main street, it is mainly the tinkle of bicycles that reaches the Unicef and Oxfam officials settling down to dinner. The killing fields are over the hill, the bones still bound with wire. Infamous Tuol Sleng is around the corner, an ordinary schoolhouse where the cadres tortured each other to death in front of blackboards.

On other rooftops, under the full moon, adolescents are recklessly abseiling on old firehoses. Little girls play hopscotch. Kittens bat, bougainvillea covers the scars of the wounded boulevards. Unlike Ho'ville, there are none of the beggars, muggers and street-sleepers to invoke the tourist's twitch of guilt. Have the Vietnamese hidden them?

As the yellow moon rises high and huge, it silhouettes boys playing football on rail-less balconies over semi-deserted main roads. The children show no fear of space, heights, adults or the authorities. The sign system for adults is different: lack of trust, disturbance of memory, an unease at sunset. Roger's detective novel has a skull on its cover. Whenever it is laid aside some anonymous hand turns it cover down. My Swiss knife left open on a table is stealthily closed by the hotel maids.

Palla, our guide, is thirty-five. She has a fixed smile which reveals one shimmering gold tooth. Forced into marriage, she has never seen her husband since their wedding night. She used to be an English teacher. Her main word is a nervous 'Yes.' She refers to her country as 'Kampuchea', but occasionally she slips, says 'Cambodia' and stutters. Her first European language is French, her religion is Buddhist, and she has suffered personally much more than Tung, her Vietnamese counterpart. Watching them talk is like watching a cat and a dog. Their concepts and cultures totally dissimilar, their hackles bristling with ancient ingrained antipathy, and the need, imposed by others, to get along, they talk in phrase-book English, with 'but' as the principal conjunctive.

Our next guide, Venlap, is the same. He is an amputee. He doesn't want to discuss it. He apologizes immediately for his English, and is happy to seize upon Quiquer and me as translators. He now has two wives, one returned from the dead from two years labouring on a Khmer Rouge farm, and ten children. He ignores Tung. Tung absents himself and reappears, dreaming of his own recent marriage. Already reprimanded for not collecting extra photographs and failing to register us as aliens, his final crime has been to allow Roger and me to get away with our outrageous plans for Angkor. He has faded into the background. He says quietly: 'The man in the white shirt is a Vietnamese policeman. The other two are Kampuchean police. I am asking you to be careful. Can you please speak to the group and tell them?' On planes and buses he has talked to me privately about family pressures to leave Vietnam, to send back the consumer treasures which he imagines America and Australia dispensing from their dragon hoards. He has refused. He loves his wife, he likes his job. When I start to outline the perils of boat-people, refugee camps and divided communities, he nods.

'Yes. They are anti-communist, that is all.'

'Mr Tung, I must tell you that I have visited many communist societies from the Soviet Union to China. None of them works. It is very sad.'

'Then you are a capitalist.'

'No. I detest capitalism. I am a sceptic.'

'I do not understand that.'

Of course not.

We lounge on the steps of the museum, talking to Palla and one of the attendants. Politics are discussed frankly, but in low voices. Patiently they answer our most irritating questions. Slowly it's becoming clear. The Khmer Rouge are alive and well. Even to use the term is like saying 'the French Revolution'. What part exactly do you mean? Saloth Sar's political studies in the '40s? Sihanouk's state of 1975? The Terror of 1976? The disaffected cadres of 1979? Or the guerillas entrenched in the border mountains in 1989? Or round Angkor Wat, the place we're heading?

Our probing continues. Are the Vietnamese vicious colonizers and oppressors of the Kampuchean people? No. Do the Kampucheans wish they'd get out? Yes. Yes. Do the Vietnamese want to get out? Yes. Do the Russians want to get out? Yes. How do you think they feel after the debacle in Afghanistan? Is it possible that after they withdraw, elements of the Khmer Rouge will come back into power? Do tigers lose their stripes?

The scenario sounds gloomy. An eternal fake French Revolution, with Pol Pot as Marat, Sihanouk playing Napoleon III, Hun Sen and Son Sann alternating as Louis Philippe, and the Khmer Rouge filling in for everything from the Commune to Vichy. In the border hills behind Angkor Wat, where we have persuaded Tung to get us a boat tomorrow, factions are stockpiling food and weapons, waiting for the monsoons. They fight best in the wet. It is called leech warfare. Step in the river and you'll feel it. 'There are cobras too, and green watersnakes,' laughs Palla mechanically. 'But I think they will not attack you.' Time to go, to walk down the steps towards the swirling river. We are all feeling the same: the incongruity of this golden light, this mauve foliage, with war.

In the floodwater's swell we assemble to take the ferry. It is a modern Vietnamese military launch and it speeds and bounces up the furious Mekong and onto the lake. Miles of mangroves ripple as our wash submerges them. Fisherman look up angrily because we ruffle their nets. The shores are wide enough for some of us to have brought cassettes to while away the time. The other side is distant and gold. Our tapes are all the same: Haydn, Rameau, Mozart, Albinoni, Dylan. It is to these musics that the silver scales flash in the nets, an abundance of good food from the bounty of this beautiful river. After an hour of gliding to our goal, there is a problem. Tung, Venlap and our new Cambodian guide Tuc are trembling in argument. Tuc nervously indicates our cassettes and points to the distance where the waters lie as flat as a squashed snake. Tung sits beside me, depressed and anxious. 'He is saying that it is too dangerous, that we will be attacked by pirates.' Tuc joins us, also whispering in high-pitched French; Tung leaves.

'Monsieur, that man has not explained that many Vietnamese people have been settled here against our wishes. To Kampucheans a boat like this is a provocation. And you cannot bring those recorders. Cameras, yes. The captain has been radioed by his own superiors. It is best if we take a helicopter and you will eat at the Siem Reap hotel.' The boat turns and speeds to a landing-stage with a helipad beyond.

Even as we fly over the shining waters a melancholy drifts through the group. Travelling has assumed the feeling of urgency, of elegy. We've all been to the great places of the earth, stood on the Great Wall, the temple peaks of Machu Picchu, the Valley of the Kings. We collect small objects of dead or dying cultures; what have we brought in return except our own desire to return to the past?

As you move forward to the five towers of Ankor Wat, that is exactly what happens. King Suryavaram II built this temple-mountain with its moat as a model of the world, a record of kingdoms and Hindu myths, an observatory in which the past would always be present and the future predicted. Each step forward makes the stone wings surround the periphery of the eyes until you become lost in its dream, almost unconscious with awe.

Then in the Bayon, the centre of the labyrinth of Angkor Thom, with giant Khmer faces dimpling down, we nine Western tourists suddenly stop and look at each other. In the stifling heat, we feel an equal chill. A loud, deep, dead explosion has just ripped the air apart. It is followed by rifle fire, and in the hills in the far distance a billow of black smoke. Everyone knows. But we ask the guide just the same. He has started to sweat. 'They're killing mosquitoes,' he says in French. 'Moustiques, mon oeil!' mutters Quiquer. The others turn to me. 'What did he say? What is it?' What the hell do you think it is? We move on through the ancient galleries, shadowed by the Marat-pockmarked police. Boy soldiers in green have their rifles stacked in the ancient towers. From courtyard to immense courtyard, don't walk on the grass. It's full of mines. The only other foreigners, a group of ten Japanese, climb indefatigably onward up the ceremonial steps. Their guide hurries them. We have persuaded ours to spend five hours longer than planned. He has agreed but is jittery. When I produce a battery-driven fan and hold it to my face his eyes widen in terror. 'Is it microphone?' he stutters. I let him feel the cool air. 'Ah.' At least a million Japanese tourists visit these ruins every year. Of course it's safe.

But what if the airport mini–bus has a puncture on the jungle road? We must be out of here by nightfall. The guides are arguing. We are wasting time. At a whisper from Dominique, I again become Group Leader. The phrase seems to have some mystic power, like 'Peoples' Republic'. We want the whole day, and we will leave before night. The Cambodian guide despairs. 'Please explain. Messieurs. I have guided many groups. It is very hot. It is exhausting climbing the steps. There is no shade, no food.'

'Thank you, Monsieur Tuc. We know. That is why we are wearing hats and carrying bread.'

'But not all your people feel like that, perhaps? Could you not order them?' Berthe is sulking and wandering off to pat a buffalo. I try to demonstrate my responsibility. 'Berthe, those fields really are mined. A peasant had his legs blown off on Tuesday. Stick to the guide. Are we agreed?' I ask.

Cambodian and Vietnamese together despair.

By 1.30 pm half the group is seated gasping in porticos where Sprite is sold. Sprite?! The cowards!

My eyes instead are in perpetual movement up the central mountains of stone, rising from the world-ocean of the 160-metre-wide moat. I never want to leave this tower of the four faces. The four aspects of the god-king Jayavarman VII smile enigmatically: mercy, compassion, clemency, impartiality. Everywhere you turn a corner, those half-open eyes are lazily watching, as if it were 1190 and he had just created the final touches to his predecessor's world.

The bas-reliefs, sharper than those of the Parthenon, more fluid than Chartres or Thebes, narrate their history for mile after mile, war after war. Unlike their Aztec or Assyrian coun-terparts, they breathe not so much fierce gloating as fiery pride in everyday life. Buffaloes bear, elephants trumpet, little dogs yap, monkeys curl, the tortoises that still inhabit Tonle Lake paddle. And live geckoes inhabit these stone lions, dart in the nagas' hoods, chirrup from the layered arches. Another rattle of machine-gun and light artillery. But look at that exquisite bas-relief over there. It has an enormous elephant with a sway-ing palanquin seat. I must see it. Isn't that King Suryavarman riding into battle against the kingdom of Cham?

Ignoring the sententious advice I have given everyone else, I charge along the pillared gallery. My Super 8 camera pans, shifts focus; I track with it. I pull out the Polaroid for a close-up of the court acrobats balancing on their cartwheels. And before I know it, I am overtaken. Out of the towers, up from the stairwells, emerging behind the pillars, a dozen men and one woman surround me and tug me around by the shirt. 'Photo. Photo,' they cry. They are snatching at my cameras. 'I am Kampuchean soldier!' one caws; and from a holster on his waist he pulls out a gun and waves it in the air.

'OK. OK. For friendship. OK. Everything OK. No problems. Don't pull. OK. OK. *Pour l'amitié. L'Amitié entre le Cambodge et L'Australie!'*

Goes over like a lead balloon. As I am about to go as well. Because the pediment onto which they have tugged me has a sheer drop of at least a hundred feet. And the self-identified Kampuchean soldier now hugging, or rather heavily patting, my torso reeks of whisky. The others are drunk too. They are all reeling and proudly displaying their guns for the comrade who has been left in the tower to take the Polaroid. The single woman won't come. In response to my beckoning, her face is as stony as the ancient queens of Khmer. Our photographer is also drunk. As we pose, he drops the camera, and it bursts into flash. Safe back on the portico, I take two extra photos of the soldiers, give them over with bows and nods, and run down the steps clutching for support at the rippling scales of the stone snake nagas.

Roger, also an art fanatic, is repositioning his tripod in the flagged courtyard. His stiff English jaw has never looked so welcome.

'What the hell was going on up there?' he says.

'Let's get out of here. Quick. Wave. Smile. *Amitié. Vive le Cambodge.'* Distant sarcastic laughter.

'You think we've deployed our delaying tactics long enough? Enough?'

'Yes, Roger. Enough. Let's just go.'

Count Dracula's castle. Must be out by nightfall. From the corbelled arches the bats are already diving and screaming. The Khmer artillery pulses softly and then explodes.

It is the next day. Persuaded by Cornelius, I have taken a cab out to the killing fields at Cheung Ek. This has been a mistake. Eighty thousand skulls are on display, arranged in piled triangles like the triumphs of the Mayans, or the Scythians described by Herodotus. I feel a jumble of emotions: gruesomely fascinated, appalled, at the same time angry with the Vietnamese for making a show of it, and the Cambodians for being such stooges. I felt equally disturbed on my visit to the waxworks in the Museum of Atheism in Petersburg Cathedral. No longer Catholic, I resented nonetheless the display of Inquisitorial atrocities, which I knew was being done under the name of another 'liberation' still itself an atrocity.

One of the most callow actions I ever committed was to send a Jewish friend a postcard from Dachau saying 'Wish you were here.' Renate thought it was hilarious, but her parents never allowed me in their house again. I've changed since then. But Cornelius is excited. Because of hotel confusions, Palla has found Cornelius and me student digs in town above a shop. Lázló is ill with age and exertion. Everyone is inclined to ignore him, so I have given him my room. Lázló kissed me. Berthe sneered.

Cornelius is still buzzing with the experience at Angkor. 'They were Khmer Rouge, those ones at the end. Did you notice their red-checked kerchiefs? I bet they have a deal with some of the Vietnamese. There's a civil war going on here, man.' He has a proposal. Instead of flying back to Saigon we could travel overland. Last night he met this guy who would drive us for the equivalent of $50 each to the border at Moc Bai. The road crosses the Mekong and there is a ferry. He will do photo-journalism on the countryside for *National Geographic* and I can film whatever I want.

'But that's exactly the route the Vietnamese are taking for their withdrawal,' I point out.

'No. They're going north through Laos.'

'Nonsense. You'll never get an overland visa in any direction.'

'This guy can arrange it. And we could get some great stuff on Battambang.'

For a moment I consider. 'Who will grant the visa? We only got in as a group.'

'The Vietnamese. They run the place, for Chrissake.'

'What will I tell Palla and Tung? They think I'm Boy Scout Leader No. 1.'

'That gives you an even better chance.'

I say no. Despite my protests that Palla and Tung are already in enough trouble, and my unvoiced fear that somehow this will expose Quiquer and Dominique, Cornelius decides to go ahead. Tung tells me that whoever Cornelius has met is either a big secret policeman or a criminal, because the visa comes through. Or perhaps the unknown coachman is part of the groups always vigilant for a hostage. For once I'm glad I could have gone on a great adventure somewhere, but didn't.

CONGO IV

As the Stag to the Waters

Out of courtesy to the others, at dinner Fergus and I spoke French even with each other. Our conversation, which frequently took the form of mild quarrels, dominated the table. Rather than taking malicious pleasure from this, as did Biharzi, Dubrois would listen for a pause between our sarcasms and then push further discussion by questions on our views of history, religion, politics. The rest of the table, rather than using Lingala or Swahili, also spoke polite French. Dubrois considered religion of all kinds part of Zaire's heritage. Where the President had thoroughly won support was in his respect and ceremonialization of his mother, Mama Yemo, just as Christ had honoured his Mother the Virgin. Dubois said this quite neutrally, without a hint of either praise or derogation.

Despite our vociferous differences about colonialism, in which Fergus refused to see any similarity between Scotland and Australia, and instead informed the table that Australians were themselves natural oppressors of blacks, we had sense enough to observe a shared silence about Mobuto. We offered no criticism of Zaire. Instead, like Dubrois, we encouraged discussion of Zaire's diamond and mineral riches, the effects of post-colonialism and civil war, the difficulties to be overcome. It was both diplomatic and dishonest. 'You realise we've probably sentenced Hans and Hendrijk to hard labour,' I hissed after one long dinner in which we joined forces to praise Roger Casement's denunciation of King Leopold II, and his subsequent martyrdom by the English. Dubrois absorbed it like a sponge sifting plankton. When he learned that Fergus and I were ex-Catholics, he told us that we should on no account miss Sunday mass on the *Lokokele*.

On Saturday night there was a wild party which ran the length of both the *Lokokele* and the *Bangala*. Drums, flutes and xylophones played music that drifted up to the *Ebeya* like alluring treacle borne on the air. Zaire is the centre of African music. Even the hip street-rap of Nigeria, the spiritual harmonies of Côte d'Ivoire and the wild and graceful songs of Mali pay homage to its brilliant rhythms. When we gulped dinner and ran down, the celebration was bubbling. The ice-caves were open, and their inhabitants were serving beers by the dozen, as well as palm-wine and glasses of distilled spirits mixed with soft drinks and chipped ice. People had cleared their mats to the side of the enormous room, and those who sat writhed in sympathy on the piles of sacking.

The central space was occupied by a massive human python that bulged and coiled while the music beat down on it. For a second it would tighten into a ball, then split in every direction and lash its tail of outflung hands. Women of all ages formed a swaying, clapping cage, but most of the dancers were men. Every part of their bodies undulated in a wave that passed through toes, calves, thighs, bellies and shoulders up to faces agape with ecstasy. I spotted Bryan rocking in the midst of them. Simonetta and Daniele were twining about each other like an erotic sculpture. The music wasn't just catchy, it was irresistible. I joined in, and was soon swept into the spiral, pumping and grinding in the crush of bodies.

Over the jerking heads I caught glimpses of Fergus bobbing up and down in a highland fling. When Bryan tried jiving he bumped into other dancers and was irritably pushed back. For me, the dips, clicks and whirlings of rembetika are the basis for all entries into the circle of dance. I can whirl, leap, spin. I spun so much that I was soon knocking into other men, who snapped in Lingala and pushed me off. But when I reached the outside of the whirling ellipse, I caught sight of sous-préfet Dubrois. He defused the fiery Zairians and they allowed me back into the riot. When I came out for a drink, he was smiling broadly. 'You dance like an African.'

The day had been oppressively hot, and the stomach of the *Lokokele* seemed to have digested it. Like many other dancers, I squirmed outside to the walkway to catch a breeze, but the air was hot and still. Madame Hortense must have had heat-detectors instead of eyes. Dressed in her best turban and tiger-waisted full frock, she pounced. She wanted to dance, and when I protested exhaustion, she insisted. It wasn't hard to give in. For a large woman in her forties she could certainly bop. She rolled her eyes and hips, ground her pelvis against mine, and when there were disapproving looks, waved merrily at Dubrois, who waved back. She smiled, she shook, she took my hand and let me twirl her under while she preformed mincing steps like a minuet. We got so drunk that only the crush of the bodies kept us on our feet, bending and curling back in waves that passed through the revelling pack like the shudder of one giant body in orgasm.

We were still dancing when the storm hit. The first clap of thunder was louder than the drumming and yelling, which you would have thought could drown out the apocalypse. A few of us stopped and were almost knocked over by the continuing celebration. Wary of being out of control on the barges, I staggered back to the *Ebeya* with Madame Hortense in pursuit.

As we reached the deck lightning flickered like filaments forking in a jar. Then one great bolt hit a tree, which exploded. A torrent of rain, a nuclear wind of rain, swept through the boat. In the *Ebeya's* searchlights the rain was silver like a fireworks display, *eaux d'artifice* and *feux d'artifice* combined. Trudeau had to reform the barges into a rectangle; then a quadrilateral. The *Bangala* started to waltz by itself, the shadows of the dancers carved on the wheelhouse walls. As the rain and wind worsened, we had to cut them loose. There they drifted, out beyond the rainspores, the music still playing, their lights still calling.

Next day the decks were slippery. People grabbed at the railing and each other. The *Bangala* was recovered, her party floor swept clean by the rain. I filmed the Europeans dancing in celebration on the roof. As we neared Bumba, the produce brought from the pirogues became more abundant. Some pirogues had outboard motors; in others, adults and children poled like gondoliers. Tortoises, a blue and green iguana, seething half-gourds of gigantic grubs covered with straw, squealing pigs were hauled over the sides of the barges. Goats, brown, white and black, were tethered to the iron stanchions. More guinea fowl, small antelopes and even smaller gazelles were pressed like fish into wicker plaits. Inevitably two young chimpanzees were immediately adopted by the white colony. The most exotic captives were three green crocodiles. The largest, a three metre monster, was purchased on the spot by Monsieur Kissinger. It seemed appropriate.

The bell rang for Sunday mass, answered by antiphonal bells on the barges. When we arrived, the congregation was already well into the Introit. The priests were robed in green silk chasubles, and had just turned to kiss the altar, a bare table covered with Belgian lace and two candles in saucers. Powerful and pitiful in its centre hung a naked black African Christ of ebony. Acolytes in lace surplices held aluminium bowls. A choir of women wearing bright *kilkwembe,* wraparound fabrics in zig-zag patterns of white and orange, swung and clapped in a semi-circle. Two others shook yellow gourds. The Kyrie began with an *a capella* chorus swaying from side to side and shuffling their bare feet two steps backwards and forward. Four men then punctuated the rhythm with sharp 'pock!' sounds from little tom-toms, and added their bass voices to the clapping and chanting of the women. The pink-palmed hands opened and closed to a plainsong of two descending notes, while about them the rattles and tom-toms wove a three-measured polyphony on the repeated words. *Kembo! Kembo!* Thank you, Lord, thank you.

The celebrant, who was young and earnest, had a bird-like voice that sang as he spoke, betraying his efforts to use its baritone register by running upwards into a melodic boyish chat-

ter. In his full lips French turned into a language whose naturally rising intonation and fluid elisions sprang into rap, not the
pushing deadpan prose of black America, but a metered verse
which jumped a startling scale, exploding with consonants and
snapping off with a regular counter-tenor cry that was both a
question and a quarrel. He reminded us that this was the feast
of Saint Bonaventure, follower of that Saint Francis who made
his theology out of joy. Only love permitted us to enter into
the knowledge of Christ. And Christ did not give the lamb,
but became that immaculate animal. So our souls should sing
joyously with the Prophet, 'Like a stag to the water'.

Immune as I thought I was to the wiles of religion, the setting of the psalm by Palestrina floated across the waters of
memory and made me tremble with longing. The Gospel was
read by one of the young women from the chorus, whom I
recognized as Joseph's friend Professor Aimée. Her voice, more
powerful than the priest's, used a similar scale and made
Matthew's words an address to all on the boat.

'You are the salt of the earth. But if the salt lose its savour,
in what way shall it be salted? You are the light of the world,
and a city seated on a mountain cannot be hid. Neither do
men light a candle and put it under a bush, but upon a can-
dlestick that it may shine to all that are in the house. So let
your light shine upon humanity.'

The Gloria was an even higher chant. The sermon was
exhortative and too long. The second class saloon was packed
and rapidly heating. The congregation let the celebrant know
by beginning to shuffle their feet and again call out the words
of the Gloria in preparation for Communion. During the
Agnus Dei the Holy Ghost sent in tongues of fire in the form
of butterflies which fastened on our foreheads and fed on the
sweat. As we swayed, the priest's hands opened and closed
against each other, four beats to three, syncopating the rhythm.

From this floating cathedral, I wandered to the sound of the
evangelical protestant service on the *Bangala*. The drumming
of a more rapid beat was led by a preacher who stalked the
middle of a circle of nodding people, wagging his finger. The
other whites were also attending both services, Hans and

Hendrijk as usual in the background.

Christopher Marlowe was right, I reflected. 'If there be any God or good religion, then it is in the papists, because the service is performed with more ceremonies, as elevation of the Mass, organs, singing, etc., and all protestants are hypocritical asses.'

I kept these intolerant sentiments to myself. But the others had also been won over by the Catholics' ritual. Simonetta and Daniele were absorbed by the naked black Christ.

'It's like a Michelangelo,' said Daniele. 'You know the ones in the Brera.'

'No, there's another Renaissance one,' said Simonetta. Perhaps Cellini. Completely nude like that. I can't remember where I saw it.'

Both of them collected African artefacts. They had more tact than Fergus, who asked the priest if we could buy it.

The glaring absence was Kitty. We found her huddled in Bryan's bunk. Now she had three chimpanzees. She sneezed continually and apologized. 'This is so silly. But I think, I have had the richard. I'm going to have to get off at Bumba. Captain Trudeau has contacted them by radio. They're going to put me on a stretcher. Isn't that funny?' Kitty couldn't walk. She was so weak that Bryan had brought her stuff down from the roof and given up his bed.

In mid-afternoon Bumba slid into view, a substantial town sprawled along the river. The foreshore was packed with people and waiting cargo. I could see why the villagers upstream had made such an effort to get in first, because the amount of produce on the deck looked like the spoils of an empire. Embarking passengers sat among their baggage and retinue. Sacks and crates were being piled by gangs of workmen into pyramids of heavy nets. Vendors rushed the boat and were pushed back by the police.

Bumba was the entrepôt for the riches of Haut Zaire, and it intended to spread them onto the *Ebeya* and the barges till they were glutted. All night we loaded. Kitty gave last instructions from her stretcher. 'I've sold the chimps to Kissinger. Make sure he looks after them.' She burst alternately into tears and bright laughter. 'I'm not an idiot, you know. Not a complete idiot.' When Fergus put his hand on her golden forehead and said 'Goodbye, baby,' she shrilled, 'I'm not a baby, just get that into your brains. I'm not anyone's baby.' Byran delivered her into the hands of two porters, directed by nuns. I tried to kiss her good-bye. 'Don't. I'm probably ravingly infectious. I'll write to you … I'm really going to make it, you know … I'm not completely crazy, but this is my parents' address just in case.'

I had seen Kitty's passport. She was sixteen. I still think of her, because she wrote me several times, and I was amazed at her capacity to survive and continue to travel. She reminded me of myself at her age. I worried about her lack of wisdom. Perhaps it was rather a question of the faith one has at sixteen, and the morass of sense and caution that all of us sink into as we get older. I also didn't yet know that Fergus had fallen fool-ishly, passionately in love with her. Her first letter reached me in Abidjan.

Hope this finds you well and happy and with all equipment you started with! I write to say thanks for your company & use of cabin on the boat! Wasn't it great? Well, with the 'flu it took five days back to Kisangani, where I finally put the canoe trip together! Yes, it worked out! – it was the time of my life. I really hope you enjoyed the rest of the trip on the boat and got the shots you wanted (& kept them!) At the end of the river trip I tried to catch up with Captain Trudeau and the *Ebeya*, but there was a general strike and all Onatra boats were recalled to Kinshasa. Rumour has it that Kissinger was sacked for embezzling, but who knows! In Zaire anything can happen! I'm now headed for Zimbabwe & on to Botswana. Very much hope that Zaire doesn't have civil war over the elections, as Kinshasa was in turmoil when I got there, and I want to go back!

Anyway, Noel, happy adventures.

Big cuddles,
Kit

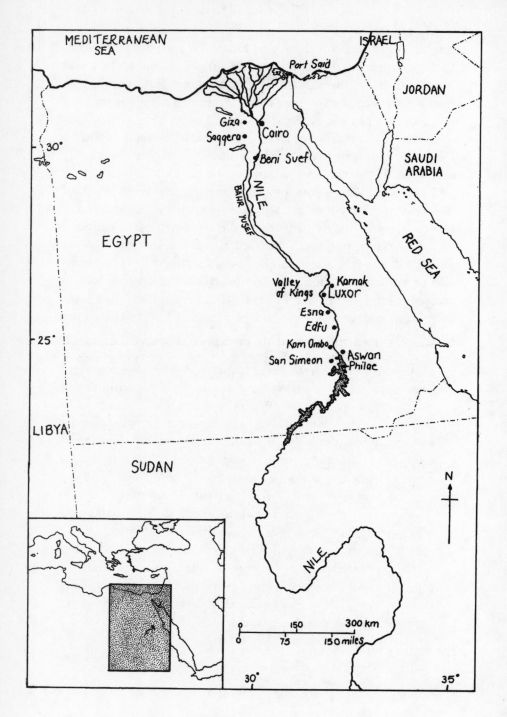

MEDITERRANEAN
SEA

ISRAEL

Port Said

JORDAN

Giza
Saqqera
Cairo

30°

SAUDI
ARABIA

Beni Suef

NILE

BAHR YUSEF

EGYPT

RED SEA

Valley
of Kings
Karnak
Luxor

Esna

Edfu

25°

Kom Ombo
San Simeon
Aswan
Philae

LIBYA

SUDAN

NILE

N

30°

35°

150	300 km
75	150 miles

NILE

NILE I

Of Karnak and Kings

The Nile is the longest river in the world; 6,690 kilometres of its waters fed farmers and tormented explorers until they found its unexpected source far below the Sudan in the mountains of Uganda. This parent of rivers took me to her amorous breast in 1963 when, ignoring all sensible advice, I inspected a shadoof, an ancient water-raising lever, and fell in. How delicious she was, cool and dirty, and how welcoming, despite my shipmates' apprehension when they joined me in her embrace. Our ship the *Neptunia* was jammed in one of the Suez Canal's perennial arguments. For Australians on a long voyage to Europe this was unexpected party-time. We were given a date a week later on which we must re-embark at Port Said and hired a bus at Suez to roam around the Nile.

You can't do that any more. But in 1963 the captain, relieved to be out of Massawa with a complement of expelled Italian settlers safe and sound except for the occasional stoning, made no objection. While he crawled through the canal, we revelled about the desert, the reeds of the Delta and the souks of Cairo, and were ferried aboard just in time to see the lights of Port Said usher us into the Mediterranean. So I knew a little about Egypt and I had always longed to return.

Twenty-three years later I was with friend and fellow-lec-
turer Shane McNeil enroute to the Venice Film Festival. We
had allowed ourselves one special excursion. What better
chance for a stopover in Cairo and a journey down the Nile?

At Giza, happy to sit with an essential mineral water under
an awning, I switched on an automatic pilot that calmly
repeated 'No, thanks' to anyone who approached with offers
of rugs, drugs, girls, boys or hermaphrodites. From the shade
I watched Shane enter the side door of the pyramid Khufu,
the robber's entrance above the seal of 4,500 years. And I
remembered what had happened in 1963.

We had been crawling up the long, steep corridor, its roof
so low that standing is impossible. Someone further up had a
fit of claustrophobia; they must have been within reach of the
Great Gallery leading another fifty metres to the King's
Chamber when blind unreason caused total loss of control.
The feeling swept back along the line. Choked inarticulate
noises became cries. Everyone shifted uneasily and tried to
turn to see how many people were behind them. The shaft was
jammed. From above came thudding sounds, squeals of pain as
fingers were crushed and faces bumped. The source of the
panic could be seen in a flashing hydra of arms. Voices in several languages protested and tried to reassure. But the unfortunate woman who was the subject of the attack had only one
objective – to get out; and she scrambled and sobbed and
crushed people against the wall until some sensible voice fifteen bodies above shouted that everyone below should start
crawling back to the entrance. It took fifteen sweaty minutes
of terror before we got out and another five before the dishevelled woman, her arms flopping and her face purple, was delivered into the arms of the guides. Children were crying, and a
man had his glasses smashed. A brave few began to enter the
corridor again. There was more space now and we all made it
to the centre, breathing the cooler air of the chamber and its
empty sarcophagus with gratitude before waiting for the shaft
to clear so we might descend.

I had no desire to do it again. While the others gave them-

selves claustrophobia, I plotted our itinerary. The source book
I carried was heavy but worth its weight in Tutenkhamon's
gold. It was an atlas of Ancient Egypt by my old friend from
Florence, John Baines, now professsor of Egyptology at
Oxford. Instead of obediently racing through a pitstop course,
we would relax and see the unusual, the difficult, the forbidden. Emerging into glaring light, Shane did a Mel Gibson lap
of honour from the base of the Sphinx to the Great Pyramid
in patriotic memory of *Gallipoli*. It made me think of my
grandfather Murray Macmillan's last sepia postcard showing
the same scene.

> 'To my dearest. The nurses here are swell but they're
> never as pretty as you are, my darling Jess, the Flower
> of Dunblane.'

Shane was quicksilver. He sipped experience and let it irrigate a receptive mind. His playful ability to switch roles kept
us in a state of such exhuberance throughout the journey that
we barely noticed the heat and irritations that often make travellers intolerant. I felt familiar enough with the Arab world,
and excited about seeing more of the Pharaonic one. The most
archaeologically important river on earth was amazing as we
flew directly above it; green to the left and later a range of rid-
dled mountains, brown to the right, a bolt of wrinkled silk in
the middle.

Within an hour we were in Luxor. Clean air, good dry
heat. The HS *Hotp* was waiting near the old Winter Palace. Its
compact size meant that we rapidly met our fellow passengers.
There was Dave McIntyre from Maroochydore. His wife
Marilyn wore matching Hawaiian shirts and shorts and was
disposed to be friendly. Each time she tried, however, Mr
McIntyre advised her to keep her nose where it belonged. Our
closest friend was Jacqui, a cultivated woman in her twenties.

But our Jewel of the Nile was Desmond. Desmond dressed
with the misplaced attention that makes all unconsciously
laughable people lovable. He turned up for dinner in sports-

clothes preserved from the sixties, buttoned into the wrong
hole of the only two possible. His daywear had different depic-
tions of the word AUSTRALIA, flourished across wattled bars
of music or unevenly printed as if with a child's crayon. But his
favourite outfit was a T-shirt printed with a boxing kangaroo,
a white towelling hat and a snug pair of yellow stubbie shorts
which displayed his perfectly bandy legs to advantage. He was
one of those people who enter a room and instantly pull off a
light-switch, debonairly shake hands with a woman by grabbing at her breasts, or tear holes in the lining of swimming
pools with their nose. Because he liked leaning familiarly
against statues while Jacqui took a shot implying he'd just had
a schooner with them, we daily expected to hear that he had
toppled a colossus of Rameses II.

His camera-tote bore a set of accessories which zoomed,
flashed and had to be individually wrapped in aluminium foil
after use. Convinced that everything he was doing was illegal,
he was both circumspect and courageous, kneeling inconspic-
uously on the ground like an alert squirrel while he raked
his bag, or stalking an obelisk with eyes darting nervously
and mouth ready to proclaim that it was all research for the
annual Cronulla Egyptian Pageant.

As a photographer Desmond had the knack of capturing
everything but his subject. His slide evenings are probably
accompanied by commentaries such as 'Blank sky near Karnak
with departed Ibises'; 'Tourist policeman concealing statue of
Ra'; 'Kiddies' hands curious about my Nikon at Edfu' or 'Abu
Simbel: plane's wing.' One certainly said 'Rare tree – cobra's
egg, Aswan,' because Shane found half a ping-pong ball on
Kitchener's Island and mischievously planted it in a date-palm.

At lunch we met our guide. Mustafa Said was an archaeology lecturer at Cairo university. Tall, thin, with a neatly
clipped moustache, his reserved presence conveyed the message that he was our source of information on antiquities, not
a shepherd or a head-counter. I asked if he knew John Baines.
He looked down and acknowledged the connection with professional probity, commenting that his work on decipherment

was highly regarded. Jacqui and the others borrowed the book. I told them that even at university, John used to make an ordinary car-drive a linguistic discovery by interpreting the license plates of the cars in front. This impaired his concentration on the road, but built his Middle Kingdom vocabulary to conversational level. 'Mmn … look, there's *HRW, Horus.* I wonder if these drivers are part of a cartouche division. Gosh, this one's local. *NKK III: You fuck all the time.* What a shocker.'

It was 8.00 am at Luxor. Shane and I were standing in the ferry packed to the rails with other tourists and bicycles, stuffing our faces with cheese, eggs and rolls pinched from the boat's buffet, determined to be first on the waiting Pullman to begin the tortuous journey round the Valley. I'd been warned about the sepulchral traffic jams in the Valley of the Kings. 'Don't even both with Tutenkhamon. It's a five hour walk through an empty cellar.' Armed with a torch, figs, dates, photocopied maps and six bottles of mineral water, we were set for underground operations. Ten tombs were on our hit-list of Kings, with a contingency for five Queens and Nobles.

We found the track that led to Seti while our fellows dutifully queued for hours to get inside Tut. Rameses IX gave the first taste of the long deep descent to the burial room, the Book of Night watched by Nut drawing the mummy's boat through the skies. At the tomb of Meneptah we flew down corridors themselves flying with vultures. Rameses VI and Amenhotep were deep and tricky, with fake chambers and sunken pits. Everywhere were clustered stars and animal-headed gods leading us deeper into the underworld. Seti I was the longest and most thrilling, with entire pillared halls and yet more steps that seemed to be tunnelling all the way under the Nile towards Thebes.

Back on the bus we drove north to the Temple of Hatshepsut, dazzled by the mighty approach to the causeway and triple terraces, and the brilliant use her architect lover had made of the landscape's cliff-bay theatre, so that the whole complex would look across the river to Luxor. Another fifteen minutes in the bus let off those who wanted to go back to the boat for lunch, but we stayed on till it wound further south to the Valley of the Queens. And there, after assuring Mustafa we would hire a donkey and make our own way back before nightfall, we spent the rest of the afternoon exploring. The Ramessid tombs were hidden and almost deserted. They have the most audacious combinations of colours, swathes of black and white and red. The torch gave an eerie sense of discovery in the dimly lit corridors, where giant jackals suddenly bared their fangs in its beam. We saw more tombs than Lord Carnarvon. Shane and I chanted ritually:

'Can you see anything?'

'Yes. Wonderful things.'

Everywhere the images took their forms from the great texts of the Book of the Dead and the Book of the Gates. These sources of the iconography of the dead person's voyage through the underworld were also ordinary calendars of the progress of the night. The goddess of night was Nut. Attended by her hand-maidens, she had been the object of our fascinated gaze throughout the subterranean day. Now it was night in our world as well.

Evening stood on tip-toe. When Venus appeared behind the after-glimmer of the dying sun, Nut arched a sinuous back. Her calves and thighs tightened with a generous display of nudity that led to her unreachable sex. Taut and stretched, she bent her lovely hips; offered and still denied the earth's desire to meet her. Tomorrow perhaps; too late now, because she curved her buttocks further upwards and used the balance to lean forward into night. More stars appeared and rode her thighs: Betelguese, Aldebran, the Pleiades. They marked the muscles where they tensed, femoralis into gluteus. When she was sure the sun was darkly disappeared, she gave one last voluptuous sigh and vanished; vanished herself and left instead an imprint that men might read and lust and fear. The Milky Way traced the invisible curve.

We lay back on the roof of the boat and abandoned ourselves to the spaces above. As the goddess arched her starry body over the earth, the boat of the sun sailed up her legs into the realm of death and down her extended arms into the dawn. Seen on its outer spin was Sagittarius, firing his arrows from the centre of the galaxy

This was the way the Old Kingdom people watched the skies and waited. Tonight was near the new moon, perfect for viewing. One of my most treasured travelling gadgets is a slid-ing circle from which the position of the stars may be calcu-lated in every season and every latitude in the world. Through the foot-long 12x80 binoculars it was possible to pick out all sorts of nebulae. We sat wrapped in blankets, and I showed Shane how to travel down the Milky Way to Orion and his belt. Shane's cries of 'Wow!' as he found the Great Nebula made up for the weight of the binoculars in our luggage.

At Karnak that July night two thousand years after the Egyptians first displayed the constellation of Leo on their domes, the unmistakeable form of Sirius blazed. I guided Shane's eyes away from Orion. And there it was: Alpha Canis Majoris, a brilliant white giant quite near the Earth, brighter than the planets. The Dog Star was rising in the sky. The inun-dation of the Nile came with regularity each time Sirius/Isis completed her wanderings and returned above the obelisks of Karnak and Kings. And though the Nile was now held back by the Aswan Dam, in the inverted bowl of night she held the memory of her flood.

CONGO V
Forbidden Images

Despite the perils, equatorial Africa seemed to be harbouring tribes of mad white youth who had joined camel-trains outside Cairo, kayaked down the Ubangi, cycled from Bangui, or hitched rides in lorries from Gabon. Beside the thrills came the terrors: devotees of The Lonely Planet ambushed in the midst of serene coast or savanna, turned upon by truckdrivers who a second ago had been their brothers. It could, of course, happen in any continent in the world. It did, and it does, in the national parks of Australia, in the canyons of Arizona, in the drug set-ups of Thailand. Would that have stopped me travelling at that age? Never. And may the young continue to keep their faith in others. But I watched Kitty leave then as if I were seeing Ophelia taken to gather her rue and rosemary.

Her departure was followed by the noise of pulleys lowering barrels of oil. Joseph was perturbed about the amount going off. 'I hope Trudeau's got enough fuel for the boat. It's always hard to get, even in Kinshasa. They must need it here bad.' All night we loaded. Bryan and Fergus went ashore to check on Kitty. She was comfortable and was confident she could get back to Kisangani by motor-pirogue. In an emergency there was also an airport. The black nuns who fussed

91

over her were adamant that she must get to a hospital. Bryan wasn't interested in the nuns; he spent the evening banging his head off in a brothel, and came back with a satisfied grin and lubricous stories. Fergus had wandered off by himself. The other whites on the barges tried the only restaurant as a respite from stews and porridge. Its specialties were stews and porridge. I talked to Madame Hortense, who had a new bruise on her arm, and to Joseph and Aimée 'Luhasa, who were passionate about the future of their country. I had written out for Joseph, as far as I could remember it, the first quatrain of Nerval's 'El Desdichado', which I now gave him.

Madame Aimée was an astonishingly beautiful woman who wore her hair pulled back and coiffured into buns as long and rounded as loaves. There was also something faintly intimidating about her. Perhaps it was because she never smiled, and yet during conversation stared directly into your eyes.

'Joseph tells me you were asking about Zairian intellectuals,' she began. 'Do you know Kabongo?'

I shook my head.

'You should. Ilunga Kabongo. I'll write it down for you. He explains our situation quite specifically.'

'You mean corruption and bribery?'

'Oh, no. It's much more complicated than that. It's the way they are alternated with "good works", both internally and externally. And the worst thing is watching your countries support it.'

'I don't quite understand.'

'Oh, the way the concept of African poverty is actually created and manipulated so that it makes our position impossible. Aid, *quelle blague!*'

I was silent.

'You're a university lecturer, aren't you?'

God, this was like being quizzed by your mother about a broken toy.

'So am I,' she continued, 'in economics. But that isn't your subject, is it? Don't worry. I don't think it's anybody else's either. Especially not at the Fac. It's a complete joke. If you

ever try to teach properly or have a department policy, you end
up in gaol.'

'Has that happened to you?'

'Twice. Then they invited me back and raised my salary.'

'Well, I'm sorry to hear the first, but I'm glad about your
salary.'

'Yes. It means I can afford 5000Z for my boat ticket, isn't
that marvellous? Excuse me a moment. There's that poor idiot
from the bank. He was sent on the same useless trip I was.'

I looked up to see her link arms with the Gomese banker,
who was murmuring, 'It's not fair, you know, Madame. Not a
decent way to repay loyalty ...'

'She's very bitter,' I winced at Joseph.

'She's also very intelligent. She was — they did bad things to
her in prison.'

'Why did they give her back such an important job, then?'

'That's the way it works.'

I could see Biharzi approaching. 'Why does she wear her
hair like that?'

'She's from Shaba. That's the style. It's also where her parents were killed during the time of Patrice Lubumba. Now it's
starting to happen again ...' Joseph suddenly got to his feet.
'Thanks for the poem. *A la prochaine.*' Biharzi continued his
stroll, pointedly looking at Joseph's back.

Glad to have the cabin to myself, I employed the full apparatus of plugs, masks and fans, and went off to an early sleep. I
woke before dawn and had a shower. I know what the bottom
of the Congo looks like, because I have seen it descending on
my head in thick brown drops. From the look of the cabin,
that too had descended to the depths, probably sometime in
the forties, judging by the rippled line on the wallpaper. Every
time I went into the bathroom I felt the threat that one day it
might do it again. On his return Fergus was irritable and irritating. 'Can't you just feel the bilharzia soaking into your
pores? Which reminds me that *le commissaire* came by when
I got back last night. Do you think he was named after the
disease, or the disease after him?'

The boat was completely overladen. On the top companionway, sweating his gold silk robes into shreds, a furious Sous-gouverneur du Zone, already annoyed that he hadn't been permitted to board the previous night, was standing cabinless in the middle of his wives and their six children, and some twelve trunks hauled aboard by his servants. The cheery Kissinger fell on me as he passed.

'Excellence, let me introduce Professeur Noël. He can tell you there really are no cabins.'

'Poor Monsieur Kissinger. Always your fault, isn't it?' I said with a straight face.

The vice-governor shoved back his gorgeous sleeves and wobbled his neck like an old turkey. Eventually, with his habitual legerdemain, Kissinger procured a double cabin on the upper deck, displacing several indignant civilian families who found themselves transported to second class. There the potentate reigned unstably, avoiding the dining-room and insisting on food brought to his cabin by Kissinger's nephew Sammy. Whenever I met him on the deck he acknowledged me with a haughty nod, drew up his sleeves like a surgeon preparing to be disinfected, held his head high and walked on.

'He thinks he's the Prince of all Africa,' Sammy told me, hoisting his little cousin Nehru and preventing his nappy from squirting its contents down my shirt. 'Just wait till we get to Kinshasa. He's in for a big surprise.'

The disrespect towards this eminent figure was confirmed by Madame Hortense and Joseph. 'They will make an example of him. He's corrupt.'

Now the horror stories started in earnest: beheaded French rafters, vanished planes. Hendrijk whispered that six months ago two Belgian boys had been killed and eaten by the Egombe, who were cannibals. Leah was travelling alone because two of her girlfriends were still in hospital in Dar-Es-Salaam. They had been attacked on a beach near Lamu, their rucksacks hacked from their backs with pangas. One had her shoulder-blade sliced as well. Both were raped. Hans told the worse news of all. I knew that the AIDS virus had appeared in the

seventies along the borders of Uganda and Zaire, and had prepared myself for months of living inside a giant condom, if I
dared open one at all.

What I didn't know about was ebola. Like other new viruses, it first erupted virulently just 100 kilometres from this port,
killed entire villages with bloody dispatch, and then spread to
the doctors and nurses, who died as they fled to Kinshasa as if
consumed by something from *Alien*. Had he really seen any of
that? He hesitated. Not the twenty-four hour form. But there
were other strains. And there were occasional cases at Ubundu,
but most of them survived. I developed a terror of contagion;
I wished he hadn't told us. Fergus quoted Pliny. *Ex Africa sem-
per aliquid novus.* Something new was always coming out of
Africa; new life, because viruses too were life; new death.

We prepared to leave Bumba in subdued spirits. God only
knew what would happen to Kitty. The main street lost itself
in the forest a couple of kilometres from the town. Byran had
a terrible hangover, and when I went to see him he was still
sleeping in underpants with a wet shirt over his head.

The river broadened until we could scarcely see the shores.
Even its dark spacious waters had become so familiar that there
was not much to see except the occasional pirogue. Concentration turned inward. At dinner Fergus and I argued in a manner that made even Monsieur Dubrois raise his brows. The
cabin became a pit. From this point on, the sheets, towels and
pillow-cases were never changed, and the stewards dropped all
pretence of cleaning. We did our own laundry and hung it in
the bathroom along with dingy nappies and buckets of soaking
clothing left by our neighbours. The necessity of clicking the
lock on the shared facilities, and arguing about who was
monopolising them, became a daily trial.

But there were new luxuries to compensate. Among the
ingenious merchandise of Bumba were tables and deck-chairs.
The people of Bumba were fine carpenters. Rattan stools,
divans, and kitchen furniture that could comfortably fill an
Australian beach house were sold for the equivalent of twelve
dollars. The chairs were both elaborate and comfortable. They

were providential and welcome. Fergus and I bought a set between us. All day long we sat in them with our feet up on the table. Our lives turned a little from the cabin outside onto the deck. At night the moths and insects threw themselves like paint splashed by Jackson Pollack at the wire-bound lights to form drunken ellipses of yellow and black.

Bridge parties were arranged in the first-class salon. The Africans played a complicated card game called Banda. We told each other stories. Pirogues made isolated attempts to sell their varieties of dried and cured fish, monkeys on spits with their teeth locked in a death grin. I took short bursts of footage. There was a light tap on my shoulder.

'Who gave you authorisation to film the people in the pirogues?'

'What special authorisation do you need for that? I'm filming the whole river.'

'You deny you took film of people?'

'No. The pirogues came into view, and people were on them.'

'Come to my cabin. Bring your apparatus and your documents.' Biharzi dismissed his guard and his women. He spread his table with claw-locked volumes and smaller files of printed and stamped documents, their empty dotted lines obvious invitations for criminal details and signatures.

'So what and where is your permission?'

I produced the form from Goma.

'That is for photographs.'

'It says *filmer* quite clearly. That means more than *photographie*. And the document was drawn up by one of the President's personal bodyguards.'

'Really? What was his name? It appears nowhere on the permit.'

I wouldn't remember the lieutenant's name, having no wish to implicate him.

'He had no such authority. And it certainly doesn't give you license to film naked people so that you can show in your cinemas what savages Zairians are.'

I protested that I had absolutely no intention of doing that; the pirogues appeared and disappeared with such rapidity that I shot whatever was happening.

'Like women with naked breasts?' What big eyes he had.

'It all seemed pretty ordinary to me.' I said.

His real concern was probably that I might have filmed something really barbarous. (As it was to turn out, he must have been planning ahead.)

'Your equipment is confiscated.'

The loaded roll contained the volcanoes of Ruhengeri, the departure from Kisangani, the scenes on the barges.

'Commissaire, these are for my family as a souvenir. They will never be shown in a cinema.' But off it went, along with tripod, light meter, and my permit.

Fergus, Simonetta and Daniele had gathered outside. The Italians were consoling. Fergus said, 'I thought the bit about your family was pathetic. Who would have thought you'd end up grovelling?' For the rest of the afternoon I fumed, milking sympathy from anyone who passed our new deck furniture, detesting Fergus for his mimicry of my abjection, and telling all our neighbours about the injustice. Madame Celeste was alarmed. 'O Dieu, he'll do the same to me.' Kissinger was placatory. 'At least you still have your instant camera. You can take many photos of us,' he beamed.

Daniele and Simonetta had suffered the loss of their camcorder at the Sudanese border. They had been trying to film animal life in a national park which turned out to be a dustbowl.

'Have you noticed that there are no hippos in this river? I haven't even seen a single elephant.'

I assured them that in Zimbabwe they'd see multitudes on the Zambezi.

'But why not here? If they've hunted them like the monkeys and antelopes they bring abroad, they've probably extinguished all the life in the forest.'

'Monkeys are inexhaustible,' said Fergus.

Even then, as Trudeau chose a channel near the bank,

monkeys rippled through the treetops like a wind through telegraph wires.

'Those are mangabey and colubus,' said Simonetta. 'They're natural survivors from here to Gabon.'

The river grew so broad that it was impossible on either side to see its banks. It was like sailing in the middle of Lake Alexandrina, with similar onslaughts by locusts, flies and gnats. After the rituals of lunch and dinner we sat at our bamboo table and drank.

Halfway between Bumba and Lisala we reached a nadir of boredom. I talked with Joseph and his friends Madame 'Luhasa and Jean-Baptiste, who appeared now not to care what they said. Joseph was wearing a Che Guevara T-shirt. When I expressed caution he said excitedly, 'But he was here! Didn't you know that?'

I didn't.

'We have a club at the university.'

'Aren't you worried that Biharzi will identify you as a communist?'

Professor 'Lhosa leant back with her elbows on the rail.

'Biharzi already has all the information he needs. He'd have to invent something not directly political. Dubrois is the source of intelligence on this boat. As long as he doesn't think it necessary, Biharzi won't do a thing. That's how Mobuto works. The police and the army and his private army never know where they stand. He sets them all against each other. Sometimes he simply doesn't pay them for months. That's why they all live on bribes. Then they can be accused of corruption. The person who investigates then himself becomes public and vulnerable to charges of corruption. And on it goes.

'Just north of here the lunatic has built a showplace city with the money he forces ministers to vote him. It's ultra-modern, with television, airports, boutiques. And all around people are undernourished.

'Kinshasa gets worse every week. Even Kisangani used once to be an attractive city. You've seen what it's like now. The roads aren't maintained. People have no way to get their produce to a market except by this boat. A lot simply give up. In Kinshasa people are moving back into the bush just to subsist. It will soon cease to operate as a capital in any sense. Mobuto likes it that way.'

We were interrupted by the sight of Monsieur Dubrois approaching. He took in the group and smiled pleasantly.

'I see the professors have met each other. Well, I won't join your academic discussion. Your hair is charming, *Madame la Professeuse.*'

Lisala floated on hills in the grassy distance. Lisala Gomba it's called, Lisala of the mountains. We woke from our trance. The boat glided on the channel. Compared with the Amazon, which can be monotonously flat for hundreds of miles, the Congo has an infinitely greater variety of scenery. Sometimes it produces marvellous little island roundels turning with the boat and the incessant Mayeno music, like verdant carousels. And though no one who has read Conrad will believe it, it can be an infinitely gentler river. It can even be cooler, as it was here. It flows more slowly and its sloping hills are graced by gentle fairways. A Louisiana mansion announced itself, coming into view like a folly carefully planned by a gardener of genius, graciously set above clipped lawns. The man I was talking to at the window pointed out the palace. He had trained in America, Israel and Germany. Something suspicious about all that.

'Ah, what do you do?'

'I'm the President's bodyguard. I am Ngande'

I didn't tell him about the encounter in Goma. This one wore a revolver. My eyes ran over his stocky body.

'Ah bon.'

Bryan was going out on the town in Lisala, and in his unique blend of infantilism and randiness, announced his intention of *playing in the the trees near that big house*. Lisala had even better brothels than Bumba. I grabbed him and asked if he was using condoms. He dithered. I outdid Father Knows Best and gave him a ream of Ansell Checkmates. By 7.30 pm the mist lifted and we were at berth.

Breakfast. The sun was already higher than the trees. Lisala at 11 o'clock, after the darkness of the night and the jungle, looked beautiful. A grass town laid out with an entire botanical garden of palm trees, walkways and street lighting, it burst into technicolour with another high-pillared mansion taking shape on the peak of the slope. The President, Joseph told me with contempt, was born here.

Once again the shore was reached by a pontoon of rusty barges ending finally with the lower decks of the Colonel's brother ship, the *General Isangi,* which had been grounded, then refloated and moored here for three weeks. The last of the sacks of beans was finally loaded by the sweating navvies. The ship's bell clanged and the barges settled beside their parent.

At the signal for embarkation the swarms poured over the rails, up the planks, dragging bleating goats and pigs. The few wealthy Zairian passengers had almost naked porters staggering after them with steel cabin-trunks sloping down their backs. At the last moment, another hundred people poured over the sides. The police drove some of them back, but most escaped into the alleys of the barges. The foreign colony gathered to watch outside *numèro 8.* Some merciful forest deity had caused Bryan to fall down a hole while stoned and still on the boat, though he had bravely managed to stagger as far as the brothel. The others had sensibly decided not to go ashore and 'play in the trees'. We glided along in the peaceful, overcast morning.

As usual the barges were nearest the shore. Half an hour later from the *Makongo* there was a distant commotion which grew to a roar. When we leant over the side, we saw green-clad soldiers leaping up through the hatches as if practising reverse paratrooping. They were armed with Uzis. We decided to stay away.

Minutes later we could only look at each other wide-eyed as a train of boys and young men, bound with coarse rope around their wrists and necks, were shoved up our companionway with guns pressed to their backs. Biharzi and his men, glaring at us in passing, pushed them down the steps to police headquarters. The thuds and screams lasted for a long time.

Commissaire Biharzi had his uniform on, and so did several of the inhabitants of the cabins around him. They were now unarguably police. The captives were driven, falling over each other, up to the bridge. The police used rhinoceros whips to encourage them. Most were youths and young men, with a few spike-haired women roped in the middle. We watched in horror. The captives moaned and begged, until lashes of the whip drove them up the companionway. Screams followed. One boy suffered two slashes across his face.

Leah and I rushed up to the bridge and were held back at the door by guards. Inside we could see Trudeau handing the wheel over to one of his sailors, and standing stiffly while he was harangued, and in turn abused the stowaways. After ten minutes we were pushed aside and asked to return to our cabins. The captives, roped in a chain, were led past. Unlike the treatment of the thieves, this time no-one pelted the victims with fruit or abused them with stones. We made a rush for the bridge. Trudeau had returned to the wheel. In passionately incoherent French we denounced the police. Trudeau kept his eyes on the river; his face was set and his eyes were weary. He advised us to follow Biharzi's orders and return to our cabins. There was nothing we could do. It was a police affair. Second class passengers had also thronged the decks of the *Ebeya*, and there was a continuing uproar on the barge.

We ran aft in time to see the line of youths and girls, still roped together, marched to the stern of the ship, and with pushes and lashes cast screaming and protesting into the water. The weight of the yoked bodies pulled them over like ninepins. The stern bubbled with the wake of the propellors. Their heads bobbed, gasping and twitching. As we rounded the island they disappeared from view.

'Oh, Noel's exaggerating,' said Fergus, who had only witnessed the scenes on deck. 'Thrown to the Crocodiles by

J.M. Barrie. They were just pushed off … they'll make it back to the shore in a few minutes.'

'I didn't say they were thrown to the crocodiles, Fergus,' I retorted. 'I said I saw them thrown in while they were still tied up. They could drown. As any idiot who's been on the under-deck or looked at the banks knows, the river is full of bloody crocodiles. Maybe we should toss you in to see whether they can stand unwashed Scottish socks.'

'Oh, he is a nasty man. Anyway, who else saw?'

'I did,' said Leah in a whisper.

Simonetta and Daniele were sitting horrified. I asked in Italian if they'd seen.

'Yes. Oh God. What can we do? Doesn't he understand that the greatest cause of death from wild animals in Africa isn't lions or leopards. It's crocodiles.' On the Zambezi a schoolboy had been taken near Livingstone the day before I arrived.

So of course we did exactly what we could do. Nothing. The next port at which we were due to dock was Mbandaka, which boasted a police station, a warehouse, a schoolhouse and a whorehouse. Daniele tried to tell the police, who ignored her because she couldn't speak French. I told the schoolmaster, who sighed, so I gave him my Swahili New Testament. And Bryan told the whores, who laughed.

MEKONG III
Banquet's Ghost

The intrigues of war take their toll. Like Martin Sheen's Marlowe in *Apocalypse Now*, I stare at the ceiling fan with its choppers whirling the insidious attraction of aggression. Lázló the Hungarian came to thank me for giving up my room; he even tried some Italian: 'You behaved nobly'. A strange concept. Perhaps it's because he himself bears an ancient name: Esterházy. The Swiss relief-worker's flat which I have been assigned by the Cambodian authorities is a typical student's room. He has pasted together a photoboard of himself with children, old men; some woman he obviously loves, sitting on look-outs together; smiling for a friend's camera. There are also terrible things: pictures of the dead still chained to their beds in the chambers of Tonle. His bookshelves include Foucault and De Sade, who explained it all. An abjection born of confusion makes me miserable. Khmer Rouge. Khmer Sanguinaire. Tomorrow we are supposed to go to Tonle Sap.

Staring at the fan, I feel despair for humanity. For three days I have been living on rice, salt and mineral water. What can it be like for a month? A year? It scarcely bears thinking about. Everywhere we've been, banquets of delicious-looking food have been prepared, as it to imply that famine never touched this country. But my body and my unconscious have ganged up to play a dirty trick: 'You think you can travel here and EAT, you pig!' I recall the compulsory jolly dinners of Moscow. After one of them I sailed into a chandelier-laden metro and executed a grand jeté which banged my head on the door. As I lay on the floor the guide had said remorsefully: 'Now you see the results of your Individualism.' Who needs Catholicism when the State's moral punishment is universal?

There is a knock at the door. It is Palla, worried that I haven't turned up at the banquet because it will reflect on her. She touches, more than the Thai or the Vietnamese do; gentle frightened touches on the hairs of the Western man's arm: 'You do not come on my tour? Why?' Because I'll be sick. 'Yes.' She has found me in a bath-towel, licking salt from the palm of my hand, and reading Becker's *Les Larmes du Cambodge*. What does she do at the end of the day? Take three valium and have a quiet lie-down in front of the KGB? When her whole body is leaking?

'I do what you do,' she says, 'I drink so much water and I eat salt. Like an animal. Same way as you.'

The war may officially have ended but its hidden reminders are everywhere. From the forest floor at Cu-Chi you can hear nothing but the insects and the honeyeaters. But we know they are somewhere down there, the humps, the blind ends, the intersections. I have already gone under for about 200 yards, led by Private Ny who now stands beside me. Ny was thirteen when he first went into the tunnels. More than slightly claustrophobic, I have declined the offer to be led through even deeper tunnels by Commander Dong. The calm blue day keeps its silence. Suddenly two of the group burst out of a leaf-strewn trapdoor six feet away, spluttering, red-faced, gasping. As the others emerge they are gabbling excitedly, laughing in embarrassment. Like the woman in the pyramid at Giza, Berthe panicked: she reached a dead end, she began to scream and fight her way back over the bodies of the others, who caught the hysteria in chain reaction. They are still panting and looking gratefully at the sky. Commander Dong lived in those tunnels, moved through their 200 kilometres, for three years.

Whatever the Americans thought they had besieged or captured on the ground, these Vietcong moles could literally bypass or undermine. When the Americans brought in sniffer dogs, the 'Cong used pepper. They dragged their wounded to underground hospitals The peasants fed them when they surfaced.

The American dentist is by no means a communist. Certainly he is red, at least in the face; he was the one who got clawed by Berthe. Just possibly because he is also deeply moved by Dong's story, he makes a speech in reply, and asks for it to be translated. He admires the fortitude, the skill and the intelligence of the Vietcong resistance. He shakes Dong's hand and tells him, 'In our whole history the Americans have never fought braver people. Thank you for what you have shown us today.'

Here the forest has grown back. Flying over the Mekong, we see huge areas still defoliated. At least Congress and the American people were able to put a stop to General Westmoreland and presidential madness. But what about the evil lords still among the Cambodians and the Vietnamese themselves? Some wounds are healed. Other bodies will never be pieced together. Driving along these paddy fields, surely I have seen all this before? Wasn't there a naked little girl running screaming towards me, covered with napalm?

No. The avenues of tamarinds are growing back to touch each other and conceal her. Ho Chi Minh bears a strange resemblance to an imagined city called Saigon. At Madame Dai's, from a lotus-sprouting centrepiece that might have been designed by Lalique, steaming delicacies offer themselves: squid stuffed with pork, cellophane noodles, lotus roots, and an extraordinary food which Madame explains is sugar cane coated with pounded shrimp, then baked and roasted. We have only got in by the skin of Quiquer's charm, and the fact that a group of Russians are leaving early. Otherwise you must book days ahead. And it is no nonsense, because this woman is a superb cook. Every lovely salad herb, lemon grass, coriander, basil, Asian parsley, is freshly washed in potassium permanganate by her husband, who is a doctor.

Sarah, an editor of *L'Epicure,* is recovering from the bellythat-walks. But the good smells overwhelm us. This is brilliant cuisine. The wines are French, an easy Bordeaux, and a glowing Côtes du Rhone. Under their influence, Sarah and I eat everything, basil and coriander and shrimp-balls included, and declare ourselves cured of all diseases.

Now Roger is wilting, but he won't admit it because of his background in the navy. He fought in the Falklands War. This has already led to some sharp exchanges between us. Dominique scoffs everything down in perfect Breton manner, and demands more bottles. Quiquer has got into a discussion about aid to children and is lost to all of us except to Madame Dai and her vocations.

She was a republican fighter, a senator; she holds a doctorate in law from Montpelier. Her mother is a licensed cordon bleu cook. The cyclo-rickshaw drivers call her Madame Cat. She looks like a grey creation by Von Sternberg, Dietrich's keeper in some Shanghai mystery. It is rumoured that the elegant serving dishes are bugged. She has lined her tiny restaurant with bookshelves of *Le Droit Civil* in ribbed bindings. Her younger sister, who bears an uncanny resemblance to Chiang Ching, sits sourly at a table in the corner and pretends to do accounts.

Quiquer is committing himself to a fund for orphans, Dominique is merry, Sarah is saying she thinks Fergie is a cow, and that Charles and Diana are both off the planet. Roger is trying to convince us, despite my assurances to Quiquer, that 'My eye' is not an English expression. By the next bottle of Côtes du Rhone, the argument has deteriorated. 'Mon oeil,' says Quiquer, and winks. We all drunkenly chorus 'MY EYE!' Madame Dai is pleased. Obviously the tonal monosyllables mean something completely different in Vietnamese. The microphones, like the food, must be jammed with unexpected condiments.

Sailing five abreast in our cyclos, sated and mellow, we arrogantly take up the whole boulevarde. A breeze hits us from the river and ruffles the tamarinds. We are idle adventurers from the thirties, lazily joking from one carriage to the other. All the horrors never happened.

I have been invited to the opera, where Marguerite has American dollars thrown like acid in her face. She sinks mortified to the stage like a piece of burning paper, curled and black. A red spot freezes her, and a wailing 'Nam rock lament has the audience whistling and reaching for another cigarette. By the end of the second act, Marguerite isn't the only one coughing. *La Dame aux Camelias* has been set in a Sixties Saigon brothel whose decor mirrors the taste in the Presidential Palace: red padded bar, plush curtains, kitsch chairs and mobiles on the wing flats. The Deco lights buzz and hiss to accompany the crackling of the mike system. The large theatre, full to the ceiling balconies, echoes with appreciation. My hostess invites me backstage.

She is one of Vietnam's few woman directors. When I tell her my wife Julie is also a director, she excitedly asks me to sit in at the Drama Academy. The next day, anxious women teachers shepherd in their class of girls, eager for my observations to be relayed to Jules. In pink and white, frail and pretty, they perform fierce martial arts transformed to the weightless dance of apsaras, serene young female spirits.

On the way back from the theatre, with curfew descending along Dong Khoi Boulevarde, a bike wobbles to a halt and two teenagers spill off, The Doors blaring from their transistor.

'You American?' they cry eagerly. Soon I am surrounded by half a dozen freckle-faced fair-headed boys.

'My father American. You American?'

No, kid. I'm not your father. Do you know your father? What's his name?

'My father's name Michael.' Crumpled pieces of paper and cards are produced: Rob Rafelson, Relator, Sacramento.

'My father's name Joe.' Another card: James Gilros, Attorney-at-Law.

'It says your father's name is James.'

'Yes, Joe!'

'And yours is Rob, not Michael.'

A hulk with tight black curls above his polished face says, 'My father American too.'

They're pulling my leg. I laugh. 'No, you can't be American. You must be from Kampuchea.' How ready and forgetful is racism. The boy insists, humiliated, 'My father American. He works for Army.'

Sorry kid; yes, now I see your black drafted father. Poor grunt.

'How old are you?'

'Fifteen.'

'And you?'

'Fifteen.'

And on it goes. Even the one who looks about seventeen is fifteen, and he speaks the best English. As the last bombs were dropped, the last seeds were sown.

The seventeen/fifteen year old walks me back to the hotel, knowing, like the university tutors I invited to lunch yesterday, that he won't be allowed in. After extracting the information most important to him, he shakes my hand in the yellow door-light. He won't have the imaginary fathers of the others, constructed from bits of paper and shreds of documents. He refuses my card. 'You could never be my father. I hate my father,' he says evenly. 'I never want to see him. He was a killer.'

At the bar of the Cu Long Hotel, Sven Nielsen, the local U.N. director of the emigration programme, is sick of reporters asking about AmAsian kids. A journalist from *The Washington Post* is hovering behind us. Sven grabs me firmly.

'Keep talking to me, for God's sake. You'd think the evacuation of Amerasians was the only problem in this place. It's you bloody tourists, too, taking up every available plane seat. Besides, the media obviously haven't the faintest idea of genetics. Through natural selection the kids could equally inherit slant eyes and buck teeth, and those sensationalist bastards wouldn't even notice them. But the result would still be half-American.'

We have another beer and talk about Australia, the upsurge of racism. He tells me that on the steps of Melbourne Railway Station, a Vietnamese has been beaten to death. *The Washington Post* slides in, interviews Sven and asks my name while his photographer pops. He's been listening to everything. He clicks off his cassette and leaves.

'You'll be quoted, you know: "Informed Australian sources say ..." They do it all the time. That's why I'm careful about saying anything at all to them. The guy's scum.' I can see the subbing: Vietnamese Emigration Prevented by Flaring Australian Racism.

Escaping the tour group at last I sail around on my cyclo, visit People's Hotels with ticket-dancer girls, and eat at street stalls. A round-eyed little seraph of about three toddles steadily towards my stool, clasps his legs about my lap, puts his face into mine and strokes my beard. He says something which makes everyone burst out laughing. His mother translates: 'He says your fur soft, like cat.' Maudlin on two shots of Mekong whisky, I hug him tightly, thinking wildly for a second, of adoption. Jules would love that. And afterwards?

Then at the university, they tell me there is a girl leaving for Adelaide. Could I give her my address? Of course. She is brought out from the throngs in the pre-fab classrooms, a young white flower in ao dai. Proudly her teachers write down her address. It is a P.O. Box number in Berri.

'There are any Vietnamese already there?'

I shake my head. 'I don't think so. It's not in Adelaide. It's a little town on the Murray. On the river.'

They beam. 'Yes. We looked it up on the map. River!'

Near a river: her life is guaranteed.

CONGO VI

Prozac for Crocodiles

By the time we were grinding past the islands where the Congo splits into several equally enormous rivers and turns south to the equator, our convoy had swollen into a city of two and a half thousand people. The boats seemed scarcely to move. Several times we started from our torpor and looked at each other as the *Ebeya* groaned and the props churned up geysers of mud.

During lunch, plates crashed, bottles spilled, and we fell against each other as directly below an almighty thump pulled everything to a halt. Trudeau churned the engines. The hull creaked and began to stammer; for a moment the boat seemed to move back slightly. Then with another lurch that knocked the waiters over, a stillness descended over the ship that was absolute. There was another odd sensation. Silence. You could hear the swish of water, the grumbling of iron and wood, a dropped spoon.

We were grounded. The propeller churned sand. We had taken the wrong channel after all, the one channel that is probably called in fluvial mythology 'the Devil of Sandbars', since hundreds stretched ahead, yellow patches in the afternoon sunlight as far as the eye could see. The barges behaved like blind children. Their momentum carried them until they crumpled against each other and their different weights and sizes made some curl around the *Ebeya's* bow, while others howled in protest as they were stretched and racked at the side.

The crew hurtled onto each barge and lowered themselves to the waterline of the *Ebeya*. They glistened and shouted, and managed to pull away the *Wemba*. On other barges passengers were sent into a crisis of damage control. The termites' nests burst open as they streamed or were pushed from vessel to vessel. The *Lokokele* started screaming as she felt the strain on her cables. Captain Trudeau came from the wheelhouse and stood on the A deck watching his crew manoeuvre. We left the salon and crowded round. He was tense, but showed no more emotion than to growl 'S'il vous plaît' when passengers obstructed his view. And what a view. The shoal we had hit was just visible above the water to the stern, far to starboard and miles away from the shore. From bank to bank and straight ahead the river showed a deceptive immensity. Refracted images of trees danced around the edge like flames on a gas-ring. Further to stern was one of the islands we had passed at dawn. The shoal was on a bend. Through binoculars I could see it diving underwater away to the right.

On the port side, where the barges were evidently in deeper water, they continued their concertina. The scene was chaos. The *Mongo* had now pushed the *Wema* almost across the prow of the *Ebeya*. In the process another gash had been ripped in the plates: plantains and broken boxes eddied in the water between. The *Mangbetu* and the *Myanza* held so many fugitives that they looked like Delhi trams, with people bursting out of the compartments at such pressure that they bulged three-deep, clutching each other and twisting their legs to get a grip on anything available. The *Lokokele* and the *Bangala* were at least in no danger of tearing apart or crushing each other. Crewmen, some only in underpants, raced along the decks winching chains round capstans and unlocking walkway bridges. The shopkeepers, fearful of their goods being stolen, had refused to move, as had many women with bundles of baggage in the open saloons. This occasioned a lot of mutual shoving and furious arguments which sounded, in the absence of the engines, like a city block in Harlem on the edge of riot.

Trudeau tried the engines again. The *Ebeya* juddered so much that our teeth chattered. A cut and another surge. The boat rocked. But we were stuck. The crew rearranged the barges, and people surged to reclaim their territories. Inevitably there were more arguments, with little physical violence but plenty of finger-wagging, headthrust oratory, and stand-offs with poles and saucepans. As the passage of people round the townships recommenced, rumour walked beside. We had hit a hippo. Trudeau was drunk. It was a plot by the military to get rid of the passengers on the *Wema*. In fact Trudeau, rather than risking the old diesel tubes or the chipped propeller further, had done the most sensible thing he could. The only other boat of this size on the river was the *Ebeya's* brother ship the *Isangi-Sangi,* and he had radioed its captain to come to our rescue and tow us off. Meanwhile we would wait.

By afternoon in mid-river the heat was scorching. It exacerbated the ill temper on the barges. Volleys of vituperation could be heard crackling like bushfire. We sat in our rattan chairs with towels over our heads, too enervated to talk, waiting for the bar to open so we could at least get a cool drink. Sometimes I heard the whistle of a kite or eagle, but when I dragged myself to the rails could never see it. As evening approached and the sun fell boiling into the water, swarms of mosquitoes added themselves to the giant moths and beetles. Insect repellent was no deterrent to the dense clouds that sucked at ears or eyes; putting on more clothes was impossible because of the heat. We were driven inside, where it was even more stifling. Sheets were soaked and we lay with them plastered like shrouds from forehead to ankles.

Dinner gave some relief because of the air-conditioning. The food was mush; there was little chilled wine or mineral water, only beer. In their need for liquid, everyone got rotten drunk and went back to collapse in their cabins, where at least the alcohol ensured that people slept. I woke with the sheet bone-dry and my face on fire. In the darkness there was a split second where I didn't know where I was. Then reality. That was the first morning I felt a deep fear trickling towards the surface. 'Oh, God, please don't let me be still on the Congo.' Even the hateful engine noise would have calmed me. Its absence meant we were still marooned and it would be another day of hell, even supposing the *Isangi* got here without itself being grounded.

We were one degree above the Equator. By 8.00 am the ship was already an oven. Madame Celeste confessed shamefacedly that she had such bad diarrhoea that she felt like dying. I gave her two Imodium and she went back to bed. I prowled the deck with my binoculars. Biharzi passed. I no longer acknowledged him, but he tried to stare me down with a smirk.

The shores looked closer now that the haze had ceased to make them dance. Or rather what I thought was a distant bank turned out under magnification to be an artificial line created by the reeds of an enormous marsh. Now I could see the birds. This lifted my mood a little and I climbed the bridge and asked Captain Trudeau if I might join him. He was drinking a great mug of coffee and studying a chart with reading glasses. After motioning me in, he tipped half the coffee into a glass for me, made the slightest grimace and turned back to the chart. I waited for him to speak, and when he didn't, said brightly,

'People have been saying that they haven't seen any hippos and elephants about the river.'

'Then it's lucky they're not steering the boat, isn't it? Or we'd be in worse trouble. There are hippopotamus everywhere. There was a family over there ahead of us this morning. I keep well clear of them for many reasons, one of them being that it means the water is SHALLOW.' His deadpan delivery amplified with a twist of the knob. 'And elephants!' he snorted. 'Who said that? Those conservationists? I suppose their atlases tell them that elephants live in the middle of rainforest and nest in the top of the trees?' Despite the signs of his strain, this image, as such images always do, made me chuckle.

He asked the helmsman to get more coffee.

'Is the Darling like this?' he asked.

'It's not really very navigable. But when it floods it makes seas hundreds of kilometres wide. This is more like the Murray, though unimaginably larger.'

'Does this sort of thing happen much?'

'Too often. But the boats, even the big steamers, are mostly pleasure craft. Sometimes the mouth closes over completely with a bar.'

He looked at me as though I were an idiot. 'Then how does it embouch?'

'Sometimes it doesn't. It seeps or dries up.'

He smacked the wheel. 'Rivers! They're either giants or fairies. The passages have changed completely. This is the third time in a month. You can be sure they'll blame me. For everything.'

'For the people who were thrown overboard?'

He threw back his head and laughed, someone who has finally heard a question so foolish that he can afford to let go completely.

'I have no control over things like that. Don't you understand? That's a ceremony. A charade. It's the police and the army who control this boat, them and Monsieur Kissinger. It's all business, business. That's all they care about. And they've already accused me of profiteering. "The captain is responsible," they say to Dubrois, "not us." '

'You should tell the Company.'

I was clearly providing him with some long-needed relief.

'The army and the police *are* the Company,' he laughed, then wiped his eyes and turned back to the charts. '*Oh, la la. Oh, Dieux*. No disrespect to Com. Biharzi. Care, eh? Those stowaways were also bad people. This is a bad place to be stranded, and thanks to Monsieur Kissinger we are so overloaded anything could happen. And I … I am the great cretin who used to love this river. Please, with your permission.' The helmsman returned. Trudeau called in a couple of the crew. I took the hint and left.

On Friday we were still stuck. Not one plate of the hull had budged. Not one mean little grain of sand had shifted. There came a distant hum. It grew into a churning sound, and a bell clanged upriver. The *Isangi* loomed. Never had a rotten old hulk looked more beautiful as he steamed towards us. First he pulled off the *Bangala* and the *Mangbetu*. Trudeau made desperate steam, and we shuddered from side to side. It was not enough. Now it was the *Myanza's* turn to be dragged off. Reluctantly the unwieldy barge groaned away, dragging its even more lumbering children. And at last the *Ebeya* moved, churned like a paddleboat, completed a turn ... and we were free!

Life picked up. There was a breeze. On the barges, civic services were re-established. The *Ebeya's* less hardy passengers flopped in their deck-chairs. At least Madame Celeste was better. The Imodium did its work, and the chloroquine sent her to sleep. Her sister the third wife of Kissinger now wanted to marry me, convinced not only of my extraordinary medical powers but by a bedside manner which had clearly been turned on a bit thick. Slices of land mid-river slid past each other like the cellophane landscapes in an animated cartoon, while women with calabashes passed in front of the deck chairs selling bananas, avocados and pineapples. Teenage girls sat in groups plaiting each other's hair into topsy spikes. Men on the barge-roofs, using each other's faces as mirrors, carefully groomed and shaved.

As in any small and enclosed community, rumours flew. From now on we would sail through the night. We'll be in Mbandaka tomorrow. *Non.* We have to take the left-hand channel and it will be at least two weeks to Kinshasa. The blancs blanched. Trudeau was ill. All the whites were going to be turned out of their cabins. Now, while the cabins were in fact designed to roast the human body slowly rather than microwave it immediately as in second class, they were at least large, had bathrooms, and Fergus and I were the only Europeans in possession of one. In the destructive element by all means immerse oneself. But watch out for those crocodiles and the possibility of never coming to the surface. Fergus was forced to cultivate the purser.

With whatever motives, Kissinger induced Fergus to study the boat's cache of crocodiles. I watched in amusement as the tartaned laird insisted they were alligators, and started back with a shriek when one lunged at him. 'That's Reagan,' Kissenger said proudly. 'And his brother Gorbachev.' The crocodiles were greener than their Australian relatives. They were sloshed frequently with water. Their eyes were green, the black slit of the iris and the rows of serrated scales making them look like dragons. Kissinger got the crewmen to loosen the bindings round their snouts and pushed in monkey meat into which he had crushed white pills.

'What are you giving them?' asked Fergus.

'Prozac. Now we all calm, aren't we?'

117

NILE II

Incident at Edfu

There is a place where you climb up the Nile's banks, enter a stadium of enormous Old Kingdom walls, and find yourself enclosed by a temple more grandiose and complete than any other in Egypt. Its compact and perfect pylons announce its alignment with the river southwards, and the inner walls are as high and secret as the maze of corridors in the Forbidden City at Beijing. The temple is Ptolemaic, but it recapitulates more ancient history with a wealth of mythological hieroglyphs and figures of the gods Horus and his enemy Seth. Edfu needs no *son et lumière* because it is already a masterpiece of theatre. Horus was always my favourite god, the hawk-headed child of Isis and Osiris, the perfection of vision, protector against evil. He was represented everywhere here, moving freely as the *ka*, the double self. His eternal antagonist was his own brother Seth, frequently shown and hunted as a hippopotamus. Perverse as people are, the Egyptians had worshipped him as well.

Lofty date-palm capitals top the columns, and suggest the vegetation around. Colossal statues of Horus hawks announce the secret courtyards. Tourists approach with surprise. Here, halfway between Luxor and Aswan, it seems almost a reconstruction, too good to be true; in a way it is, a sort of postmodernist Ptolemaic imitation of the past. As you walk along the great wall on the left, you are already in shadow. And as I walked along its unending trap, I was not merely in shadow but trouble.

We had spent the morning in the town of Esna. While the *Htop* went through the barrage we sensibly decked ourselves in suncream and sunhats and rode in shaded calèches. I loved Esna. Its temple rose from the middle of a crater forty feet deep, where the soil of centuries had buried it as effectively as the lava of Herculaneum. I wanted to pull down the rest of the town and excavate it instantly. I had to be satisfied with exploring for several hours instead. Hungry with clambering and discussing the astrological ceiling with Shane, lured by the clarinets in the market alleys, I made the Fatal Mistake.

It was like being in Tangiers in the sixties again. The souk was jammed with veiled women, and smelled of saffron, cummin and cardamon. I ate alluring, sizzling meatballs fried in tempura shells in the bazaar, and drank the lethal Juice of Pomegranates. I know it was the pomegranates because there had been a suspicion of over-cold water which could only mean unpurified ice. There was later forensic evidence as well in the form of mashed seeds.

Now at Edfu the Revenge of the Mad Pomegranate attacked. I fell behind the group, and made a lightning run to the nearest rock. Horus stared resolutely and discreetly ahead. For this relief much thanks, good Horus, and when I had time to realize there was no paper I blessed him further for the miraculous provision of an old book half-buried in the sands. Rabelais may rave about the comfort of an obliging goose, or other instruments of voluptuous fantasy, but I fell upon that book for personal salvation. I reached for another page.

Around the corner came the full group. I scuttled sideways like a crab. Horus fixed them with a stern gaze, but it was towards Horus they were coming. The eye of Horus may have watched my ancient human act with tolerant vigilance, but the twenty tourists who came round the temple pylon did not. I skidded like a crab on rollerboards behind the nearest heap of rubble. But it was too late. My name now began with M and ended in D.

Mustafa spotted me first, and raised his eyes to Allah. But the eyes of Mr McIntyre were fixed on my distinctive cream shirt and kepi, dragged by a tell-tale sunburnt arm further behind the monument. My credit was gone; all reputation, honour, dignity, lectureship, masculinity, humanity, charm, drama-training and breathing-exercises, all down the spout. Farewell the tranquil mind. Farewell content. As the group passed in solemn procession, everyone, except for Shane, Jacqui and Desmond, who stared with fascination, let me know that heaven had been pleased to try me with affliction, and that I didn't exist.

Ah, Ozymandias! Look on my works, ye mighty, and perspire. I did. I mopped my brow with my shirt. All around, the lone and desert sands stretched far away. The rest of the book was savagely used, at least two chapters. To this day, Shane swears that everyone instantly recognized it as a rare papyrus.

I ran in the opposite direction to the group, vaguely knowing the temple's plan, and was soothed by its play of light and shade, especially those corners of total darkness. Perhaps it should have been done, and done quickly, in here. No, what desecration. Besides, there were the usual pillar fellaheen performing their mysterious syncopated appearances. In so far as one can in the flick of a nervous eye, I assimilated every detail of fourteenth dynasty architecture and incised gods, and fled onwards to rejoin the group. I caught up with them in another courtyard. Mustafa was on the point of taking a photo with everyone's camera in turn. Please take me back. Here I am. Finally Mustafa slipped my camera over his wrist, stepped back and clicked. Mr McIntyre guffawed, like a hearty sportsmaster, 'Caught short, sport?' at the wrong moment, and the photo shows the result: a group of humans surrounding the enraged hippopotamus demon, profaner of Horus.

As we left, Horus' twin regarded us, eagle-eyed as he was meant to. O great father, forgive. I never meant all that, you know, … stuff, and the other bits with spears and everything that Seth did to you. And besides the book really was a Frog publication, probably by enemies of Ra. Horus winked.

'I suppose it's just as well it wasn't a copy of the Quran,' I whispered to Mustafa.

'Don't even joke about it,' he muttered. 'Your head would-n't look very attractive on a pike and I'd lose my job.'

Shane gave up pretending that he had distinctly seen hiero-glyphs through the binoculars.

'I think it's time to give you my lecture on stage two of infantile development. At this rate you'll soon be wiping out the Rosetta Stone.'

'The text I was all-so-leisurely scanning was about French military tactics, so it must have been post-Napoleonic. At least 1820.'

'Ah. Only 160 years old. We must wire the university librarian. He'll be glad to know there's some of it left: Special Collection. Dirty Books. Purdon Bequest.'

We sailed on to Kom Ombo, standing dramatically at sun-set on the bend of the river. This was a healing temple, like those rest-cure clinics dedicated to Aesculapius in Greece. Mustafa pointed out carvings of a box of surgical instruments. Fortunately the group's wonder at what I might do for my next trick was distracted by a cage of mummified crocodiles. The steps leading to the Nilometer were also a crowd-puller. While they drew into its spiral I looked out over the dunes and the comforting acres of cultivated land. Below us were carpet-sellers, stalls with reed mats, men in galabechs touting donkey-carts and taxis. Mustafa called me over to show the portrait of the architect laying out the temple. Horus was satisfied. And his local friend Sobek, for a crocodile god, was especially kind. Mr McIntyre disappeared while bargaining for a rug, and his wife, cautioned so constantly about being a stickybeak, failed to report it till Aswan. There are no crocodiles in this part of the Nile anymore. Perhaps Sobek just took him up on the pediment and ate him.

CONGO VII
Mask of Fire

The river had subtly changed. Its colours ranged from bright yellow to velvet brown. In the early morning it was often coiled with mist. At evening, the sky dissolved and took on the colours of the steaming rainforest beneath. The vendors became more persistent. The delay had upset their economy. I was lazily watching the purple liana vines that groped for the sun over the forest canopy, imagining Stanley making his way through that wilderness, and wondering whether the Mbonge, through whose lands we were passing, really were cannibals, when there was a huge and sudden thud. Please God, NO! The engines cut immediately.

This time we were really stuck. A haggard Trudeau radioed again for help. But the *Isangi* was now miles upriver and itself afraid of grounding. The boats settled into the sand. We were totally isolated. No pirogues had appeared for days. Everyone was counting on arriving at Mbandaka tomorrow and replenishing. Meanwhile we all wanted to live. And that meant that eating and drinking, and not getting sick, were paramount.

Monkeys and bats were smoked over vents and charcoal fires by the cooks on the barges. The three-storied forward wall became plastered with splayed carcases until it resembled a medieval monument decorated with red and black

123

escutcheons. The dead animals clung to it like shields. Despite the smoking they stank. In the still air they radiated a pungent smell of charred flesh that made it impossible to go on deck without holding your nose. *Nature morte.* Still nature. Dead nature. Still life. One of the smaller crocodiles was skinned, hacked apart and roasted on a spit. Cooks made soups from water-snakes and catfish. More reluctantly they slaughtered fowls and pigs, supposedly for the first class saloon.

Even here dinner was reduced to a succession of stews with mealie mixed with heavily salted and shredded pieces of unidentifiable flesh. I ate out of sheer hunger. When Joseph told me that they were actually monkey and bat I was horrified. The salon was the only refuge from the heat, however, so god knows what I ate. When I asked the chief steward he just pointed to his head and laughed. 'Very good for the brains.' But I could hardly bear the thought of connecting the displays of other primates, constantly moved by the crew on sliding ladders, with the brown mess served at table.

Toinette persuaded me to try the toasted caterpillars, which, once they were crisp, were the best food aboard. They tasted like witchetty grubs. I snacked on them throughout the day and made do in the evening salon with rice and boiled cassava. As the food shortage increased in second and third class, others also had recourse to cassava, pounded into balls and turned to Pechee-pechee with the addition of garlic, oil and peppers.

The main problem was drink. Mineral water was finished, and soft drinks were unobtainable. Wine and beer were available, at inflated prices. The first class passengers got stuck into every liquor and liqueur that stood on the mirrored shelves as ornaments. Dinnertime consisted of unfinished plates, little green, red and orange bottles, and tottering passengers. I persuaded Madame Celeste that vodka tasted just like water once it had bananas squeezed into it, and she swayed round the decks saying 'Ooo la la.' Even Madame Hortense got sick of unadulterated rum, and boisterously abused the Second Noël until he produced cans of Fanta. That meant the stewards were holding back. Their resources were the barges. Refrigeration had failed over the entire convoy, but the fast-melting recesses of the *Lokokele* still held crates of soft drink. We bought them at extortionate rates and guarded them like the Rothschilds' cellar masters. Our thirst was insatiable. We were marooned at a point just before the Lulonga joins the main river, about 0.5 degrees above the equator, and we dripped and dehydrated rapidly. The stalls sold amulets against sickness; the large numbers of pregnant women wore them about their necks and waists.

The intense humidity made it impossible for cooling sweat to evaporate. Alcohol gave immediate euphoria for depression and parched throats, but exacted its vengeance in headaches, and cancelled its liquidity in urine. We all needed litres of water. If we were lucky we were getting pints. As a city of two and a half thousand people we were running out of every resource. The Congolese doggedly hauled buckets from the river. As with the consumption of monkey flesh, I recoiled from the thought of drinking water into which thousands of people were daily excreting enough bacillae to cause a cholera epidemic. For a time I tried out my iodine tablets. The result was life-saving but unpalatable. I tried them with pekoe tea-bags, which made the liquid turn black and taste like boots; and with powdered coffee, which made it taste like the mixture it was: primal and processed mud.

The days go by in a haze; the dancing heat on the waters, the nightly screaming of birds and animals from the forest, the slide of bravado into fear. Every time I appear on deck, the children of the first-class officials are waiting for my cabin-curtains to open. They are pretty children, mostly young girls in their spikes, their faces shining black as if polished, their cotton dresses clean and printed with flowers. *Ah, père Noël, père Noël,* they chant. Where are you going? Well, I'm going up the companionway to see if I can get anything resembling breakfast, aren't I? *Ah, père Noël,* you're naughty. It's too late. You get up too late. Maybe you drink too much beer last night.

A quick look shows that both the cane chairs and the table we bought in Bumba have vanished. I swipe a chair from next door. Zoulde comes and sits on my knee. She strokes my hair and offers to plait it.

'How old are you, père Noël?'

'I'm forty-eight.'

'You're old.'

'And you're impudent. And don't use *tu* to me unless I give you permission.'

She wriggles in my lap. She turns up big eyes and says sweetly, 'I ask your permission.'

'Well you can't have it. Get off me.'

'You call me *tu*.'

'That's because you're a child.'

That makes her jump off more effectively than anything I could have devised.

'I'm not. I'm engaged. You let the boys call you *tu*.'

'That's because they're university students and they're my friends.'

'If you don't want to be my friend you can't call me *tu* anymore. I hate you.' She bursts into tears and runs to her parents' cabin. All I need. But now I notice that this chair isn't the one we bought either. The one outside her parents' cabin is.

We baked and reeked in the rays of the pitiless copper star. When the sky had finished flaming, the moon brought millions of insects to torment, clogging nostrils and descending throats. The bar closed again, and the salon was opened only for lunch and dinner, which still consisted of monkey and bat-meat. Fergus and I gobbled it down. The absence of liquid was more serious. The Europeans gathered in my cabin to use the distiller. We watched it like vampires attending a blood drip. The constant use of the bathroom provoked violent exchanges with our neighbours on the starboard. If anyone occupied the bathroom too long, we banged and banged at the communicating door, and exchanged curses about the condition of the baths and lavatories and the washing of clothes. The bathroom became a rolling, sloshing mess which the drains refused to empty. The previously good-natured girls who washed infinite nappies glared as they unclicked the door. The whites who rushed in on the point of fouling their pants were heard squirting and grunting, and sarcastically laughed at.

Fergus irritated me beyond measure. He had become obsessed with the idea that Kitty had been sleeping with Bryan.

'I know it can't have been you, since you're married, or gay or both. You wouldn't do such a thing, would you?'

'If you really want to know, Kitty was fucking everyone on the ship, especially Kissinger.' That backfired by giving him more to be obsessed about.

'It's just that Bryan is so careless. You know what I mean.' I thought of the innumerable condoms I had doled out, with no sexual satisfaction to myself. I looked with disgust at his sprawled body. He had an ulcer on his leg, besides the lice that made him scratch. He lay on his bed like a fixture of the boat. Our books had started to mildew. He had finished *Heart of Darkness* and was now reading *Lord Jim*. One morning I walked twice around the deck and slouched back into the cabin.

'Do you think that narrative is important in Conrad?'

He was surprised, pleased. This was the kind of conversation he wanted to have with me.

'Of course.'

'Where are you up to?'

'Well, after the *Patna*, Jim has met Stein and found a community, and a lover he can protect. Ah, the second engineer from the *Patna* has left him in peace. He's now called Tuan in this remote little place.'

'You mean the Malay people he infects with his stupid attempts to be good? Well, Tuan Jim has brought with him every evil pirate in the region, and it all ends in disaster. For him. For her. For the whole community. They're killed.'

There was a moment's silence before he said. 'That was exceedingly spiteful. That was cruel.'

'Good,' I said. 'Now you have at least an inkling of what we're actually living in. And we only needed fiction to establish it.'

There were other crises of European behaviour. As conditions got worse in the barges, Bryan had deposited his food-box under Fergus' bed. Fergus plundered and ate it, and blamed me. Bryan smacked his face.

For five days we sat on that hateful bank, a prefabricated city on the point of collapse. The crew transferred a mountain of cargo in order to redistribute weight. Food speckled and putrefied. Fruit rotted and blackened as in a time-lapse film. We were in the doldrums. Over each afternoon spread a torpor held in place by the fiery heat, until we longed for the air-conditioning of the salon. One night when even the salon was hot, and the tables had been cleared for card-games, we lingered on a couch with the other foreigners. Each opening of the door brought a blast from a furnace. The lights dimmed and sheet lightening silently took its place about the river. By the time we went on deck, the sky was convulsed with its display. Sheets of livid white flickered soundlessly from rim to rim of the horizon, succeeded by stabs of even brighter light shooting from one invisible stormcloud to another. But no rain followed.

One day there was hot water in the showers. The only trouble was that it came out in spits and was scalding. We woke to find everything in fog, the forested bank a dado of grey bush, the river steaming. To get rid of the accumulated rubbish and blood-spattered straw and bones Trudeau had ordered the decks sprayed with fire-hoses. The barges were in full swing, bubbling with chants and xylophones, and the seething sounds of humanity. The decks were awash. People were hauling up buckets and sloshing themselves. Yells came from the men and women on the underdecks as they received a dousing. Insults were traded in Lingala, Swahili and French like buckets of slop.

I went in search of something to drink. The links between the barges were slippery this morning, and people were skidding with their tubs and bundles, and landing with a thud on cassava bags and outraged pigs. I slipped for a full six feet, riding it like a skateboarder, enjoying the trip until I saw that it was about to end by contacting the belly of a three-metre crocodile. Fortunately it had its mouth taped, but one evil tooth had gashed its way upwards. Kissinger continued to amuse his intimates by ordering the crocodiles' snouts unbound, and tossing them live chickens which they snapped in mid-air.

On the fifth day the weather changed. Cumulus built in the west and cirrus breezes enticed us onto the decks. Little frills of waves danced on the river. By sunset the sky was purple, and darker clouds pushed lower towards the boat. We sat fanning ourselves and watching the steady creep of the clouds. A few premature spots of rain sliced at the deck like needles. For another fifteen minutes there was nothing. No sign of rain; simply the clouds growing in volume and compressed shades of grey and black. Streaks appeared between the upper and lower clouds, twisting like the cones of a tornado.

Then it hit. The sky was convulsed with lightning. The whole atmosphere was churning like a firestorm on Jupiter or Venus. No longer was the planet recognizable as our familiar Earth. We were caught whirling in space encircled by a gigantic and dangerous electric current. As one we held our breaths. And then the world and the river broke. A thick yellow bolt struck a tree on the shore. Its fragments were illuminated as they exploded in thunder. We were in the very centre of the storm, and instinctively gathered together as Nature crashed and tore herself apart. The rain fell as thick as bullets. Sheets of it tore at the forest, whipped the trees and roared through the boat. The animal carcases were plucked from the wall. Awnings flew. Cooks hastily doused fires that were groping and raping nets and fabrics. The stallholders pulled their braziers inside and tried in vain to stop their displays from toppling.

This vicious, life-saving rain continued for hours. When the gale abated, the downpour continued. Water spouted in fountains from the roofs of the barges, jetted from the vents. Within a few hours, as the level of the river rose, the barges began a crazy heavy dance. We lay gratefully in the cool; adjoining passengers successfully persuading their neighbours to open connecting doors and savour the sprinkled draughts. Just after midnight we all felt it; the surge in the stomach; the lift. The *Ebeya* was afloat.

Trudeau had no time for careful manipulations. He started the engines, threw them into reverse and ordered crew onto each barge, slackening cables and starting to pull whichever of his convoy could follow. In the searchlights people could be seen darting and leaping from one barge to whichever seemed to be moving. Baggage and animals circled in a frenzied carousel. But we were afloat! We were afloat! The *Mongo* seemed to have got itself stuck again. Sheets of wet torn plastic flapped and blinded it. Its passengers screamed as the crew cut it loose. Some threw goods onto the *Myanza* and leapt in and swam. Even as we severed links completely someone managed to haul a dead antelope the size of a horse onto the deck. It hung there like the horse in Eisenstein's *October* as the *Ebeya* shuddered and backed away.

Next morning was a strange sight. The *Myanza* was now immediately alongside. The crew had worked through the night, securing the others. We had lost the *Mongo*. But it was too risky to go back. On every roof and lines strung across the promenades, wet clothes and mats were hanging. Some passengers had crawled onto the roofs to sleep and dry off in their clothes. The *Myanza* displayed an apparent field of Jonestown bodies, as if fresh from a massive dose of lethal Kool-Aid.

By the time we came to Mbandaka, I didn't care about anything except getting off the boat. Mbandaka was the largest town we'd reached. It was ugly, almost industrial, but it had a factory, a spired church, and an enormous dock. When I found out from Monsieur Dubrois, who was disembarking, that the local hotel had ceiling fans, I left Fergus in charge of my bag, and went ashore. Kissinger warned jovially, 'This is the place where the President offered the populace a railway, a mine, or a brewery. You know what they chose? The brewery! That shows you what the people of this region are like.'

But in the Hotel des Masques I slept well, falling into unconsciousness while my eyes stared at a severe, icy cold mask above my bed. It gazed at me serenely, indifferently, with eye-brows and long nose arched in an expression of chalky self-possession. The eyes were close together, pin-pricks of calm vision. And it was completely white. I had confused dreams in which it had been stolen from me, possibly an indication of the extent to which I desired it. It was ice, an iceberg on which I could leap. When at breakfast I asked the proprietor about its impression of beautifully frigid calm, he replied, 'Ah, that's not surprising, it is the mask of Fire.'

NILE III
Aswan

Aswan is already Nubian, African, a beautiful, intricate town like a series of harbours. Skins are darker, spices more pungent; strange birds sing at night. The displaced inhabitants of the valley of the Aswan Dam roam the town like the survivors of Atlantis. At this end of the Nile, even more than at Cairo, it's like coming into port. The main island, Elephantine, had been a garrison on the way to the wilderness, a Saint Louis, bearing the traces of Jewish colonies, of change and reshaping. It was here that Eratosthenes calculated the circumference of the earth. The present town is more than an oasis. The tombs of the nobles high on the red cliffs descend to Roman cemeteries, and the earth breaks into green. The promenade sweeping the shores is cool with shelters where citizens play backgammon. Sails slap over the waters of its many gardened islands. But it's all an artifice.

For starters, Aswan's centrepiece Philae really isn't the ancient cataract island anymore. It's a reconstructed site whose soil is that of its former neighbour Agilkia. Augustus, Hadrian and Trajan would have bestowed villas upon the modern engineers who painstakingly reassembled its temples and kiosks. Isis the restorer and Hathor the guardian of these first cataracts before Nubia would also have been satisfied. The last hieroglyphs were carved in the fourth century AD. Visitors began adding graffiti in the fifth century and didn't stop for another fifteen hundred, just as they finished the work of the hewers in the quarries by obligingly polishing the granite obelisks and mummy faces to a reverent glow, like unknown elephants rubbing the tusks of their ancestors. The graffitists in demotic Latin, Greek, French, English and German obviously had more time than a flashy vandal with a spray-can. The incisions are deep and devoted. Christians started first with some easy noughts and crosses. Napoleon's soldiers managed a few little ones before his scholars smacked them and, like Denon, added their own more academic design. 1836 was a good year for the English Holroyd and Langton. Zuccolo, Robertson and Mure must have had an industrious morning in 1868, when they were joined by some aristocrat of the double eagle. Rimbaud had mercifully relieved himself further downstream. When I pretended to be making my own additions with a biro, Jacqui muttered, 'What fresh lunacy is he up to now?'

While some of the group entrusted themselves to a flight to Abu Simbel, and others settled for the pink mausoleum of the Agha Khan, we decided to spend the weekend relaxing in the town itself. Shane charmed the family of Rashad, one of the many Nubians settled there, and we hired a felucca to visit the sites along the northern shore. When we embarked, the kids did everything except run along behind like Brandon de Wilde crying, 'Shane! Come back!'

Having no devotion to the Agha Khan, and very little to Saint Simeon except that he was centuries older, we asked Rashad to moor downstream, far from a tourist group among whom we could distinguish some of our own party descending a bus before the sepulchre on the hill. Deftly Rashad tacked with the winds into a rock cove where three or four drivers and their camels sat under a date-palm.

It was now late afternoon, and if 35°C can be considered cool, it was cooler. The camels were doubled-saddled. After Shane and I mounted, the animal rose to its feet beneath the driver's stick and groaned with every indication that at least one of us should go on a diet. Rashad fixed a price for the camel. He would wait one hour, because he had been booked by a party for an evening cruise at 7.00 pm. Tapped by the driver, the resentful beast picked its way up the rubble of a dry ravine and opened our view onto desert. Dunes concealed the monastery, which we reached after fifteen minutes. We were the only visitors.

The monastery was of considerable size, well-preserved, its stone courtyards, basilica and staircases entire. They led to upper rooms which had been cells and dormitories for 300 monks, and to side chancels marked with Coptic crosses and headless Apostles. I filmed the arches of light that pierced the darkness, disregarding the offers of guidance from men who sprang from the exterior masonry, and followed my map. Like many Christian sites from Ireland to India, this was not the province, or even the tomb, of the saint who endowed it with his name.

The redoubtable Simeon who sat on a pole for thirty-six years had chosen Syria for his stunt. Despite flocks of imitators, some of whom improved on his act by doing it naked and descending every now and then to freak people out and give them theology lectures, the Saint Simeon who lived here was a common or desert ascetic, and the monastery wasn't even built until the seventh century.

I have seen candid snaps of these anchorites by Breughel and Bosch, and their homes are generally not inviting. Visited by people wearing teapots and funnels on their heads, and ladies whose lingerie couldn't conceal the odd claw or tail, they dramatically shortened the food chain with teams of anchorettes and anchorlings who poked gruel in one end of their cells and cleaned it out the other. You can't stop people doing this sort of thing to themselves. It saves Prozac and wear and tear on relatives' nerves; and it prevents them from going into welfare or prison services and doing it unto others.

But it is not endearing. The only tolerable anchorites I would have come within a mile of were Saint Anthony, and maybe the real Saint Simeon, just to see how he said Mass at the top of the pole. But this fourth century Simeon wasn't even called Simeon. He was a certain Anba Hadra who finked out on his wife the day after their marriage and decided to take a felucca and be celibate. No record remained of the Byzantine or Orthodox militancy which led Sidi Anba or his successors to martyrdom. But there was no doubt that this outpost of a monastery was conceived as a fortress. Iron wall-brackets were still in place. Huge oil, grain and wine-jars lay round the cloisters. Intact amphorae, gently fallen from their tripods, nestled in the sand. The place was so untouched, unrestored and full of artefacts that I was torn between writing an indignant letter to the Department of Antiquities, and asking the camel-driver whether a six foot amphora or two might not be attached to the saddle.

I needn't have bothered. Shane's watch reminded us that we had already enjoyed this place for an hour, and had better hurry to the felucca. The behaviour of the guardians and camel-master helped. Despite having paid their entrance fees, our scurrying bodies were pursued from the temple by a tribulet of money-gatherers. They had seen me filming. That was extra. We had gone where no tourist had been allowed to go before; that was double-extra.

'What's Arabic for "camel-shit"?' I asked Shane. Fortunately he didn't answer, because the camel-master then joined whole-heartedly in the clamour.

'We're late. Please go,' we shouted, pointing in the possible direction of the river, since the sun was now glowing red to our right. But that controller of animals had turned into a master of men. He too must now be paid extra for taking us back.

'Not one shekel,' I replied.

The argument grew louder. In that case we could stay in the desert. OK. One shekel. Maybe more shekels. But only for the guards of the monastery. Otherwise, he, the camel-driver, could sort it out with Rashad, because we had paid him fairly (true), and left all our money with him (not so true). We departed with curses at our backs and a last astonished look at the camel-man as he lashed the camel and sent us hurtling into the desert. I have the film. You've probably seen camels galloping. Unless you've volunteered as a jockey in some Territorian derby, I doubt you've felt in your entrails the sensations of interplanetary flight that accompanies them. Free of its master, avenging years of human abuse, the deranged beast galumphed. The sun jumped up and down like a bouncing orange. Shane valiantly clung with one hand while he filmed bits of my hat, sky and sand in the manner of early Godard. I pulled the reins down and back till the camel dangerously twisted its head, and revealed a mouth whose every tooth said, 'Try that again, molester-of-dromedaries, and we'll crash.'

The crazed bolt continued till we topped a dune and could see the Nile below the rocky ravine.

'Chee-suss!'

'And by Saint Simeon's bones!'

In the sudden quiet we could hear shrill whistles. We looked for the driver. No sign. Perhaps the bastard had programmed his creature by subsonic control. We kicked its sides. I loosened the reins and made encouraging clucks. Not a budge. The lightning streaker of yestermoment might have been stuffed; if I possessed taxidermic skills, it would have been. But soon its master appeared, his teeth as malicious as the camel's. He was so sorry, *effendi,* but sometimes camels did that. He led us with great solicitation down to the river. Oh, look at that, there was a nasty boulder; lucky he was there to guide us and control this mother of atrocity. The camel sneezed in disdain.

When we neared the felucca, Rashad came into view, made exasperated displays and pointed at his watch. We in turn pointed at the driver, dismounted with a double-thump, and set in motion an argument that went four ways and ended with Rashad inviting the driver to the mint-tea he had waiting. Furious gestures became folded arms, then relaxed hands holding glasses. The sensation of everything going up and down continued way beyond the gentle swaying of the boat. All was resolved. Rashad would drop us off at the Oberoi jetty, because we were so late. We would have to get back to the *Hotp* by

ferry. He asked if we'd enjoyed our day. We thanked him
enthusiastically. As we reached the dock, the sun was liquefy-
ing over Elephantine Island. About us the sky was green,
merging to purple and scarlet where the great star flared as it
sank into the underworld behind the Aswan Dam. Rashad
suggested we might view it better by taking a taxi to the top.

'No, thanks, Rashad. We've already seen it,' I said. 'It was
beautiful.'

'... and very moving,' added Shane, his head still bobbing.

The next day was the last on the boat. Everything went
smoothly, except that we recognised with a pang at lunch that
the *Hotp* was no longer ours. It had managed to wriggle
around, facing downstream, and looked as if it had dunked
itself in the Nile. The decks swam, the lavatories were sluicing
water, the boutiques closed, the cabins locked. Lunch was
coldly furnished forth. The buffet salads looked as if they had
been dressed with eau de Nil, and the kofta and kebbah might
have been brought down in a basket from the Tombs of the
Nobles. 'I wouldn't touch it,' said Shane. 'Let's eat at the Old
Cataract and ask Mustafa to pick us up when they've finished
shopping.'

We did. After the incident at Edfu, though Montezuma was
clearly in the wrong place to have his revenge, I had mine.
Whether it was the lettuce à la cholera or the Old Kingdom
Kofta, the entire group spent the afternoon at Lake Nasser
bribing guards to let them into the engine rooms, generators,
construction sheds or the nearest rocks. Despite my discovery
of a deep interest in hydroelectric systems and their inhabitants, I merely peeked at the venues, and my camera, though
not the twinkle in my eye, was sealed.

DANUBE

DANUBE I
The Flood

The Danube traverses nine countries – Germany, Austria, Slovakia, Hungary, Croatia, Serbia, Romania, Bulgaria and the Ukraine – and if the Balkans aren't careful, it will cut through a few more until its marshes merge with the Black Sea. Apart from the Volga, at 2,850 kilometres it's the longest river in Europe. Connected by canal with the Main and the Rhine, it draws the northern line of an ellipse completed southward by the Mediterranean. For centuries it defined the Roman boundary of all that was meant by civilization.

Whenever Europeans have faced major temporal or spatial changes in this enclosure of reason, they have resorted to thoughts of annihilation and the apocalypse. We're about to do it again because of the Millennium. Deranged cults, miraculous happenings, the cracking of nations into tribes, daily life as spasms of fright, the landscape of Hieronymus Bosch. Among previous favourite images have been those of global madness and the breaking of God's covenant: the Deluge.

At Regensburg in July 1997, ironic Renaissance humanists like Erasmus, and the astronomer Johannes Kepler, who had actually lived there in a period of ideological hysteria (his

141

mother was almost burned as a witch), might have been chuckling up their posthumous sleeves.

Because, to start with, there was a flood. That meant the river was there but the boat wasn't. In fact, the river was very much there. The Brown Danube curled round the pylons of the Donaumarkt, and the sailors had spent the last week swimming between the bridges in Budapest trying to lift anchor and get back to Germany. That's why the boat wasn't in Regensburg but in Passau. And that was partly why many of the passengers weren't there either.

There were rumours that a contingent had been sighted in Dusseldorf in wheelchairs. The passengers who were in Regensburg were divided between sympathy for these paraplegics because they were disabled, and a secret suspicion that they had caused the floods. The Regensburg passengers had faithfully arrived at the German dock at noon, foregoing the delights of coffee in the Domplatz and a stroll beneath the Roman walls in order to kick things around the deserted market, in the middle of which stood an inauspiciously immobile bus.

I had spent a pleasant day meandering from Nürnberg to this more congenial city because my ticket clearly said: 'Embarkation will begin at the Donaumarkt at 5.00 pm – followed by drinks and dinner.' The seething masses in the bus clearly did not have such tickets. They obviously had tickets which said, 'Be here at noon or the boat will go away and you will be as starvelings in the wilderness', and they were as pissed off as Wagner's Niebelüngen after a bad day at Bayreuth.

So when I wheeled my bag down the Gichtigasse at 5.30 pm, with the guidance Saint James the traveller's patron extends to those who carry his cockleshell (and also buy streetmaps), they fell upon me with joy. The joy was because one more person out of the missing seven had turned up. That meant that the bus to Passau might soon receive its full complement and leave. The only thing that annoyed them was that I wasn't a family and showed no signs of being crippled, and therefore couldn't be part of the missing gang last seen trying to get their wheel-chairs into taxis at Dusseldorf.

The company representative was an olive-skinned young woman called Giulia, dressed in naval uniform with an Armani scarf. People honed in on her to talk sternly in German. She made frequent use of a mobile phone. After watching and lis-tening with some admiration and growing suspicion, I tried it out. 'Ma come mai una donzella come lei deve prendere la responsililità per quest' imbroglio?' *Donzella* is a courtly Tuscan word, but she picked up the compliment, 'How come a nice girl like you has to take responsibility for all this mess?' She practically embraced me, 'Sei Italiano?' We worked on mutu-al explanations. My years in Florence. Venice. The Biennale. 'You're the first one ever on these cruises who speaks Italian. Germans, French, English, Dutch, Scandinavians, even Spaniards and Portuguese. But never Italian.'

She was from Torcello, the youngest and most independent child of the Veneto, the Queen of Waters. Did any of the oth-ers speak Italian? No. We made a pact to have *conversazioni intime* whenever necessary. I couldn't understand the hassle. Floods? I like floods. The more water, the nicer the river.

Just a week ago I had seen the Danube emerge from its declared source in a fountain at Donaueschingen. Germany boasted a new train called the Kleber Express, after the family who ran the old post-routes. It ran once daily between Munich and Freiburg. The last part of its route was right along the Danube. Its young conductor Thomas was so proud of his first job that he collected timetables and maps, and set me off at the little station at Donaueschingen. The train would be back on its home run in two hours – just enough time to lunch beside the famous natal fountain, and rejoin the train as far as Tüttlingen. The old post-inn there had a camping ground which hired canoes. Thomas, as impulsive as I was, had already booked me a room and a boat. I could stay the night, catch the swift current as far as the cliffs of Sigmaringen, leave the canoe at the post-inn there, and be ready to catch the

Kleber at lunchtime tomorrow. Back aboard I could see more of the Danube Valley as we hugged its banks, change trains for Ulm and be on the river all the way to Regensberg.

It was bliss. The heavy rain of the past fortnight had ceased. The sun twinkled through the Black Forest and burst on the Donaueschingen Palace gardens, turning the spray into God's guaranteed rainbow. The spray became a trickle. The trickle became a brook; and the brook became the Danube. As the limpid little stream curved through white chalk gorges, I drifted happy as a trout over pebbles to Sigmaringen. Under the crystal water the stones looked like opals. When my arms got tired of steering I gratefully accepted a tow from a couple in a twin kayak.

It all went exacly to plan, though I just made the 12.26 train in time. The conductor's manic figure greeted me with a lunch-pack of chicken and riesling prepared by the incumbent Herr Kleber himself. Thomas was so impressed by our strategies that he gave me a souvenir. During the last stop he unscrewed the name plate on the carriage. I hope Herr Kleber didn't mind.

At Ulm, after climbing the cathedral spire – the tallest in the world and yielding a view of the Danube to infinity – I took the ferry as far as Günzburg, because from there the river really becomes knotted and turbulent; and you can see that Ortelius knew so too, because it's on the front cover of this book.

So of course I'd heard about the floods. My family made sure of that every night after the news. 'But there are sandbags on the Oder in Poland and Germany ...' With the last batteries in my mobile I assured them that the distinguishing feature of boats was that they floated, that I was already on one leading to a bigger vessel at Regensburg and that the Danube was a snap. Only one had the cheek to mutter: 'Remember the Congo.'

It should have occurred to me that rivers have tributaries, and that three hundred of the little monsters were busy melting Alpine glaciers, turning the Carpathians and Moravian plateau into oceans, and emptying it all into the biggest river they could find, their gargantuan child – the Danube. Those measuring signs of previous water-levels six feet above your head in the quaint little villages weren't put there by Dürer as an exercise in draughtsmanship. Giulia explained that the river was so high that the dams were almost breached and that the boat couldn't pass under the bridge at Deggendorf. Even if we had been able to start at Regensburg we might be stuck for weeks, and never see the royal palace of Estergom, the towers of Visegrad, let alone the famous bend of the Danube Knee and the splendours of Vienna and Budapest. But more urgently there was the bus. What was she going to do about the bus?

The bus, on closer inspection, seethed with forty or so European wasps with more or less human faces. I stayed outside, chatting with an English family from Lincolnshire who were treating it with sang-froid, except for the mother's chain-smoking. A taxi arrived, disgorging an elegant but unfortunately unmaimed French couple called Severin. Once they too had been interrogated about Dusseldorf and informed of the expected arrivals, they chose to get in the bus and be part of the Seething, except à la parisienne. European languages being such a bag of tricks, sheer cold-bloodedness doesn't mean sang froid. It means Seventh Arrondissement Ice, and this pair had obviously won a contest to spread it abroad like performances of Corneille.

Giulia looked harassed as she fought off various suggestions and demands. Abandon the disabled couple. What was their name anyway? She consulted her list. They were called Patates and they were English. That divided the passengers even further. How could they be English if they were called Patates? They were obviously Lebanese or other üntermensch. A company sign should be left for them on the mooring in at least one of those barbarous tongues and we should go.

The trouble with that idea was Giulia needed the sign for the bus, and there wasn't a mooring because it was underwater. A log hit the nearest pylon and everyone jumped. The English mother lit up another one. An elderly German with a

cane hawked deeply with every indication that he was about
to die of emphysema. From the bus appeared his raw-boned
son Hermann. Using the steps as a podium, he harangued
the small crowd and disagreed with everything everyone else
suggested.

Finally the English father and I tricked him into disagree-
ing with himself. Duncan Elwood showed signs of being a
logician. Even he had been swayed by the possibility that the
Patates weren't English. Duncan calmly pointed out the complete unreality of the crippled couple at Dusseldorf railway station. Item One: Dusseldorf was hundreds of miles away and on
the Rhine, not the Danube. Item Two: If the Patates had any
intention of coming to Regensburg they would have been at
Regensburg railway station or at least at Munich. Hermann
muttered darkly about the arrogance of the English, even if
their name was Potatoes, and complained that if we went to
Passau by bus we would miss the Doric Parthenon at Valhalla
and the mansion of Hermann Goering.

Duncan and I sized each other up. Duncan clearly sailed. I
could see him on the Broads, the sort of phlegmatic man who
only strangled people when they failed to furl the sheets properly. By the same inscrutable sense, he could tell that I was the
sort used to having others take notes while I discoursed on
Renaissance water-imagery and giving them a D minus if they
didn't listen. We made an unspoken agreement to combine
forces. Giulia said that things could get worse. Like how? It
could, for example, start to rain.

Then it did start to rain. Giulia was plucky. She loved the
Countess Erzsébet, she said with tears in her eyes. Was that
because she had been on it continuously for three weeks during the floods? No, she choked, she had been on for three
years. She called the company again on her mobile. An official
in Köln crackled out a Brechtian patter-song in which I could
catch the words *sechs und dreisig* repeated at high volume.
Wherever the Patates were, we were to get on the bus at
6.30 pm and go to Passau. Everyone consulted their watches.
Giulia surrendered the sign, Hermann taped it to a rubbish

skip, and even Duncan and I treacherously agreed to abandon the cripples in favour of dry clothes and dinner. Later, when I was the Patates' best friend, Hermann revenged himself by telling them that I was Reichsfuhrer of the plot to abandon them to the river.

The driver revved his engine. The rain announced its intention of flooding everything east of Zurich. The spire of Regensburg cathedral disappeared in the mist. The passengers grumbled with content. And wailing along the quay came a Volkswagon with two gesticulating people, who hauled luggage and ran dripping to the bus. Giulia stood with her clipboard and the pneumatic doors hissed open. Two frantic people were enveloped and the doors closed. Check. The Potatoes had arrived. They had been wandering around the upper banks for hours, wondering where the boat or even the mooring was, since the lower river–walk was invisible to all but fish.

The female Potato was called Joan and was shaking with nerves. She was an outgoing woman, and her black fringe bobbed as she made every effort to apologise for her blameless crime and establish herself with the group. Her husband stared out the window and occasionally turned a tired face wrinkled with the marks of many years of smiling. She picked up papers from the floor. 'Has anyone dropped these?' No one had. No one cared, not even Giulia, who was more than slightly annoyed by Hermann grabbing the microphone. Because we did pass Valhalla, and Hermann offered a Wagnerian commentary.

It got worse when we sped past the Nazi villas. After his English spiel was greeted with appalled silence, he did it in German. 'And now Giulia will tell you all about it …' Giulia, for one so young and under pressure, set her face into alabaster.

'*Cazzo*,' she muttered.

'Can someone let me in on the secret …?' said Joan.

But everyone let her in on the silence instead. A gigantic frost descended on the bus like an invention of the Brothers Grimm. And grim was the word for the majority of its German passengers, the Jungreisesgruppe, named, I think, for their local Lutheran psychiatrist rather than their age, since the youngest was a stripling of seventy and considered sprightly for the way in which he flourished his walking stick. The silence held. There were baroque churches aplenty. My photos of them show well-focused close-ups of traffic lights; then, at the last great globe of red on photo number twelve, a mighty bridge and a town that appeared to be on an island.

The riverbanks at Passau were thronged. Between the wooded mountains and the pastel town it looked like a sort of upper-class refugee centre. Every ship from the Rhine to the Black Sea seemed to be moored or sitting in the swollen river, the *Moldavia,* the *Lorelei,* tankers with Cyrillic letters, the *Mozart.* And there she was, the MV *Countess Erzsébet,* spick and span with polished decks and a beaming uniformed crew, who went into speed-up motion to install us in our cabins. When my steward Gisela opened the door I knew I had reached Rabelais' Abbey of Do-As-You-Will. Instead of a porthole, a large window opened onto the waters and the grassy bank. Then she showed me the mini-bar. I emerged thirty minutes later much refreshed and with my tie on backwards, but otherwise dressed for dinner amid an equally transformed group of elegant ladies and gentlemen.

The maitre d' led me to a table for four. Joan was still apologising, '*Entschuldigen,* I don't mind where we sit.' It was thus I made the acquaintance of the Potatoes. They turned out to be wonderful table companions and their real name was Patatares. We were joined by another passenger travelling on his own. He was Finnish and his name, I think, was Antoii Pööwö. I'm fairly sure of that because I had an electronic translator with twelve languages, and the Patatares and I took turns punching in useful phrases such as, 'What is your name?' and 'Is that your best price?' He spoke no language other than his definitely non-Indo European, though he did point out some helpful liquid crystal displays such as, 'The golf-course is damp.'

The next table contained two couples. One member of each was in the early stages of dementia, and their partners were being patient. The demented wife alternatively insisted that it was Sunday and Wednesday. The undemented husband was saying, 'Well, what day do you want it to be?' and the undemented wife demurely helped herself to soup when her spouse suddenly stood up and began singing. The pianist launched into Strauss, but his elder rival had a firmer grip on Handel's *Messiah*. Giulia appeared in a red cat suit and four inch clogs, and smilingly helped him sit down. '*Ciao, bella!*' I called. Well-bred Northern Italian girls don't wink. They simply close both eyes for a moment and open them again like a cat sharing a mystery; and that's what Giulia did, with an indecipherable smile.

CONGO VIII
The Secret Agent

It was at Mbandaka that the man called Monsieur Kele came aboard. At first I took no particular notice of him, fascinated with the manoeuvres by which Kissinger displaced the Governor and his harem from their cabin to the space in front of the salon. They were permitted to put down their bundled mats. After a furious argument, an iron bed was brought. The Governor, throwing back his ample sleeves and gown, argued. He argued loudly and in a haughty French that resembled that of the Côte d'Ivoire more than Zaire. Why were the cabins full of piddling police fluviale and their sluts, while he, the Sous-Gouverneur of Haut Zaire, outranked them? The commissaire smiled nastily. Kissinger apologised. Unless Monsieur Noël would give up his cabin. No way. From an ample tribal sleeve to a rolled-up shirt thick bundles of notes were passed. Not enough. Perhaps one more bed and that was it. Wives wept. Children howled. The Governor demanded to speak to the captain. He did, and that was the last message they exchanged until we reached Kinshasa.

Meanwhile Monsieur Kele, tall and austere in an immaculate European silk suit, was being ushered into the cabin which had formerly been the governor's. In contrast to the gubernatorial potentate he had little luggage, and his only companion was a small girl of about five or six, dressed in pink, a ribbon tying her hair so severely that she looked almost bald. I had seen them at breakfast in the Hotel des Masques. Monsieur Dubrois was about to set off for an assignment, he explained as he farewelled me, then crossed over to salute the tall man in black.

Professor 'Luhasa arched her eyebrows ironically as she saw me reboarding an hour later through the barges in the company of a gang of people toting cages fluttering with brightly coloured birds. Kissinger and his cohorts had bought an Ark of animals to be sold either live or for their skins in Kinshasa. There were always Lebanese with wallets ready to take over a chimpanzee, parrot, python or twelve foot crocodile. Unlike the departed Dubrois, Kissinger lived on the boat, his main wife, slob son, infant daughter and nephew sharing his downstairs cabin, and the annexe ready for wives who took his fancy along the route. He was unctuously wary of Kele. Kissinger could have played a perfect Iago, face always shining with bonhomie, teeth flashing. Kele's face was dignified and sad. He never responded to the purser's overtures. I caught Kissinger staring at the tall man's back with an expression of unguarded resentment.

Able to use the salon again, I sat there to write. Kele did the same. We acknowledged each other with a nod, since Kissinger had avoided any effort at introduction. But someone obviously told Kele about me. One morning after the increasingly frequent meetings of the ship's staff over which he presided, he came out last. I was waiting by the door in my usual attempt to persuade the steward to leave it unlocked. He shook his head wordlessly. Kele's eyes went from my disappointed face to the biro and sheaves of notes.

'So you are writing about African cinema?'

'And trying to learn about the countries and people.'

'Then you must be very disillusioned.'

I shrugged.

'I'm afraid we have to keep the salon locked. It is certainly the only tolerable place to write.'

'I notice that you write yourself, Monsieur. On what?'

'I am writing a report.'

'About what?'

'About everything.'

He spoke with calm and authority. Then we did introduce ourselves, and he added. 'If you feel like some refreshment at noon, come to my cabin and meet my child Marie-Louise. At least the fan works.'

I brought my camera. Kele offered mineral water, and stood to pose for a photo with the little girl in pink. The difference in their heights was so disproportionate that a Polaroid would never display their faces. 'You will have to sit. And hold Marie-Louise by your side, with the lamp on your face.'

The photo smoked into brown, then full colour and detail. They looked dignified and composed. I took several others, and he was pleased.

'Your accent is excellent, for an Englishman,' he said.

'Not really. Only in Polynesia or the colonies do they tell me that.'

His face had the ghost of a smile. 'So, only those who are themselves not French ... like me.'

I laughed. 'No. In Marseilles, they were so surprised when I told them I was Australian that they said *"un chapeau pour le français"*. I think it's because they thought I was Italian.' More mineral water, poured as graciously as if it were La Veuve.

'And what are your impressions of Zaire?'

'I detest colonizers. The Belgians were probably among the worst. Your country is of extraordinary beauty. But ...' I seized the opportunity, 'petty tyranny is always disgusting; white or black.'

His face met mine coolly, as I described the stowaways and the confiscation of the movie camera.

'So now I make do with these Polaroids. I've given them practically all away. I have only one pack left.'

'Who confiscated your camera?'

'Commissaire Biharzi.'

'Why?'

'He claimed I was filming forbidden subjects.'

'Do you have a camera permit?'

'Of course. I got one in Goma.'

He ushered me to the door. 'Thank Mr Noël for the photos, chèrie … On my behalf too.' Marie-Louise shifted her polished shoes and curtsied perfectly.

Next morning I was summoned to Biharzi's cabin. A woman lying on a bed harshly pulled a curtain to the back, and a soldier sat on the bunk opposite and smoked. My camera lay beside him. Biharzi was laboriously writing an official procés-verbal. Any emotion he felt was concealed by the bureaucratic formulae of the document. He read aloud as he filled in the form:

Region: Kinshasa
Division: Enquetes
Department: Reseau Fluviale
Bureau: A Bord I.T. Ebeya
Detachment: Navigation et Convoyage
Reference P.V.J.: 089/5B–Ebeya/90

When he got to the substance of the restitution, the soldier began to snigger and play alternatively with my camera and the gun in his holster. Biharzi read his statement aloud. 'Je, le Sujet Monsieur Purdon-Noël-Francis de nationalité australienne ticket no. 0650158, target de Siami-Siami-Kinshasha, en declarant que je comprends parfaitement Lingala …'

I interrupted. 'That's nonsense. I don't speak Lingala. I'm not going to sign that.'

The soldier cackled, and Biharzi curved his lips. 'What an error! I meant: 'que je comprends parfaitement le français de Monsieur Kele …' Soldier-boy had a fit. Biharzi snapped like a mamba. 'What's amusing you? Get out.' He proceeded to the restitution of the object designated 'un appareil photo-caméra de marque Canon 310 x 6', called in another soldier to witness my 'je jure que le present PV est sincère' and handed me the camera. It rattled. I held my eye to the viewfinder. The frame tilted at forty-five degrees.

'You've broken it. Put that in the document too.'

'My subordinates, I'm afraid, are careless when they examine things. The document contains no more space except for your signature, "après lecture faite persisté et signé avec nous". Otherwise you may leave the camera here, along with the patronising magic-box with which you entertain the natives.'

We played canasta, so relieved that there was refreshment again that we asked the barman Noel to put a dozen beers on ice. We drank them all. Kele sat at a table behind us. He seemed to be doing accounts, slowly checking the pages of one book against another. Two soldiers lounged behind him. I regaled the European gang with polymorphous sexual adventures, first in French, then with even more gusto in Italian. While demonstrating one particularly vigorous *amour* I knocked the heavy ashtray on the floor. Madame Hortense and her friends looked over from the bar, also drunk and grinning, but seeming somehow dirty, drugged and sleepy, as we all were. When I picked up the cracked tray, Kele's eyes rose for a second. Looking again at his books, he said, 'Noël, you drink too much. You smoke too much. And you talk too much.'

I felt aggressive, expansive.

'Yes, that's true. But I suppose you, like Robespierre, have no vices at all. Indifferent, watching your magnificent country's wealth exploited by idiots. *Le jour n'est plus pur que le fond de mon coeur ...*' I mocked.

The police stiffened. Kele looked up from his notes, calm and quiet. He didn't raise his voice. There were bags under his eyes.

'Go to bed, Monsieur Noël.'

'That was a quote, Monsieur Kele, from Racine. Perhaps my poor French renders it unrecognisable.'

'You are too vehement. In three days we will be in Kinshasa. I believe you are comparing me to Hippolyte in *Phèdre,* also unjustly accused. And I wager you don't know the first line of that couplet ... Go to bed, please. Take the other Europeans with you. Good night.'

We threw in our canasta hands, gathered the unfinished

bottles and left. Simonetta, Daniele, and Bryan to find their
ways back to the *Lokokele*, Hans and Hendrijk to the *Bangala*,
and Fergus and I to totter below. Fergus explained my diatribe
to Bryan. Erroneously, he said it was about incest.

'Christ, you're lucky,' said Bryan. 'It's a wonder he didn't
shoot you.'

I swaggered and staggered.

'I reckon he fancies his daughter,' Fergus said. 'If she is his
daughter.'

'Oh for God's sake,' we all said.

'He's the head of the Secret Police.'

'Balls.'

'He's someone important. Even that Governor and that shit
of a commissaire watch out for him.'

'He is the head of the Secret Police,' repeated Bryan.
'Everyone on the *Myanaza* says so. He walks about there sometimes. He's taken over from Dubrois.'

'I'm going to find out,' I declared; and despite the others'
attempts to stop me, charged up the companionway.

Steward Noël was coming out with a tray and some bottles.

'It's locked,' he said. 'Finished.' The lights were still on
inside.

'Who is Kele really?' I asked my namesake.

'He's Mister Mbili.'

'And who's that?'

The barman giggled. 'Mister Mbili Number ABC,' he
teased and vanished.

Fergus was lying on his bed, sullenly reading.

'Have you got a Lingala phrase-book?' I asked.

'No. Only Swahili. And no concordance to Racine, in case
you want to ruin the play by declaiming the end.'

Mbili was right at the front. It meant 'two'.

Fergus was more surprised than I was. 'God. Maybe he is.'
I was starting to feel for Kele the kind of love that the tortured
are said to feel for their torturers. Despite my outburst I
respected him. In some way I thought he respected me as well.

'He's educated,' said Fergus. 'He recognised the Racine

straight off. It was, wasn't it? Did you know the line before?'

I didn't. I checked it up in the library at Abidjan. It made sense. *'On sait de mes chagrins l'inflexible rigueur.'* Like the Mask of Fire from whose sanctuary Kele had emerged at Mbandaka his angry grief was exactly that; calm, icy, incorruptible.

Early next morning we reached the junction of the Ubangi, here as mighty as the Congo. Its blacker, swifter waters encouraged rainforest right down to the banks, and eddies and whirlpools which Trudeau determinedly avoided. By now everything was clammy, festering, scaly. Walking on the bottom deck was more perilous than ever, because it had become an ice-rink of fish-scales, soap, blood and oil. Clothes stuck to the body. Fergus's bed was covered in lice. The ulcer on his leg was puffed and purple. Night sweats and fevers stalked the ship. 'Eight people died from poisoning on the *Bangala*,' Joseph whispered.

One evening the saloon was unexpectedly opened to all. A video projector was produced from its hiding-place. *Les gorilles dans la brume* was screened to a packed audience. A half-witted boy leaning through the windows drooled and made mooing noises whenever the misty gorillas appeared. The film had been dubbed into French, with a clever attempt at catching the accents. Madame Celeste turned and laughed during one of Bryan Brown's monologues. 'He sounds just like your friend on the *Lokokele*.' But any movement towards amiability jammed when Diane Fossey was stalked by her former black friends and killed by the poachers. A cheer went up from the adolescent audience, and there was clapping. I left.

With the rotting iron, the pestilent vapours of dead and dying animals, it was all beginning to assume the proportions of a nightmare, a concentration camp. There was an increasingly visible delight in cruelty. The retarded boy moaned and slobbered while he was baited. The animals were kicked and squashed. The landscape opened, turned from forest to savanna. There were now sand dunes and hills on either side. I still patrolled the decks.

'Jour Noël, ça va, Père?' and then hideous laughter.

'J'ai pas craqué,' I said defiantly.

But on the barges it was enough to make anyone crack.

There was no mistaking the general air of hostility that now pervaded the ship. The officers enclosed themselves for hours in the salon and forbad entry. Our last tables and deck chairs disappeared. When we saw the others still firmly placed outside the cabins of Madame Celeste, Hortense and Kissinger we argued that they were ours, hopelessly and without evidence, because they all looked the same. Madame Celeste burst into tears that I could think such a thing, and Fergus was knocked against a post by a jabbering Sammy. Leah, miserable as she was about Bryan, who was increasingly immobile and dependent, was also baited and physically attacked by teenage boys on her barge until Kele stopped it. Trudeau was tight-lipped and concentrated on his navigating. He returned my binoculars. On the shore cattle stations were visible, freshly gashed roads leading to the river. A splendidly appointed boat, half the size of the *Ebeya* but with slanted perspex windows, was moored at the side.

'That's what the mongrel uses to entertain his British and American guests,' muttered Professor Aimée. 'Look how empty it is. They all come away saying what a wonderful trip on the Congo they had. And look at us.'

The *Myanza* was the tallest of the barges. Now that their configuration had been shifted, its top deck and roof were immediately opposite my cabin. Its passengers were among the poorest and most ragged of the convoy, with whom Biharzi no longer bothered now that Kele was aboard, many of them homeless or abandoned children for whom a life on the boat was at least a greater chance of survival than fending for themselves in the forest or the cities. Most were wizened. Since food supplies were short after our last grounding, they could be seen scrounging the skin and bones of other people's meals, or tearing like little rats into the grainsacks. Rejected even by the youths who aggressively bartered jetsam fished from the floor or the river, and driven away by families only slightly less desperate than they were, they spent most of their time scrambling along the roof, squabbling over whatever dead bird or animal leg came their way. The cabins in the *Ebeya* must have seemed like luxury apartments, since these children existed without shelter or even the cardboard cartons used by others as sleeping mats. When there was nothing to scavenge, they lined the rails and stared.

Because the heat was at its most stifling, there was no question of keeping the doors closed. The first class passengers were either prostrate on their beds or sitting outside their doors fanning themselves with the giant palm-woven spades bought at Bumba. Kinsfolk with friends on the starboard side kept their doors open right through the shared bathrooms. The *Myanza* kids watched all this for hours on end.

One particular boy became my nightmare. He had polio, and sat with his twisted little legs straddling the rails not two metres from my cabin. I tried to avoid his sunken face, his eyes huge and unblinking. They pierced me. When I woke in the morning and removed my eyemask he was there, staring, unmoving, wordless. In other circumstances I might have pitied him. But he was driving me mad. Though I walked the decks with the same fixed smile I no longer knew what day it was. When Toinette or Zoulde asked me why I took so much exercise, I replied like a parrot, 'I haven't cracked yet,' and thought I heard the same mocking laughter.

As they too sickened and weakened, the other foreigners collected in my cabin. Every day we went through the water-purifying ritual, watching each precious droplet condense with the same stare with which the polio-boy watched us. Late one afternoon there was a dreadful shriek. Leah stumbled in supporting Bryan. He kept brushing his hand in front of his face. Leah was crying. Bryan muttered, 'I'm OK. Don't hassle me.' And tried to hit her and push her away. He walked out and sat on the floor of the deck, then rolled over and said, 'There's nothing there.' The rest of us looked at each other in bewilderment. It wasn't until we got him inside and lay him on my bed that we realized how disoriented he was. He made shadow-boxing movements, lay still for a moment, then arched his back and violently went into convulsions. The bed rocked as he thumped. Leah screamed. Hans left the purifier and he, Fergus and I held the thrashing body. Leah continued to cry, 'Oh, God, Bryan, Bryan. What's the matter with him?'

Hans felt his pulse and temples. 'He's very hot.'

'Could it be heatstroke?' I asked. We called his name and put a towel on his forehead. Bryan was unconscious. Leah grabbed the purifier and tried to give him some water. Hans stopped her immediately.

'No! Not while he's like that. He could choke.'

I looked at Hans fearfully. 'Could it be malaria?' Hans hesitated.

'Yes. It could. But ...'

'But what?' Leah wailed. 'You're a nurse. Noel has those pills. What?'

Hendrijk came over. 'Has he had diarrhoea or been vomiting?'

'No,' said Leah. 'He just said he had a terrible headache and then started talking funny and said he felt dizzy and wanted to get off the boat.'

Leah didn't understand French; Fergus relayed the conference. The Damianos sat apprehensively in the corner.

Then Hendrijk said softly, 'If it's malaria, the only form it could be with symptoms like that is cerebral malaria, which is the worst.'

I lost my temper. 'Where's that fucking useless doctor?' With Fergus I stormed out and banged on the air-conditioned door. We were still thumping when Trudeau appeared looking sleepy and irritated from the next cabin. We explained what had happened.

'Dr Boileau's not there; he's at his clinic on the Wema.'

Since Kele's arrival and observation of so many sick people on the barges, he had ordered the doctor to work. Leah came running round the corner.

'Bryan's conscious. He feels OK, but he doesn't know what's happened.'

Bryan was on his feet. We decided, despite the squeeze and the distance, to get him to the doctor at once. And so we did, past the impassive watchers on the *Myanza* down the steps to the *Lokokele*, through the *Bangala* following the directions people gave us to the clinic. The *Wema* had a kind of brig in its bulkhead. This was the clinic. In the dark interior we could make out hospital beds, gurneys, a nurse in uniform and a nervous little man in civilian clothes. A long mass of patients stretched round the bow.

No wonder the doctor wasn't often At Home. The queue included polio sufferers, most with their limbs completely anatomized of muscle, so that they drew themselves along by their hands or performed obscene sideways motions with their splayed and shrunken thighs. Others were lepers whose faces were so repulsive that you immediately and guiltily looked away. Many wore filthy bandages on which the blood was the colour of varnish. Some nursed broken limbs, perhaps the result of our sudden groundings. Heavily pregnant women snacked on grubs, the life inside them pressing and punching to come into the world, whatever that world might be.

When we tried to move Bryan to the front, there were justified complaints. The doctor looked himself sick and intimidated. It was obvious that we could neither leave Bryan on one of the gurneys nor stand with him for hours in the sun. I gave Boileau my cabin number and we dragged Bryan back. The doctor never came. Bryan slept. We were desperate for liquid. I called Sammy and asked him to get the bar open. Sammy demanded another Polaroid. When I told him they were finished, he was surly and muttered that neither he nor his uncle had a key.

'Then get Noël the barman.'

'He's not the barman anymore.'

I hauled myself upstairs and found him smoking with a couple of soldiers. I tried joking.

'Noël I needs Noël II to open the bar and get some mineral water.'

'No keys,' he turned out his pockets. 'Monsieur Kele took everything. And anyway,' he growled with the bravery of a nasty little dog that has been waiting to get a bite at a slightly

161

bigger dog, but hasn't had the chance, 'My name's not Noël. My name is Nguza.' And he spat his cigarette at my feet.

By now we were well into Stanley Pool. The enormous lake, twenty kilometres wide, had not even savanna on its shores; just red eroded cliffs on which bidonvilles were starting to sprout. We went on with the water-purifying. I looked at Bryan's fevered face, and myself felt sick. The bathroom door was locked. I hammered on it enough to dent the steel, and when it was reluctantly clicked open, I rampaged. Nappies flew in the air. Under a barrage of curses the girls retreated and clicked their side. I abused them violently. When I came out I was streaming with sweat. The others were still packed around engaged at their various tasks of life preserving.

'And YOU, you fucking parasites, get out of my cabin. GET OUT! You've done nothing but use me the whole trip. Can't you see that I'm sick too, you selfish bastards!'

They looked at me appalled. Leah and Fergus started to pick Bryan up as Daniele and Simonetta slunk out the door. Now I was appalled.

'I'm so terribly sorry,' I said stiffly. 'I don't mean it. Please come back in. I don't know what happened.'

But I did. I had cracked.

When I awoke the miasma had disappeared. But so had other things. My walking boots, socks, underpants and long shorts with their notebook-pocket were gone. At this point I wept. There is a stage of human deprivation where a symbolic removal of what has fundamentally, even ridiculously, served as a guarantee of dignity becomes a question of life or death. I was enraged. I threw back the mattress, rummaged through the case under my bed. Three boys from the rafts had climbed onto the ship rails and watched with the red eyes of rats. Madame Celeste and Zoulde came out of their cabin next door and implored. I was swearing.

'*Père Noël, Père Noël*. That's a bad impression. What has happened?'

I snarled at them. 'You're all fucking mad. You realise that? Where's the Commissaire? In his cage?'

The Commissaire seemed prepared. He dismissed the soldier lying on the bunk in his singlet and took my statement.
He had his own detective strategy. Had the boy Joseph or
Madame la Professeuse ever been to my cabin? Of course they
had. So they knew where these valuable items were kept? Oh
yes, it was very, very secret: they were hung over the edge of
the bed. And the other Europeans? They had used my cabin as
a sort of freehouse. They too would be interrogated. I lost my
temper. How dare he suspect my friends of whatever nation-
ality? Joseph was brought in, his eyes wide. Yes. He had been
to my cabin. Was that where he'd got the idea? The idea of
what? His criminal theft, his subversions. Joseph stared at me
in terror. What had I said? I yelled at Biharzi that Joseph had
nothing to do with it. By now Fergus was at the door. 'Don't
plead,' he said. 'We're about to dock. They'll pinch our bloody
cases next. Leave it. Bryan's already being taken to hospital.'

But I couldn't leave it. Joseph was arrested by the soldier in
the singlet. I signed form after form, insisting that no mention
be made of Professor Aimée. When I got back the other
Europeans were gathered in my cabin sitting on their luggage.
I was going straight to the Hotel Hieronymus. Despite the heat
I felt cold.

I hadn't reckoned on the next torment. The vast dock
warehouse had a sign reading *Douane*. As the Africans from the
barges were shoved in rows of ten past a crowd of officials who
plucked squawking chickens and other fowl from them as if
they were removing their quills, the ten foreigners were shunt-
ed into a series of high-roofed cages, each occupied by a table,
some chairs, and several officials wearing suits. We were called
in one at a time, asked whether we spoke French and request-
ed to take a seat. The smiles came at exactly the moment they
found the same deadly place in our passports. I was the third,
and had already seen the Belgian boys indignantly waving their
arms.

Our visas had expired. We had no right to enter Kinshasa.
The river was an international waterway. It didn't matter what
it was at Kisangani. Nor did the sandbanks and the groundings.

We should have thought of that. Three weeks was the maximum visa allowed. *Hélas,* what were they to do about that? Their open palms suggested an invitation to bribery or a slap.

'Then what are we supposed to do?'

One of the moustachioed young men smiled. 'Stay here until you get new visas. Or cross to Brazzaville and get one there. But you will have to go to the Congolese Embassy and get a visa to go to Brazzaville first. Or, of course, there's always gaol.'

I asked him to excuse me a moment and ran back along the quay, yelling out the disastrous news to Fergus, who was next, and asking him to watch my luggage. Burly, almost naked porters and packers were unloading the cargo. I dodged them. 'Where's the captain?' I asked every member of the crew I could recognise. The malicious barman laughed. 'Probably in gaol.' I tore onwards towards the boat. Governor Bangola and his retinue were being ushered aboard an open-backed truck. He huffed like an outraged rooster to avoid contact with the soldiers.

'Excellence,' I implored him, 'Where is Monsieur Kele?'

'On the boat, of course, waiting for his limousine,' he sniffed.

I ran up the gangway, cursed by porters unloading the chests of loot amassed by the wives of the police. Then I saw little Marie-Louise, dressed in a communion-like frock of white. She sat timidly on a chair outside the saloon. 'Where's papa?' She pointed solemnly inside. Kele was also wearing immaculate white. Before him stood Trudeau, a sweating Kissinger and his nephew. Kele frowned at the interruption. I myself was drenched with sweat and my Panama hung round my ears like a bandage. When I explained what was happening, his frown deepened. He spoke quietly to Commissaire Biharzi, who gave me a look of pure hatred and remained with the Kissingers. Kele picked up his folder, took Marie-Louise by the hand and marched to the customs shed. The Damiamos were the current victims. Because they spoke neither French nor English, even Fergus couldn't help them. They fell on me.

They were only in transit. Couldn't I explain? I began to, when Kele interrupted.

'It is far too hot for these people here. Let them sit down outside. Noël, would you please take Marie-Louise?'

We waited anxiously, squatting on our luggage, while Kele, his back to us, talked. One of the young officers lit a cigarette and was told to put it out. Marie-Louise stroked Simonetta's hair. After five minutes Kele emerged.

'What hotel are you staying at?' he asked.

'The Hieronymus.'

'It is quite close, but you should take a taxi. You look ill. You should stop drinking and smoking. There is a plane for Kenya tomorrow and also one for Algiers.'

'But I'm going to Nigeria.'

'All the seats on everything will be full in any case. Tell the manager of the Hieronymus that you wish to speak to Father Alain at the Redemptorist Convent. Thank you for minding my daughter. Keep all your documents relating to Zaire ready, and tell the Belgians to do the same; carry passports with you at all times. This is a difficult period for the city. In other circumstances I would say that it has been a pleasure to meet you.' He shook hands solemnly.

Then he walked back to the boat. We were summoned. An old officer with a paunch and a wheezy laugh beckoned with hooked fingers as if he were a tired but indulgent schoolmaster and we were a particularly difficult class. Simonetta and Daniele went up together. After Yukio's turn, even though his face had turned as pale as Kabuki make-up, he bowed. The younger officer asked me to tell the group there was a 1,900Z fee. As I passed I could see what was happening. The dates of the visa were undergoing perfect transformations. 1s became 7s, 6s curled into 8s. My own 2 was also augmented to a perfect 8.

'You have missed your vocation, monsieur,' I murmured.

'This is my vocation,' he chuckled.

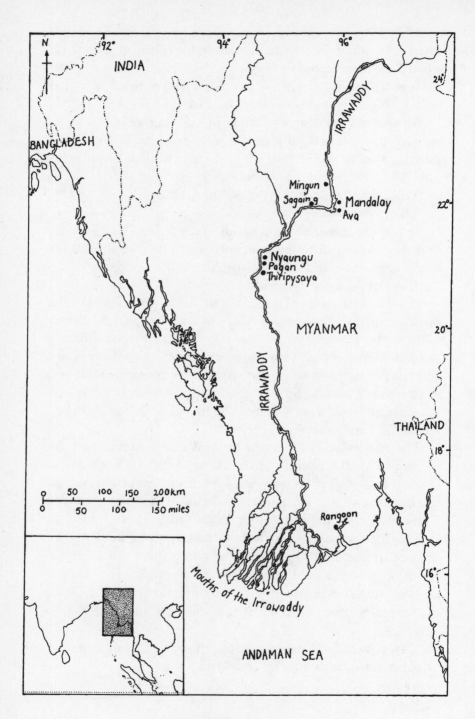

IRRAWADDY

IRRAWADDY

Steamboat to Pagan

The Irrawaddy is a pink and lemon dream drifting within a nightmare. Several thousand kilometres of its muddy waters run from the top of Burma to the Bay. Sunrise on its steamboat comes like grace abounding, not from China, but from Heaven. In 1988 sailing along it was impossible without manipulating the tentacles of Tourist Burma. The government didn't care for individual travellers – they might see too much. It liked nice groups, who would be shepherded through one or two cities and never have a close encounter even of the second kind with a Burmese.

My first view of the river came as I stepped into Mandalay from the Rangoon train: blue mountains, golden stupas glittering among clumps of palm and banyan. Paing-Paing was in one of a line of trishaws waiting outside the station. I asked him to drive me to the Mandalay Hotel.

'But they will be annoyed. They have their own transport.'

'It's too expensive and I don't want to be part of their group tours.' I offered to pay him instead, in return for being taken where I wanted. For example, Ava and Mingun.

'But Mingun is on the other side of the river.'

'That's exactly where I want to go.'

The hotel was modelled on early Soviet-Australian brutalism, a hasty horror serviced by demons and harpies trained in

167

the dreary Party meanness that characterised China in the seventies. I took one look at a poster in the lobby. 'Today the people of the Shwegon District of Pegui, assisted by the Youth Brigade, will do voluntary sanitation work on the No. 3 District Canal.' Now I knew where I was; I had sung its name in a Brecht production: Mother Goddam's House in Mandalay. Perhaps it was from here that the President ran his brothel, and that's why he kept such a low profile.

Tourists who delight in ruining Third World economies by exchanging currency at a rate which will wipe them out wouldn't have been as discouraged. This was their place. The hotel reeked of fresh, greedy cement. I had one acid exchange with the desk-staff, and refused to stay there. Since the Burmese for the numbers one, two and eight happens to be 'Tit', 'Chit' and 'Shit', I was able to do this in combinations that relieved deep feelings, and left them wondering why I had become a numerologist.

Paing, waiting within earshot outside the gate, respected the fact that I didn't want to be bossed around or speculate on the black market. Risking his safety, he took me from the hotel to his own house. He hummed and tinkled his bell as we bumped down the road, pedalling for hours, leaving me to remove my sandals and walk the temple staircases, amorous with doves and scented with jasmine incense sticks. He was perpetually meeting friends and proudly introducing me. A band of lively boatmen headed by his young nephew Nyu planned my river journey: sampan to Mingun and steamboat to Pagan.

At Mingun there are magnificent ruins half-buried by the jungle. I wandered and explored to my heart's content. Only the base of the temple survives, but it rises a solid five hundred feet among rustling trees, still mighty with its pagoda-sized bell. Bullock and pony-carts trod slowly past the village beach where women washed at a public tap and the woven houses, ramshackle as they looked, were as open to the breeze as the white temple below. The rows of snow-white lions were less fierce than their polychrome brothers across the river. Those had red tongues. These were blue-eyed and wore a look of pleased astonishment.

To find local boats to Mingun and Amarapura, you had to fend your way over the dykes. They were slow, but offered a serpentine trip around the sandbacks and pagodas. One of them let us off directly outside Paing's house near Ava, its stilts bathing in the water. Alongside banana trees, herbs flourished in the little patch of garden: garlic, coriander, spring onions, basil, ginger.

His sister-in-law Daw greeted us in the kitchen. Jars in the curved cupboard held orange chilis, yellow groundpeas, tamarind, turmeric and coconut milk. A celadon bowl of pure steaming rice, another of lentils, a cauldron for more noodles and green tea were simmering on the charcoal fire. Daw made Moh hin gha, for which I provided canned herrings from my backpack. The noodles were fogging the room, and the hot fish stew, with its prepared slices from the banana tree, was tipped from a brown bowl into each of our green ones. The colour was a deep yellow: the pickles and egg-curd, dried prawns like little roasted whitebait.

Paing's daughter brought us towels and hot water in a tin dish. Another celadon bowl of thick smoking rice was laid on the mat, followed by one of lentils. Paing's neighbour appeared with a saucepan of chicken curry fresh with great chopped leaves of coriander. Bananas and coconut milk were our dessert. I gave the family a box of cigars, and was then unfortunately obliged to smoke one with Paing's father upstairs. The old man had his meal served separately; he was dying. After the cigar, so was I. But Paing and Daw, mindful of their promise to get me on the boat to Pagan next morning, put me to sleep on a mat beside him. I fell asleep to his ancient songs.

I was miles up some dream mountain when they woke me by stroking my hands and helped me struggle into clothes. Paing put superhuman energy into the trishaw, hailed Nyu from the river path, and bundled us towards the dark shape of the *Maung Nat*. I was one of the last up the springy gangplank. The steamer was already packed with yellow-robed monks in their pongyi, high-school students off to the vocational centres downriver in Myingyan, and two other escapee tourists with rucksacks. Over the stern-well a canopy had been erected. Midship the cabins looked like bathing huts with folding wooden shutters. As we reached centre stream and the dawn began to glimmer, people emerged sleepy-eyed, scratched themselves and went back to their bunks. The side seats were full of passengers with sacks and poultry. I was still hardly awake. It was cold, very cold, and I was glad Daw had inserted my arms into the sweater and padded jacket. That also left more space in the rucksack for the bananas, the water-bottle and cans of salmon. But this was the third morning in a row that I'd been woken before 5.00 am, and I felt like a zombie. I could no longer see Paing on the banks; I had a moment's sharp pain that I would never see him again, and that his father would die.

As we passed under a bridge I discovered the little ricecakes Daw had wrapped in banana leaves for my breakfast, washed down with half a bottle of cool black tea. As the river curved the bend into Sagaing, pagodas stood out on its hill. The river twisted sharply. In the east the sun had cleared the descending ranges to bathe the banks with already tropical heat. Parasols opened like mushrooms: now every colour was picked out, from the boat's blue palings to the viscous brown of the river. Below the short space at the bow, where I still blundered around and got in everyone's way, the sharp prow seemed almost to be digging into the mud.

The land became completely flat; fields of pulse or sorghum were irrigated by myriad canals which sparkled among the green. At times it seemed like a vast swamp, the broad river converging twenty miles ahead. A few sampans passed, with people hanging out their washing or crouched modestly over a tub to sluice their bare brown backs. The sun was really hot now. How beautiful the Burmese looked in their longyis and soft tight little jackets, the women's short-sleeved and folded over their breasts like white gauze. Because of the diesel fumes and the monstrous cigars that all Burmese smoke from the age of seven onwards, I began to cough uncontrollably.

'He's got TB, that one,' said the captain. A fourteen year old Buddhist nun on her way to the shrine at Ananda obligingly translated and helped me out on the roof.

'TB. Yes,' I agreed, 'Tourist Burma. A hundred–per–cent mortality rate.'

Some of the people round me laughed. The middle-aged and the adolescents spoke good English; I knew I couldn't have been the first to make the pun. Now the younger men, including Nyu, removed their aingyis, the smart top jackets. They were handsome boys, round and curved and compact, their flesh the colour of honey, the hairless chests made voluptuous by the darker nipples. The girls sprawled back on the roof and surreptitiously flirted. Many of them emphasised their slightly paler skin by wearing yellow paint brushed smoothly over the entire face. Some had inscribed on each other's cheeks diagonal stripes of blue. It was a sensuous combination. Wondering if it were some mark of caste or virginity, I asked the little novice. She laughed and covered her own face.

'Oh no. It is to protect the skin. Against the sun. Would you like to wear some?'

'What is it made of?'

'Clay. Or you would say mud.'

I had a coughing spasm and fished out some suncream.

'What is that made of?' I rapidly read the ingredients. Good God, they sounded like a chemical dump. But it did say Palmolive Milk on the front.

'Er ... milk,' I mumbled and offered her a fingertip, which she laughingly declined. But she did tell the reclining girls and boys, who inspected the tube and tried some on their arms. We continued to pass low flat fields. This was the dry season, Pyatho, the tenth moon on the Burmese calendar.

'Last night we watched it rise with Phoksha,' said Nyu.

'That's the constellation we call Pisces, I think.'

He and the young novice pointed out scenes on the banks: buffalo coming to drink; water levers that reminded me of the Nile's shadoofs; excited groups of villagers thrashing a tree with smoking branches.

'It is the month of gathering honey,' smiled the nun. I asked Nyu whether there were wild animals in the stretches of forest that broke up the territories of the fields. 'Not here. Further up where you aren't allowed to go, there are bears, leopards, tigers, rhinoceros.'

'And elephants,' added a child. He asked where I was from, and then made his final addition. 'And flying foxes, as in Australia.'

'You're very clever,' I congratulated him.

'I am a geographer.'

I dozed from lack of sleep, waking with a jerk as we passed a tributary noisy with men straddling logs of teak. Nearing villages we sliced through clumps of bamboo and bracken, and stopped at market stalls that looked like an emperor's granary, hundreds of terracotta jars delicately carved and lidded, fresh from the kiln. This west side had broad beaches in front of the thatched houses. Like sensible people everywhere, the villagers went about their business carrying their jars and goods on their heads. Egrets and geese took off against the eggshell sky and the brown hills. White ibises waded in the green, undisturbed by the men checking fish traps. When the river widened it became alive with lanteen-rigged yachts, the sails of rainbow variety, stern and prow standing tall in the water like triremes. Downstream were moored boats of all sizes. Some breathtaking two-masters braved the spits of sand and took the wind near the cliffs.

The Irrawaddy near Pagan is like nothing on the face of this earth. It is probably the most extensive visible evidence of a millennium-old civilisation set in its natural landscape and used for its original purposes. Between the mountain and the river the temples extend on its blue-brown plain like a vision. When the steamboat hit that dusk, the banks were pink. By the time we reached Nyaung U the sun had set, and I could barely make out the bell-shaped cupolas of the temples. I slept on a mat at Nyu's parents' house. As with Paing's hospitality, this was illegal. Unlike the hotels it was also real. My rucksack held silk shirts, because they were light and beautifully patterned. They made wonderful gifts, as did the canned food which I no longer needed. Next morning I took a sampan the further eight kilometres to the landing below the lighthouse-like pagoda of Bupaya, pointed out by the other Westerner on the boat, an archaeologist called Timothy who had been working for a year on Hindu–Buddhist iconography.

When we stepped off the boat at Pagan, there was a festival in full progress. Caravans of covered wagons with wheels as huge as those in the temple carvings lined the route from the city gates to Htilominlo. In their niches, the brother and sister spirits of the city bade them welcome, animism co-existing with the Gautama and images of Brahma and Vishnu. The bells and chanting went on all day and night. Here the monks wore vivid scarlet, and processions of people carrying offerings on their heads and prayer-papers in their hands thronged the temples. Mei-mei, a little girl about seven of frightening thin-ness and equally frighteningly intelligent grey eyes, offered herself as a guide. She spoke English, French and Italian. 'Courrez! Courrez!' she cried after ringing all the Ananda Temple gongs at once. The outraged monks came shaking their hands towards us.

The highest circle of Paradise, the place where the angels spent most of the day simply singing, was the Irra Inn, high on the banks of the Irrawaddy near Leya. Here the management not only knew that foreigners needed to wash their clothes, but provided detergent and drying racks. The food, if you asked for it properly, was classic Burmese cuisine: tender beef, aubergine sauce, butternut soup, salads of shallots and toma-toes. The sprightly proprietor was the only Burmese I ever heard raise his voice and tell Tourist Burma exactly where they could place Forms F, G & H. His staff held their ears while he thundered over the telephone.

'Monsters,' he said when he had finished. 'Have you ever had Ame Hnat?' I didn't think so. 'It's my best curry. Except for the beef and pumpkin one, but I haven't got any pumpkin.' I promised to find him one. He pounced on my map. 'See this dot marked Manuha? That's the temple where the great Buddha lies with his arms flat beside, like this. They call it the dead Buddha, but of course it's no such thing. He is entering bliss and peace, which I bloody well wish I could do. So before you get there, see this dot marked Myinkaba. It's actually quite a large village, and there's a market.' With two and a half days to explore the vast city, I had already hired a bike, and planned to spend that day with Timothy going further south where the river curves almost at a right angle. There lay some of the ancient capitals and the most perfect stone carving. There dwelt also the king of pumpkins and I duly brought it back.

Tim and I watched the sunset from the Thatbyinnyu Temple, which rises in a series of broad terraces and has a winding staircase inside the central tower that takes you to the top of Pagan, over two hundred feet up. The bells and music pealed from the nearby Ananda; in every direction there were thousands of other stupas, pagodas and palaces.

'This one's twelfth century,' Tim explained. 'Most of the others are also eleventh to thirteenth. There used to be more. But the Irrawaddy's eating the banks. You saw how thick it is. It hits that curve just above Pebinkyaung, and takes the walls and whatever's on them. It's done about fifty so far. That's where we're working, over to the south-west. There's a complex of libraries and gateways. You're interested in iconography. Ride over.'

Pagan at night, perhaps because of the feast, had even more stalls than Mandalay, booths strung with little lights and lamps, some selling food, others bike repair outfits, the air hot with roasting peanuts. One of the puppet booths was doing the Mahabarata. The puppets were manipulated, not very dexterously, by children. Stubby little arms kept appearing from the velveteen curtains. Fingers with sticking plaster re-arranged a recalcitrant string. At first they were single puppets jigging to recorded music. The rattan booth had cane chairs for the audience, which soon filled them according to invitation. Scores more clustered outside; the next part of the show consisted of excerpts from the Ramayana, and was performed with vigour and gasps of delight at the antics of the Monkey-King. The marionettes were large, some over three feet; as well as their limbs they also moved their eyes, eyelids and mouths. Next door was the puppet-master's shop, with hundreds of Hanumans, Sitas, Ramas and Ganeshas hanging from the walls. Most were dressed in rich but faded brocades with gold-frilled trimmings.

'They are antiques,' said the old man.

'I suppose that means they're expensive.'

'It depends who you like.'

I liked Ganesh; his elephant trunk coiled and moved, and he was crowned. After a little haggling I had him.

'He is your patron, you know.'

In between the stalls were handcarts of books. It seemed as if the British on departing had left their entire educational syllabus. Texts on trigonometry, diagrams of bunsen burners were piled beside Carlyle and Ruskin. To my astonishment I found volume one of the first edition of *The Ring and the Book*. The cart-holder rummaged through shorthand and anthropometry until he fished up the other three, swirling still with their water-patterns.

Next day I cycled out to Tim at Pyathonzu, racing downhill surrounded by yellow-flowering shrubs. Now the whole place appeared as an afterworld of giant sandcastles, where a group of intelligent children had been let loose and allowed to make a thousand towers of every kind they liked. Some were pyramids, some like the bulbs of the poppy, some like umbrellas, some still curving their rings and coils inside the hands of an invisible potter. I found Tim tracing a wall-painting. He was by himself and working carefully on the figure of a floating apsara.

'I'm just recording. The stone's crumbling. We won't restore. We can't.'

'Well, I brought my carefully recorded and preserved Johnny Walker to ease your labours.'

He laughed. 'I don't drink. But if you want to give me a lunch-break I can take you to someone who certainly does.'

Mrs Ky ran a small eating pavilion in the village above. She was a toughie. While she snapped open bottles of soft-drink with her teeth and stirred her pot of noodles, she interrogated Tim in Burmese, then tossed her head at my Johnny Walker and addressed me in English.

'How much you want? And you must have nice box with label. Otherwise not worth shit.'

I had discarded the box so that I could wrap the bottle in clothes and save packing space. While she made lunch and fortified herself and me from an already open bottle of Scotch she studied me as if I were mentally retarded. Clicking her tongue and sucking her breath she continued the examination as she slugged another jamjar.

'I like shirt very much,' she finally said. It was a Thai striper with a fake Calvin Klein label on the pocket.

'I buy that. How much?'

I told the truth. I had bought it in Bangkok for ten dollars.

'Not important. You sell and I buy Johnny Walker too. Good label.' After another course of lotus and whisky slugs I agreed. She became thoughtful. 'Your shorts good quality. Please show.'

I looked to Tim for advice. He shrugged. She called, 'AAYYEE' and summoned a boy who had been bringing fresh-cut bamboo shoots to the kitchen. 'This my son.' They talked rapidly, and looked me over. 'Show me underpants.'

I goggled at Timothy. 'I thought Burmese were supposed to be modest.'

'They are. Mrs Ky's not one of them. She knows all Westerners are shameless. Do it.'

I removed my shirt, then the shorts. They found favour with the Kys, who wagged their heads and spoke cheerfully to the archaeologist.

'Apparently you don't stink. Now the underpants.'

'Great. And how am I supposed to get around Burma? Stark naked?' Timothy translated, and after some serious chuckles, Mrs Ky responded.

'You wear longyi. Fair exchange. Kalvin underpants please.

My son say excellent.'

I went behind the thatched pavilion, and Tim passed me a longyi which he later exchanged for a set of his own baggy shorts. When I emerged the deal was celebrated with another round of whisky. The transaction had paid for the meal, and bestowed upon me extra cash about which I felt morally and economically confused.

'Mrs Ky,' I said as she helped me tie the longyi, 'those clothes are not really Calvin Klein. And you have given us at least half a bottle of Johnny Walker while paying for the one you bought.'

She investigated my navel and picked at it with her fingers. She laughed.

'Many babies there. And that not Johnny Walker we drink. That whisky from Mekong. I just pour into Johnny label. Same label, same experience. And you not notice.'

At the colonial sailing club outside Rangoon were the gloating idiots who had made a fortune out of the currency black market. 'It's a brilliant way of keeping down inflation,' a Yale yuppie explained to me. 'It all comes back as consumer goods from Thailand.' From the rest-house on the lake I took a local steamer the final few miles into Rangoon. The sun was setting over the golden spire of the Shwe-Dagon temple on the hill, over the gently decaying post office, over the back alleys where torn remnants of Tennyson fluttered in the wind or floated in the gutters. And some children, only their hands visible in a park behind the hill, were flying kites, hoping to catch the breeze.

Home again in Australia I found a letter. It was in English, scrolled with the Palic flourishes used by professional scribes.

'By this month you will have returned to your own land. People call it an absurdity of mine. But every time a tourist comes round a corner, I expect it to be you. So I look for you. When you come again to Burma, perhaps you will remember me. Daw Nainng asks if you enjoyed her cooking. You were respectful of our spirits. And the spirits have reminded me to write. But perhaps you have already forgotten me. I was your trishaw driver.

Paing-Paing'

I wrote back immediately. By then it was late February. In March the massacre unleashed on the Burmese was horrendous. Mandalay was purged; 6,000 villagers of Pagan were driven out and their homes bulldozed; the students of Rangoon were shot and bayoneted by the riot police, the Lon Htien, outside the beautiful pagodas. I never heard from Paing again. But I still dream of the kites catching the breeze.

CONGO IX

Hotel Hieronymus

I woke with a fright. The heavy velvet curtain had drifted over my face. If the Kinshasa Hieronymus had seen better days, it was hiding them, perhaps behind one of the miles of doors in the panelled walls that fat chambermaids and shovel-slippered flunkies opened and closed to deposit or withdraw linen, crockery and large card-tables. My room was on the top. It had air-conditioning, even though the box wheezed like an old donkey reminding a rider of its unfair load, and the bed was large and clean. The Hieronymus was dark. Even at noon its shutters kept out the light, because the light was like the sun, hot. In the dark, Greek and Lebanese businessmen did deals over the bar and the green baize tables.

But there was another reason for the closed shutters. The hotel looked directly onto the main square, the markets beside it, and the expanse of river beyond. When I felt rested, I opened the shutters and was bathed in a breeze rising from the four mile expanse of water across to Brazzaville. I left them open, switched off the whine of the air-conditioner, and went back to bed. My doze was interrupted by yells, gunshots and screams. I ran to the window in time to see flashes of black and white disappear into the markets, and two trucks bristling with rifles. I stood watching them circle. There was a knock on the

179

door. The concierge respectfully asked me to close the shutters. It had been noticed. It was dangerous.

'What's happening?'

'It's just a *manif,* monsieur, a demonstration. Better to close the windows too. I closed the windows, took four sleeping pills, switched the air-conditioning back on, covered my face with a wet towel and went to oblivion.

I awoke long before dawn, dizzy and hot, but feeling an immense relief that I was no longer on the screaming, pullulating boat. Kele was right. I drank and smoked too much. I sat on the edge of the bath and was surprised when I started vomiting. I knelt on the tiles, shuddering with fright and disgust, then cleaned my teeth and took two more rohypnol. When I woke again I had stomach cramps. Daniele, Simonetta, Fergus and I had arranged to meet at the old market at 10.00 am.

The flu and the backache were getting worse. The humidity made movement exhausting; I didn't want to get really ill and be confined in a place whose menace had boiled to the surface. I should ring Father Alain. I collected my documents. A letter from the London Ambassade du Zaire in response to my first visa request now spelt out its full sinister meaning. It suggested that the single point of entry should be the capital, and that because of 'troubles' the only means of internal transport should be by air.

'We do not doubt that you will understand these wise measures taken simply for security reasons and to avoid unforeseeable consequences involving innocent visitors, and to save the Zairian government from shouldering any responsibility of any possible circumstance.'

A leopard's head snarled from a shield between crossed spears and an olive branch: *Justice. Paix. Travail.* I understood why Kele had arranged what seemed the strange subterfuge of the mission. Because he foresaw the 'unforeseeable', and because, whoever he was, he took responsibility.

For a city of several million people, Kinshasa was eerily empty. Few cars and fewer pedestrians traversed its broad avenues and squares. The shops were meshed with rusty grilles; behind the blinds of the tall offices people might or might not be working. There could be no question of contacting cinéastes. I was a week late at the Hieronymus, and there was no mail. The concierge recalled one phone message, but his palsied hands and quavering voice conveyed that he hadn't understood it.

I walked to the antiquarian market, taking frequent rests. Under the tree-shaded avenues Kinshasa was humid. Carved wooden figures ten feet tall, masks from all over central Africa, heavy Belgian jewellery, seventeenth century Portuguese ceramics were laid out in long lines under a tent the size of a circus big-top. Simonetta and Daniele were already there, hand in hand. There were few tourists and the vendors sat listlessly. The masks were beautiful, but I thought it would be foolish to add such heavy items to my bag when I could already hardly carry it, despite my practice of regularly posting packages home. Equally foolishly, I did buy a sixteenth century Portuguese blue-glaze jug which proved even heavier. Simonetta and Daniele bought an eerie hollow-cheeked mask, like the one I had coveted at Mbandaka, but not as ascetic. The vendor understood my description of the white calm face that had gazed on me there, but waved it away.

'Not Zairian. From the Gabon.'

At the crossroads we promised to meet for dinner before I left, and I waved back to them. We were among the few pedestrians on the main roads. Fergus hadn't bothered to show up. I asked the concierge to find the number of the convent, and tell them that I needed urgently to speak with Father Alain. The old man buzzed me twice to say that it was useless. Then, as I was drifting off to sleep, a female operator's voice announced that a priest was waiting to speak to me. His English had a Canadian accent, and he interrupted my suggestion that we to meet by saying that it was far too dangerous for travel in the city at the moment, but that there was a Lagos

flight tomorrow. He would call for me in the convent's car at
6.30 am if I could be ready. I promised with all my soul. 'Speak
in French,' he added. 'And tell a few white lies. We have seats
for you and an Igbo priest. You don't have to pretend to be a
priest. Just someone who has been a guest of the convent and
is returning to Nigeria. Do you understand?'

I was suspicious. I had expected him to be French, and
he wasn't. I started to question and he said: 'Listen. Your
friend has already contacted me. In case you're wondering, I'm
from Quebec. And from your accent, I agree with him –
you're from Marseilles.' Then he hung up, or was cut off. My
conflict of fear and hope was tempered by his joke. At lunch,
a group of Zairian businessmen wrote their addresses on the
pages of my notebook. I felt so unwell that I went upstairs,
switched on the air-conditioning and pulled a blanket round
and round.

Again at about 5.00 pm I was awoken by sirens and screams.
This time a much larger demonstration, mainly of women,
heaved across the square. They struggled with the soldiers in
the rib-backed trucks, exposing their breasts and daring them
to shoot. The soldiers did. The screams were unearthly, turning into long wails between the bursts of fire. Peeking through
the shutters I saw bodies and blood. I couldn't tell whether or
not they were dead. I hurtled downstairs, but the concierge
blocked me as he did other guests who ran into the lobby. The
staff bolted the front doors. They begged us to return to our
rooms.

I sat on my bed and wondered if I should ring Father Alain;
got up; wandered relentlessly in circles; got no sound from the
telephone; and was irresistibly drawn back to the windows.
The bodies had gone, but there were stains of blood and oil,
and what looked like palm or vegetable leaves all over the con-
crete. The concierge knocked, and when I didn't answer,
because I didn't want him to think that I had been at the window, announced that there was a *couvre-feu*. At first I didn't
understand the word, then, from somewhere – South-East
Asia? Films? – it clicked. Cover-fire. Put out the light. The sky

was bloody, a smoky apocalypse in which armies of skeletons might be advancing.

I lay in bed, greatly frightened, and planned and plotted. I could ring the convent or the British consul, but that might make things worse. Instead of being able to sneak out, I would be identified. I half-dozed, trying to breathe properly and calm myself. Headache pounded, and not even Panadeine would stop it. In this state, I was disturbed by another knock. The concierge apologized, but there was a lady downstairs at the half-grilled door who wished to see me, and he was reluctant to unbar it.

I had never seen, or imagined, Simonetta so distraught. Even in the last bad days on the boat, even at the market today when she had been subdued, her Botticelli face and graceful little body had radiated self-possession. Now she ran into the hotel, brushing off the concierge's arm, looked wildly around and sobbed as soon as she saw me.

'They'll kill him,' she shrieked. 'They've taken him away in a truck and they're going to kill him.'

I held her and made soothing noises, looking anxiously at the concierge, who had locked the door behind her. I hugged her more tightly, saying over and over, 'Calmati. Forza. Cosa c'hai?' She raved her story.

After I left them, she and Daniele had continued walking along the road. A convoy of soldiers drove past, then stopped. A group in camouflage descended and surrounded them, demanding to see their visas. Daniele produced his. Simonetta had left hers at the hotel, along with her other documents and possessions, alert to the possibility of being robbed on the eve of their escape.

The soldiers ordered her to get in the truck and come with them to the police station. Daniele protested. He wasn't a big man, but he loved his wife and certainly wasn't going to allow her to be taken off by a group of bandits in uniform. There was a struggle and Simonetta was pulled away, calling out to Daniele for help. He was being held by another soldier and arguing in Italian. When he was released he ran to the truck, and pulled out his pen to take its licence number. Having no paper, he used one of the by now worthless Zairian makuta banknotes.

Immediately shouts erupted and rifles bristled. There was much pointing at the banknote and shouting. He had defaced the picture of President Mobutu. He would go to jail for life. They abandoned Simonetta for their new prize. She ran after the truck. The station wasn't far. After more struggle, Daniele was locked in a cell and Simonetta was made to understand that he could only be released on bail for $500. They wrote it on a piece of paper and made slitting motions across their throats. The Hieronymus was the only safe place in the centre because curfew had descended. And she knew I was staying here. Could I lend her $500? Her dishevelled blonde hair was wet with rain and panic. 'And *ti prego, ti prego.* Come with me to the police station. I can only understand a few words of their French. *Per carità,* you can translate. You can explain, I'll pay you back tomorrow, you know I will. Otherwise they'll kill him. They'll torture him.'

I am ashamed I had so little courage left. After the carnage, I dreaded leaving the hotel. Simonetta was on the point of collapse, and I gave her the key to my room. I asked the hotel staff what I should do. Their eyes popped in terror. Women killed in the main square, and now tourists in trouble with the military. I cashed cheques for $200, which was all I could afford, and asked the concierge to take them to the police station. He refused. I begged him for the sake of the woman lying in tears on my bed. He conferred with the manager, then with the hotel gendarme. Perhaps $300 would be a sufficient offer in cash. Perhaps neither I nor Simonetta would need to go. The gendarme would take it. $300 would be better. I haggled, exasperated: that was all I could afford. They warned me about defacement of the President's image. I told them that I understood. It was a disgraceful accident. President Mobutu was the Saviour of Zaire. The gendarme had a car brought round and left. Simonetta fell asleep in my room. I sat dazed in an armchair watching her. There was another knock.

It was the laundry-woman, at whom I'd thrust my stained and grubby clothes. But that's not why she was returning. In a whisper she informed me that another foreigner had banged on the hotel door and needed to see me. I exulted. Daniele had been released! I followed her down the stairs, expecting to embrace him. But the man who stood wavering beside the desk was Fergus. Fergus was a wreck. His eyes were baggy and he looked as if he'd lost several kilos. He was wearing his kilt, which had a salty stain down the front.

'What happened to you? Simonetta and Daniele and I waited for you at the market for an hour.'

'Yes. Well, that's it. I'm afraid I couldn't attend the *matinée au marché*. I was locked up in a *vespasienne* at the time, and ... well, movement was limited.'

'What do you mean?'

'I was arrested.'

'For what?'

'Apparently I'm a spy and a transvestite. I was walking down to the Continentale to see Yukio. You and he are the only gentry on the boat, the distinguished Monsieur Kissinger always excepted of course. The Continentale has a swimming pool. The Europeans remaining in this gracious city live in bougainville-covered cages there, and I thought I might have a swim. But ... fatally I wandered off the road, down to the river-bank, because I thought I'd get a closer look at Brazzaville.'

'Where's Bryan?'

'Apparently he's still delirious. Try for once not to interrupt me'

'Go on then. But stop burbling.'

'Well, the next thing I know, half a dozen thugs in uniform leapt out of the bushes, held me at riflepoint, locked me in a sentry-box and told me they'd come back when I was ready to give a deposition. Can I use your bathroom?'

'Simonetta's already in my room.' I told him what had happened to her.

'Oh, Jesus,' he said, 'Can I come up? I'm about to bust.' I

lay on the bed, careful not to disturb Simonetta. When he came out his face was cleaner and clearer.

'So what happened?'

'I gave a deposition. I'm a jaywalker, second class. Pedestrianism is four years. Espionage, they just hang you. Transvestism's free.'

I laughed unwillingly.

'Like old times, isn't it?'

There was a rattle of machine-gun fire. Simonetta jumped awake and Fergus hugged her.

'Holy Jesus!'

'You were always so flippant and cynical, Fergus. You never supported me. I'm at the end of my strength. You pretended it all wasn't happening'.

The concierge again knocked apologetically. 'The shooting is on the other side of town, near the university. Don't be afraid. And come downstairs. I think everything has been regulated.'

When we reached the lobby, there he was. Daniele was pale under his tan, but wildly happy as soon as he saw Simonetta. And beside him, entering cautiously under the eyes of the gendarme, were Hans, Hendrijk and Leah. 'Colpo di fortuna!' Daniele cried, and raced into the arms of his wife.

While they tearfully embraced and soothed each other, the rest came sheepishly forward. They had all been arrested, rounded up at the fleapit hotel which had been their immediate haven. And they had all been released, thanks to quarrels between the army, the police, and the final payment of the fine for Daniele.

'God knows who is shooting whom,' said Hans. 'Sometimes it seems they're firing into the air, and sometimes at each other's trucks.'

Simonetta immediately insisted on changing traveller's cheques pooled from the rest and repaying me. Dollars were unavailable, so I settled for West African francs. We sat round a table with the gendarme, and the others got hysterically drunk while I stuck to mineral water and got high on the atmosphere. Fergus burst into a declaration of unrequited love for Kitty, and sat with his eyes watering. We drank a toast to her, and prompted by Leah, to Bryan. Then Fergus imitated Kissinger, and we had uncontrollable giggles of the kind with which a classroom of anxious children might be possessed as with the devil. If we were waiting for the Apocalypse we would have been found like the inane revellers in the Pisa frescoes, throwing dice while Death mows down their fellows. With many kisses I slid upstairs to bed.

Father Alain and his driver called at dawn. He would collect my boarding pass, and pass me over to plain-clothes men who would take me through customs. In front of the airport I must let everyone know that I had come from the convent, otherwise the other drivers would give his driver hell for fetching a fare. At least the Church still had some protection, because the President needed its international approval. There must be no mention of the river or Kele's name; just the convent and my friends there.

'Your other friend believes you will be a friend to Africa.'

I couldn't help asking: 'What's Kele's connection with the convent?'

Father Alain was silent for a moment. 'His wife passed away with us three months ago. The little girl was sent back to Mbandaka. He is a good man.'

'How on earth can he be part of Mobutu's government?'

The priest silently indicated the driver and shook his head with a warning.

'Here we are ...'

I pumped the driver's hand, and called out ostentatiously. 'And give my regards to Father Francois and Father Paul.' I did the same in the airport after Father Alain stood in line for my pass, joined from nowhere by two plain-clothed men. We all shook hands again. They ushered me through a concealed door, checked my passport and luggage, and produced some office tape, ready to seal it. One said, 'Do you have any souvenirs for us?' I was prepared. The Polaroid was starting to jam and oozed brown muck every time it developed: my cassette player was broken. I demonstrated the open/eject mechanism and the case. 'It won't work unless you put in lithium batteries. Remember. *Pilules du lithium.*' They were impressed. And what do policemen like more than their mothers? Sunglasses. Four pairs bought whenever I thought I'd lost the current ones had been churned up during packing. The police were satisfied.

I was released into the waiting hall, and astonished to see Yukio. Good old R2D2. He still bowed; still smiled.

'How did you manage it?' I asked

'Oh, I am always very polite. And I give money. The manager gave me his ticket. My friends said this was a foolish adventure, without honour. But I have honour.' He told me Leah had rung him at the Intercontinentale. 'When Bryan is better he will be arrested. Did you hear the gunfire last night?'

'Thank God we're getting out. We can't help them any more. We're lucky.'

Whatever Yukio's honour was, it was pervasive. We bowed and shook hands. I was offended to see Yukio recoil.

'Your hand is very hot. But you're shivering.'

Yes, I could feel the shivering; with the fear of something whose patience has been exhausted, lurking, ready to pounce. Not fear of the jungle, which was pristine rain forest, nor of the animals which we had seen mastered and eaten. But a fear of other humans, which is the worst fear of all; because ultimately, if you count yourself among the categories of men, it's a fear of yourself. As I boarded the plane with that archaic desire to see what lay on the other side of the river, I looked across the Congo at the towers and cubes of Brazzaville, and thought: No. I shall never go there, however curious I always am about what lies on the other side. No. This has been enough.

NIGER

NIGER I

Fever

As we flew over Mount Cameroon after fighting the heat turbulence over Kinshasa the weather changed, like a calendar flipped by the wind. Clouds boiled over dark serpentine rivers, mist and mangroves. The rainy season had arrived. The estuaries of the Niger Delta were grey and oily and spattered with refineries. The scene filled me with apprehension about getting out of humid Lagos to the drier heat of Kano. But I was lucky. My seat was next to that of a tall young man glowing with vitality and dressed like a prince. He was a Hausa merchant. When he found that I too wished to go on to Kano and was worried about making the connection because of immigration, he beamed and called for candy-sticks. 'No problem. You are my personal guest. I am Cheik Oumar El-Haj Idriss.' The Hausa are the most powerful of the three main ethnic groups which make up the two hundred tribes of Nigeria. Despite living in the north, their ancient control of the desert market has led them to invest in the oil of the south, where the Yoruba nominally control the government, but not the economy. As for the unfortunate Igbo, along whose coasts the wells smoke through the night, many are Christian converts. When they asserted themselves, they became the victims of the Biafran war.

191

But thank Allah for Cheik Oumar. It turned out that the domestic airport was ten miles from the international one. He radiated influence with the stubborn immigration officer, grabbed a taxi, and organised two ragged men to gallop with our luggage straight onto the runway, fanning himself and saying, 'Oh, my goodness.' When I had no Nigerian money to tip, he dripped bills of naira. Seated, he made a show of extravagant expressions of relief, ordered cool drinks, charmed the hostesses, and introduced me to everyone around, presenting his own cards and a bundle of mine. 'He is an Australian film director,' announced Oumar to the whole plane with cheerful inaccuracy.

For the next two days he drove me round Kano, to open-air cinemas, the Emir's palace, the dyers, the cattle market, his father's and brother's shop, and his house, where I was allowed to meet his veiled sister and wife. The sky was so white. The people all seemed dressed in blue. Oumar shone happiness. He chirped like a bird. I felt ashamed that my headaches and diarrhoea persisted, that whatever daze possessed me in Kinshasa had become worse, and that I had to keep on blowing my nose so messily in public.

Despite the dry climate, two steps saw me soaked and dizzy and wearing a clinging shirt. As Oumar strode tall and beaming in his immaculate robes I felt like a wretched little dog trotting to keep up. One evening I arrived back at my hotel, had a beer and a cigarette in the courtyard, and rising to go upstairs, felt such terrible aches in my back and legs I could hardly climb. My eyes were irritated as if they were full of sand. I sat for a minute and seemed to fall down a lift-shaft. When I came to, I was lying at the bottom. Oumar and his brother were sitting watching me gravely, slapping their fly-whisks from shoulder to shoulder. My mother sang 'The Lily of Laguna' and 'three little fishie-wishies' and became Deborah Kerr chanting endlessly 'Whenever I fear the people I fool I fear myself as well'. Why was her French so wrong? Julie and I sailed the Coorong in the freezing cold till the Antarctic winds forced us back, never to pass Cape Horn. I shook and shivered and cried. So much fluid poured from my eyes, nose and throat that I stumbled to and from the bathroom, pulling at the toilet roll and blowing my nose and spitting and wetting the paper to plaster round my face. God knows how many times I lay on the bathroom floor, even though it frightened me because I was glued to it and the window was full of lightning. But my limbs ached so much I could hardly get up again. People who have been injured or stricken with severe illness suddenly will tell you the same story. The first reaction is surprise. Perhaps it occurs as a gift of mercy. It replaces pain. You stare at the blood streaming from your mouth onto your hands and think, 'What on earth is this?'

When I crawled back into the bed, it sloped, tipping itself up an incline from which I could feel myself sliding down into hell. Sometime early in the morning I apparently had convulsions loud and long enough to dislodge the bed from its frame with a crash that woke the entire hotel and made blue men come. Now there was blood mixed with mucous round my mouth. My jaw juddered uncontrollably. I had bitten a slice off my tongue. I thought that Cheik Oumar was looking at me with disgust. He was saying something about a private clinic in the hills outside the city on the way to Jos, and ordering the men in blue to wipe me with a towel and dress me in a shirt and shorts. His brother must have packed my case. As they carried me into the car, the blue man touched his forehead and heart.

'I'm so terribly sorry, sir,' he said.

Miles of white wavy battlements, palms and fern trees, pressed against the car. The clinic was full, I remember. A score of black faces, all in those blue robes, turned to look. Then I was on some kind of bench on the other side of the partition where the doctor was bandaging wounds. I was whimpering, floating in knots like a foetus in a bottle. It must have been those sounds that brought the doctor. He was touching me everywhere, forcing my mouth open and withdrawing his hand hastily when my teeth came down like automata and bit him.

'I'm going to give you an injection,' he said.

I moaned: 'No, No. It will give me AIDS. It must be sterilised. You know they all have AIDS.'

He patted me. 'It is sterilized. I am a doctor.' There were nurses who held me. I didn't even feel the needle. I saw the tops of acacias outside the window. Maybe I was home, maybe everything would be all right. The wall loomed with an enormous lacquered Coca Cola poster. Bottles were packed in ice, one serrated cap open and bubbles starting to fizz, one simply glistening with droplets of cool water on the glass.

When the doctor came again, he sat beside me and asked how I felt. Indescribable relief and happiness. Just one thing would make it perfect. 'I would like so much that bottle of beautiful Coca Cola, with the bubbles gleaming on it. So beautifully.' The nurses brought one and then another. I started laughing, because I hate Coca Cola and never drink it. When I was conscious again, I was in an iron bed in a room with cupboards. The nurses were pulling things out of them and turning to look at me.

For the next few days I was out of my head. Every now and then I was woken by these white-eyed nurses. They crept silently to and from the cupboards, pulled sheets from under me and put on fresh ones. The bed still tilted. It made them seem miles away down the mountains of Ruwenzori. The lieutenant would come and take me. On his bike. I knew they were practising sorcery. The doctor did surgery in the clinic. They must be putting away amputated legs and secret organs from polio victims. Before I slept again, Billy Mutta's voice came out of his film *Bongo's Jinx* and told me how it was done.

On the third day, I recognised Dr Kelim when he appeared. I asked for my notebook and pencil to record these atrocities. I can hardly decipher it now. 'Kitui wants to see ju-ju. Catholic Church won't allow it. *Enfin. Enfant. J'apprends.* Sand.' The Christian cleaning woman kissed my hand and slipped holy pictures and pamphlets about Preparing for Paradise With Jesus under my pillow. Kelim was furious, and argued with her till my head exploded and he gave me another injection.

Thursday morning was a resurrection. My eyes blinked, but the blocks of mucous had cleared. Now it felt as if I had sand behind them. The nurses were adjusting the bedframe and Kelim was pulling me up to give me pills out of a crystal glass. The first thing I said was 'What a lovely glass!' He exchanged triumphant looks with the two nurses and a few brief words in Hausa, then beamed. 'It's Russian. My wife brought it back, a whole set actually. It's her holidays and she's in Russia again. This time I have demanded caviar! And as for you, you must be wanting some of your own foods. Do you want to eat?'

While I wolfed ham, eggs, cheese and baked beans on smoke-toasted bread, he introduced two children, who shook hands shyly and left the room. He chuckled. 'Don't worry. They already know you. I've had to drive them off. They think you look like John Denver. You don't, actually. But now I can make sense of it. I was bloody wondering to myself what kind of adventurer you were. We had some German hippy boys in here a month back. They tried going down the Niger River on a raft, I ask you. But you are an academic and you have a serious purpose.' I nodded dumbly. 'Oumar told me, but he is so grandiose you know, that you can't believe him. But ... your notebooks explain it.'

I was annoyed. He had been through my luggage. 'I had to, in order to make sense of you. Or in the event of contacting your wife. In any case, you threw it all round the room.' I had no memory of any such thing. He talked about himself. He had trained at Moscow on a scholarship, met his wife Raina, who was also Muslim, though neither was orthodox, and returned to Kano Province to open this clinic for the increasingly wealthy Hausa.

'Without going into a damn-awful collapse, you need to understand that you have malaria. I was concerned it was typhoid, because your symptoms are complicated. I have taken two blood tests and the parasites are still active. Many people die. You will not. I have you on an intensive course of quinine, lots of plasma and you have drunk gallons of mineral water which is enough to give an elephant stomach cramps. So you will damn well survive this malaria business or I will hang up my degree.'

I explained that I had taken my protective tablets religiously like communion wafers, and he grinned sadly. 'No use sometimes, I'm afraid. Let the quinine do his work.' He hesitated. 'And there's some other condition you have, but I cannot diagnose it. I can't test for everything here, unfortunately. Your face is very flushed, but you have no rash. Whatever it is, it's not yellow fever and you aren't infectious. You haven't eaten much, but your tongue needed two stitches, so it's probably just as well it has not been irritated. And you have stopped convulsions, what a terrible racket.'

Now his kids came and played with me every day, the nurses vigilant in case they got too boisterous. Anya and Koje were both the colour of rich honey. They missed their mother. They brought colouring books in which we decided that the people could be blue or green or yellow or any colour they liked and their clothes could be gold and red, but the sky must always be blue.

After months of speaking French, I listened to Nigerian English with the pleasure of a baby, relishing the exploding Bs, the mammary Ms, the hissing SSs, the African consonants that lie between GE and KA, TT and DD, humming and lulling. Koje and Anya spent hours inventing sounds, imitating their father by putting their hands on my chest to feel the reverberation. The language was sailing away from the main island, like American, Indian or Australian, laden with archaisms but blown by living breaths. I lay in bed lapping the elles, remembering Madame Celeste and the similar bubbles in her French, the young priest's lips like bells; and I slept.

As I sat up more, and moved around the clinic holding onto the door frames, Kelim let me go out in the yard. The colours seemed odd. Everything was yellow. The space was dazzling. Little Anya and Koje were pursuing their games with pleasure in this dry city that is constantly crumbling and renewing itself with its own earth. It seemed that I had floated on iron, flown over cities of tin, of gold, of silver. Now in these dust gullies I had reached Kano the city of mud, and it was as beautiful to me as the mysterious and inquisitive chameleons that froze on the mud walls while I watched their eyes and tongues and changing skin. I imagined my own eyes popping and sliding with lids like theirs as I sat and stared at their almost undetectable movements. Like mine. That's how I would move. Until Kelim asked the nurses or his factotum John to bring me inside.

Cheik Oumar came to visit. I had a handwritten list of films, and a letter of introduction to the head of regional television.

'I will have it typed. That is much more professional. But the typists are in a very bad neighbourhood,' he whispered, 'Christians. Don't you worry about that.' He had bought me a copy of the Quran.

'I've read it.'

'That's not what it's for, my dear. It's for lifting you up with us.' His voice beamed and broke the surface, again the shining bubbles of West African voices both French and English. I admired his gold and white gown.

'Well, I'm certainly not going to give you that. An English girl once asked if she could buy it so she could wear it to parties. I said "Oh my dear, what can you be thinking of?"' His departure left the colour of his gaiety in the room. In the afternoon he came back. 'John will drive you to meet Mr Zachary Mohammed tomorrow.'

John waited, while I shakily mounted the stairs and was greeted by a tiny, exquisitely robed man who shook my hand with nervous sympathy. 'Your man has told me. I have only been able to locate five of the films, all on video. I have set up our largest screen in my office. And please … it is at your disposal while you are stationed here.'

Listlessly I watched several studio productions with sets and actors that seemed equally on the point of collapse, a Songhai period costume drama and a superbly sarcastic production of Soyenka's *Brother Jero*. Zachary returned with John.

'Dr Kelim thinks you should come home. I hope some of these were of interest.'

'I liked the Soyenka very much. Who directed it?'

He fidgeted with the tapes and papers on his desk. 'I did.'

'Why ever didn't you make more? Your name wasn't on my list.'

'My name is probably on no-one's list. Except the wrong ones. This bloody impossible country. Excuse me. One does what one can. And one can very easily be … trapped.' I thanked him, and was helped to the car by John.

The time came when I had to move on to Mali. There were appointments with directors to keep, and the Venice film festival later in September. Doctor Kelim wasn't happy. The only way out of Nigeria was through Lagos.

'I urge you most strongly not to do *anything* in Lagos. A most terrible city in a most terrible world. The humidity alone is positively killing. Nigerians are a bloody aggressive kettle of fish. You are so weak now, you can't stand up for yourself.' Kelim was at least five inches shorter than me, but he had a pugnacious face and broad shoulders which he employed to butt me while he strutted round during his diatribe.

'Why in heaven's name don't you get yourself to a first-class hotel and just stay in bed, and don't go running around the bloody country or taking canoes up the Niger or some of the rest of your bloody nonsense. I'm going to write a letter for you; let's pray you get out of Lagos without being robbed blind. Very bad people. Very bad indeed. There is a plane tomorrow and I have taken the extreme liberty of using your ticket to get you a seat; and I'm going to give one last injection. But it is called a street-drug in Lagos, you understand? And you must have nothing to do with it. Even with their so-called doctors. Witch-doctors more likely. My opinion is you should have another blood test in Abidjan before you get to Mali. In a private clinic, too, and not wait until they cart you off to some factory of cross-infections called a hospital.

Because that's what's going to happen to you if you carry on with your foolishness'

His temper continued into the morning. But I had slept with the stuff dreams are made of, asked for another injection, and watched passively as John loaded my luggage, and, cursed continuously by Kelim, found a parking spot at the airport by bumping several smaller cars out of the way. Kelim stood in line and officiously got a boarding-pass. The other passengers and their companions smoked, bought potato crisps and plastic souvenirs, slouched on benches and read tabloid newspapers.

The women wore slabs of lipstick and rouge; the men were pomaded with sloppy suits and ties with pink nudes. It's like the western suburbs of Sydney, I thought stupidly, but they're all black. Kelim shook my hand and then smacked it. 'I've written to your wife Julie,' he warned me, and when John tried to embrace me and tripped over the case, told him not to be so bloody stupid. But when Anya and Koje clambered over me with kisses he hugged me rapidly, and let go.

The morphine lasted till we got over the plateau of Jos. I saw a reflection of myself in the window, grinning inanely. Then I felt a pressure against my thigh. A woman glistening with lipstick was leering; her vaselined male companion was pressed in turn against her legs, and inclined his head towards me with a smile. As her warm thigh was joined by a calf sliding slowly and deliberately, I felt the first stirrings of panic. The place was too small, her intimacy too intense.

I looked down at the landscape which now began to wave, and had an attack of vertigo. Panic assaulted me from within and without. I had to get off the plane … NOW. The seat-rows left no leg room. I struggled to my feet and felt further nausea. The air was thick with cigarette smoke. My companions looked like a Harlem gangster and his moll. We hit a pocket of turbulence; the hostess rolled along and asked me to sit down.

'I can't. Get me out of here. Get me OUT of here. Into some air.'

She pulled me over the astonished Nigerian couple. I fell into their laps. 'I'm terribly sorry. There's not enough air. Excuse me, excuse me.' The hostess led me to the very back of the plane, where I pulled at all the air-vents, and sat with my eyes closed until we bumped into the domestic airport. I had to squat on the floor while I waited for my case, buzzed over by a swarm of porters. I pointed it out; how pathetic it looked; two of them fought over it.

'Get a taxi to take me to the Airport Sheraton.'

I dropped naira all about, a whole bundle into the hands of the bellboy who came scuttling down the Sheraton's steps.

'Please get me a room with a bath and air-conditioning. Tell them to bring the forms and I'll do them there. What's your name?'

'Aloysius,' said the grey-haired man. 'Do you have a reservation, sir?'

'Aloysius,' I mumbled. 'Just please make them do everything. And get me a tissue. I have to blow my nose.'

My face was streaming again. My shirt and trousers were frayed from sweat at the groin and armpits. Aloysius was a sensible man.

'I'll organize everything, sir. You have a very bad cold.'

'Very bad. You mustn't call me Sir. Please ... just do it'

I cooled my head against a marble pillar while he talked at the desk and took me up to the third floor. After filling in the forms, I turned the air-conditioning on full blast, and when a maid timidly knocked and entered, yelled at her to go away. I stared at the ceiling for some time, then tried to ring the Film Commission. It was engaged. Then the airport. Engaged. Then the first three travel agents I found in the book. Engaged. Engaged. Engaged. I rang reception and asked them to try the numbers. They were either wrong or out of order, said the telephonist. 'You can never get through to the airport anyway.'

Each attempt left me exhausted. For two days after that, I just stayed in bed, or ran very hot baths where I lay for hours topping up the water and using all the sachets of bubble-bath till it was boiling and aromatic. I watched the same television programmes in English, Hausa and Yoruba, and listened to the satiric and bravely political rap on the radio. I laughed out loud. 'How ridiculous. I'm spending a fortune just to die somewhere where the temperature's controllable.' Once I stood by the window. There had been a rumbling noise for hours. Convoys of tanks were rolling down the highway from the towers of Lagos. I read the newspapers. The bodies of two ministers had been found floating in the mud and plastic off the city centre on Victoria Island. There was a war in Liberia. That's where the tanks were going.

On Friday I felt strong enough to dress, and asked Aloysius to order a taxi to the Film Commission. As he opened the revolving door, the heat hit like molten plastic. The driver got from the hotel access to the highway. The tanks thundered past in the other lane. Our own lane was jammed with cars farting black smoke. We jerked forward a few feet at a time. All the other cars were honking and the drivers leaned out and abused each other. Rubbish lay everywhere in the gaps between the tangle of roads. And from the rubbish came people. They had spotted a car with a European. In their desperation they moved fast, though some were hunched, some amputees. Worst of all, an opened oil-drum of polio-stricken children exploded like a nest of spiderlings. They crawled and hopped and spun themselves on their hands to reach the car, and soon they were climbing and crawling all over it. Hollow faces and bright eyes pressed at the windows, spider legs fastened to the hot metal, like the boy on the *Myanza*. Flies sucked at the last drops of moisture in their noses.

Horror and hatred flowed through my own body and boiled over. 'Make them get out of the way!' I cried. The driver added his honking to the rest, and inched forward to bang the bumper of the driver in front, who swore at him. The kids still clambered, starting to scratch at the window-tops with filthy nails. When we were able to move a few metres, they glued themselves to the hood.

'It's always bad on Fri ...,' began the driver.

'Just make them get out of the way,' I cried louder.

'They won't, sir.'

'Then run them over,' I howled.

In the silence that took over my mind, I started to realise what I had said, and I was frightened. But the horror of their insect limbs and faces intensified, and as I asked the driver to turn back to the hotel I closed my eyes and opened them only when Aloysius had me inside. He suggested a brandy. I took a sip and it made me sick. On the next couch an American tourist was displaying a bandage round his wrist. He had been attacked down-town with his wife and family. His wife had been pulled to the ground by her hair and her bag and jew-ellery snatched. He had his watch slashed from his arm. Their passports, cheques, money, tickets were all gone.

I had to get out. Aloysius took me up in the lift. Somehow he put a call through to the international airport. There was a flight to Adidjan in three hours, but all tickets were sold.

'I've got a ticket.'

'But there are no seats.'

'I don't care. I'm going ...'

Aloysius helped pack my scattered luggage and find Kelim's medical certificate, which I elastic-banded together with pass-port, visas, tickets and wads of naira. I paid my bill and insist-ed he call a taxi and come with me to the airport. By using backroads, we still had fifty minutes. He raced my baggage to the check-in, and had a fierce argument with the controller. There was much peering up at the clock, tapping of watches, and pointings in my direction where I sat on the floor.

'Take me to the place where they're loading the luggage.'

After more arguments a door at the back was opened. Aloysius flew with my bag down a dark corridor in the hangar, asking directions as we sped along. The luggage-controller looked up surprised as we crashed at the counter. She was a large Igbo woman of about forty. After listening to the expla-nations, she shook her head.

'Too late, sir. And you have no reservation. You should have come to the airport.'

202

'I've been trying to get through for the last week,' I croaked. 'And I am ill. I've hardly been able to move.'

'Every person says things like that.'

'No. Look. Read it ...,' and I brandished Kelim's medical certificate. She studied it, looked at my tear and sweat-covered face, and snapped into action. She told her assistant to take over, then opened the counter and led Aloysius smartly with the trolley through labyrinths of booths and counters. As each official argued she flapped open Kelim's letter and gestured. She roared like a lioness. She flirted. She got the fuselage open and my bags inside. Then she climbed the gangway and got me a seat in first-class, and gave one of the most beautiful smiles I've ever seen. When I shook her hand and she felt the wad of naira in it, she frowned.

'No. No. We're not all like that, God bless you. Take good care of yourself.'

'Then give it to Aloysius, the man who was with me. He is a saint.'

'He has the name of a saint. Most Igbo people do. Unfortunately for us, because who of us is even good?'

As we rose over the endless delta and lagoon, I stared out the window and cried. The plane climbed swiftly, clutching at the last fingers of the Niger. Then the window grew opaque as the lagoons slid beneath the clouds. The condensation in the cabin trickled down the window like a little delta over my own face. Not cracked as I had felt it finally on the Congo; here, like the vanishing delta of the Niger, dissolved.

The Hotel Ivoire had a limousine waiting at the Abidjan airport. It was for someone else. I was four days early; the expected arrivals didn't show up so I took it. As we drove past the bays of Grand Bassam I loosened up. The day was overcast and cool. The Intercontinentale had a pile of mail from my family, my wife Julie, the university, Kitty, the Centre Culturel at Abidjan, and various film-makers in Côte d'Ivoire, Mali, and Nigeria.

The room was large, just above the tallest palms where ravens called; I could see ships in the bay. I also saw with a shock an image of myself in a full-length mirror; gaunt, unrecognisable. I stripped. My skin looked sallow and there was a rash on my chest, but at least I was cool. Brother Body the Ass. Poor donkey, he'd carried me to the limit. I tore open Julie's letter.

'Thanks for the parcels and the Maasai ear-rings. But what ARE you doing! For someone who can be so cautious on behalf of others, you show a remarkable degree of lunacy over your own travels. The reports from Liberia are horrendous, closely rivalled by those from Algeria, which I assume will be your next stop. At least Venice seems relatively safe from everything except your plastic cards. Why don't you ring from Venice – reverse the charges – just so I know you've left the darkest heart?'

My mother's letter informed me that she was about to set off for Ireland.

'You seem so far away; but you are a seasoned traveller and know the ropes, which is a peculiar metaphor when you consider it ... Nadina leaves the day before we do. They are backpacking, with contacts first in Honolulu and thence onto Canada, and after that, the world for a year or so. I bought them the *Life and Crimes of Charles Sobhraj* for bed-time reading, and advised, with grandmotherly license, to practise her Karate.'

It was such a typical mixture of adventure and macabre warning that I laughed, but also felt proud. My eldest niece Nadina had something of the Kitty in her, but with infinitely more resources. (The result of her travels was a book on Alaska and the Northwestern Territories.) At that moment I wished I could set off with her and sit on a nice iceberg. I rang Julie. When she heard that I had malaria, she instantly offered to come and collect me. Her voice was soothing and practical. I imagined her comforting breasts and lovely eyes, half-way between sapphires and emeralds. Our houseboat Mutiny up the Murray, and my press-ganging her onto a freighter to the Society Islands had revealed how obstinate I could be in my travels. But she was so warm-hearted she was still ready to come to the rescue. I was very tempted. After an hour's talk I felt so cheered that I determined to clean myself up, lick my wounds, and go on.

In the afternoon, the limousine sped me across the lagoon to the best tailor on the Plateau. Within an hour I had a Parisian blue cotton shirt, new underpants, socks and trousers, and two new pairs of shoes. They were expensive but stitched so sturdily I wear them eight years later. With my old clothes in a clean bag, I introduced myself to Michele Nardi and Frédéric Convert at the French Cultural Centre, and was delighted to find they had the films I wanted, and would arrange screenings. Madame Nardi said she'd drop by in the evening. I walked up the hill to have my passport stamped with a Malian visa. Whatever Kelim's warnings, I had every intention, as long as I still had breath in my body, of going up the Niger.

Then the world fell apart. The consulate was jammed; I would have to wait four days for the visa. I stepped dizzily into the glaring street and nearly fell down a huge pothole. Abidjan, whatever its cafes and cultural centres, was a city of zones: upper-class Cocody, trashville Treichville, and the uneven Plateau where one street was richly maintained and the next a ravine. A restaurant had recently been sprayed with machine-guns and the diners bled to death in their vichysoisse. In the Ivoire's shop you could buy the *Times, Le Monde, Corriere della Sera* and the *Washington Post.* Not a mention of the shootings in Kinshasa. Too few? Too local? Perhaps not even reported. There was the vision of the hostile black faces again. I broke into a huge sweat, staggered back to the car and didn't leave my bed till I could slide over and phone for a doctor.

The test results came back in two days. Doctor Eloufin listened to my history. 'No typhoid, yellow fever, polio, HIV, all negative. If it were anything more fulminant, you wouldn't still be breathing. *Non, c'est typique.*' But what about the flu, the bleeding, the immobility, the vertigo? He was used to dealing with Europeans. He showed me a chart with indecipherable terms, asterisks and decimal points. 'The malaria is conclusive, with other febrile complications. It's no longer critical. I'll prescribe antibiotics if you like, but they won't do any good. Rest, cool, good food, refreshment.' He wrote on a pad, *'Paludisme et fièvre protiènne.'* It was only years later in Australia that a blood-test which cultivated a specimen for over a month discovered the 'protean' part. As well as malaria, I had dengue.

'*Ah, je comprends,*' said Madame Nardi as we walked in the elegant gardens of Cocody to the sounds of lawnmowers. *'Vous avez le palu.'* She said it as naturally as if I had a cold. 'That's why there'll be few Europeans at Roland's party tonight. Malaria hits us much worse than the Africans. But Bertrand should be up and about again in a couple of days. He'll go through the catalogue with you.' I was amazed.

'But it made me so sick I couldn't walk. I thought I had polio.'

She studied a passing gardener, a heavily muscled young man with his shirt rolled up.

'Yes, it always does that the first time. If you live here you get used to it. Look at that boy. You'd think he'd take his shirt off in this heat. Africans are such prudes.'

For the next few weeks, I lay like one of those Kano chameleons on the lawns near the pool, or in bed propped up on cushions, or slouched in the theatre watching the films of Timité Bassori and Gnoan M'Bala. Timité came to dinner in the pavilion on the artificial lake. We had whiting with fennel, yams and glazed carrots. It was still an effort to sit and appear at ease without feeling that I was acting. Timité was both quick and sophisticated. I opened up to him about the fear I was developing about blacks. He couldn't resist saying, 'Now you know how we feel in Paris.'

Timité is one of Africa's most sensitive authors of novels about the perception of whites by blacks. He gave me a copy of his collection, *Les bannis du village,* and arranged with

Madame Nardi to have VHS dubs made of his film *La Femme au Couteau* and M'Bala's *Ablakon*. As in Nigeria, I abandoned all plans of exploring the country, and instead saved my energies for the Niger. Besides, Timité was delightful, with a wit that could handle the most dangerous of topics. I lunched with him frequently, and every day brought a new subject.

'African narrative often appears to wander, to put things in brackets and switch purposelessly from one subject or set of characters to another. A patch of colours here. A song about feeling sick and having to work. Most people in the world feel that, you know. The story seems to refuse to come to the point.' Timité grinned. 'But it already has.'

Moved by his books and films, and by *Ablakon,* which showed the vivid contrasts between the new black bourgeoisie and the dispossessed, the sand fell out of my eyes and I began to see clearly. I told him how frightened I'd been that I had polio, and how I had reacted so violently to those who did.

'Everyone is a mess of fears. I'm frightened, for example of castration. You can see it in the beginning of *The Woman with a Knife*. Especially the sequences which I've overlaid with Beethoven.'

'Mozart,' I said automatically.

'You see. I made the film but you already know better.'

'I can't help it. I know it's Mozart's clarinet concerto. That doesn't make me a racist.'

'I didn't say it did. I was trying to explain that the conflict of cultures is the conflict of fears, and that's what makes political ideologies nonsense. They go to the deepest level, particularly in parts of the continent – which is most of it unfortunately – where the cult of the African Big Man masquerades as liberation. It makes me feel impotent but I transfer the fear to women. There's probably not a single person in the world who wouldn't feel racist if they were pushed to it by deprivation. I think many whites also have a sort of uneasy and inappropriate guilt.'

'All right. What kind of racist am I then?'

'Oh, the very nicest kind. I'm sure you didn't even suspect

it. You remind me of a friend of mine in the French Ministry of Culture. He came out, had a wonderful time, and kept on remarking how intelligent Africans were, even at films and literature, as if he still expected us to be making Benin bronzes. Then one day while we were walking in Treichville he said,

'It's so wonderful watching all these people going about their lives. Why do they all have to be black?'

I took his point, and felt a load fall from my mind.

'You great casuist. But it's still Mozart.'

I left Côte D'Ivoire refreshed. At the airport an official ran frantically to tell me there was an urgent package and a message. What last minute disaster was waiting to spring? The parcel was a video from Gnoan M'Bala, with a vote of confidence that I would never betray African cinema but promote it. The message was from Timité.

'Travel safely camarade. You were right. It is Mozart. Or at least *some* of it is.'

DANUBE II

Ship of Fools

We weighed anchor for an evening cruise about the lights of Passau, three-sided city where the Danube meets its sisters the Inn and the Ilz. The white domes and the cliff-fortress on our left shone in ribbons of pale gold and blue. The tables with their silver cutlery and salvers began to sparkle like the river. The man with Alzheimer's stood up as if in church and again bellowed the Hallelujah chorus. I thought he did it rather well. His companion in dementia was called Elspeth. Elspeth had false teeth the size of a Clydesdale's. She had perhaps suffered the onset of her condition while watching someone impersonate the Queen. 'Jolly good,' she would grin, until it looked as if her whole jaw might become detachable and neigh by itself. 'Carry on, then.' She brought what looked like a freshly electrocuted Pekinese to dinner and asked the maitre d' for an extra chair. He was inclined to object to the presence of a dog in the dining saloon: Elspeth devoured him with her choppers.

'Well do your best. One of those quinze or seize things will be perfect.' When the cushioned plush was fetched, Joan leaned across and complimented her on the dog's charm.

'Oh my dear. You must think I'm crazy to order an extra

209

chair for a dog! This is not a dog, lord knows. That's my daughter. Elizabeth.'

The crew confirmed the fact that we were an official travelling asylum by putting on a welcome show. As giant rope-headed frauleins simpered in their rouge, the ancient mystery was re-affirmed: that peculiar affinity between boats, sailors and transvestism; the equatorial rites of passage; the outburst of Carnival which makes every vessel since the Renaissance a Ship of Fools.

Captain Zylstra was Frisian, and wisely kept aloof. His sailors clog-danced, made extravagant love to each other, slapped their knees and bottoms, and then everyone else's. We were lured into the circle of clowns, until a round had formed which twirled the passengers into a gauntlet of couples who jigged two by two under the arched arms of the company. Bottom-slapping was mandatory. At least it loosened up the Jungtravellers' Group to the point where they yodelled and showed a knack for accelerated jogging beneath the bower of hands. I'm sounding so superior about this now because at the time I was breathless with Group Participation. The sailors, joined by the stewardesses and waiters, and accompanied by Ravel's *Bolero,* enacted a burlesque of promiscuous courtship, with catch-phrases from German operetta, Neapolitan belcanto and American musicals.

'God, this is almost as bad as a commedia I did for a boat on the Nile,' I puffed to Giulia. 'Who on earth devised it?'

'I did,' said Giulia with dignity. 'And I'm in Paradiso.'

At Passau next day the cathedral organist opened the trompe l'oeil heavens on the vault with enough César Franck to blast off the mud you could still smell in the alleys, and split the universe. By Linz I was quarrelling with the guide over artistic inaccuracy and the Anschluss-loving discourse I detected in her cheery commentary. The truth was that on the most primitive level I associated German-speakers not with Goethe but with Hitler. There were exceptions: Mozart was an honorary Italian, Dürer drew, Freud was really English, and Rilke could never have achieved sublimity without living in Italy and thinking in French.

Linz was Hitler's favourite town. Just a few miles down the Danube we would pass the concentration camp of Mauthausen, which apparently became invisible to the good people of Linz while slaves perished miserably in its quarries. The sensation of having stood a few days ago in Speer's Nurenberg stadium exactly in Hitler's place, imagining the roars and fires of Leni Riefenstahl's film, was still with me. But it was stupid to blame an entire language. I determined to reform. I practised my *kunsthistorische* arts secretly at dinner. Joan was genuinely interested, and she insouciantly swept through the rest of the trip murmuring 'tryptich' and 'rococo' with panache. Even Antoii the Finn beamed broadly and croaked 'baroque' at breakfast. One morning we were on deck doing onion-domes, which obligingly grew in ecclesiastical patches on both banks, when we were joined by Sir Larry the impromptu singer. Beside him were Beverley and Ted, a quiet, gentle mining engineer from Limerick. With the Danube swirling round our bows, Ted quizzed me about my travels in South America. He had seen a beautiful church near Belo Horizonte which he urged me to visit. He started to write the name, then began to stammer and excused himself in embarrassment. I thought with a rush of sympathy that perhaps he'd recently had a stroke. That would explain his slow, careful movements, his long silences, and Beverley's headfirst dives to cover them.

Sir Larry was seldom silent. He had been a diplomat in Jersey before the war. In his eighties he had a mane of immaculately barbered silver hair and a disconcerting habit of talking two inches from your face.

'So how are you, young fellow? You know, I think we got off on the wrong elbow. You're not French; you're Australian. I like Australians. Would you care to take a look at my watch?' He produced a sparkling silver fob. 'Given me in '45. Inscription's French. At Orgueil. Know what that means? That's what confused me. Thought you were one of those Gauls at the buffet, heard you carrying on about *la flotte*.

211

Notice anything peculiar about it?'

'Er ... the numerals are Roman.'

'Exactly. Probably why the hands don't move!'

The hands were moving, and I pointed out the second hand clicking up to the VII.

'No. Big chap up there. Never budges. Same all over the ship. You take a good look. Captain's chronometer up to the same trick. Nice chap though. Dutch. Had them all over Jersey. You'd think they were good with clocks, wouldn't you? Bells chiming all over the place and can't even keep time with a metronome.'

Giulia joined us to discuss the excursions. As we passed great medieval castles high on their rocks we plotted to teach Hermann the foulest *parolacce* and turn him loose on the next Italian we encountered. Sir Larry and Giulia bantered, Sir Larry drinking in her vivacity and Giulia naughtily shifting her shoulders. When she left, Larry was smiling foolishly. 'Lovely chap, that one.'

If the *Ebeya* was male, the *Countess* insisted on her femininity. One of the oldest and smallest ships on the central European river circuit, she still had her scrolled pillars, her starboard reading room, her pianist reminding her of Bizet's 'Love is just a gypsy child'. I could see why Giulia enjoyed being her attendant. Like the towns and cities which were her mooring places, she had more than a touch of the rococo, and like her passengers she knew the full indulgence of an excursion into the baroque.

We could see one of her favourite destinations, the exuberant Abbey of Melk, long before we reached it. The monastery dug into the cliff rising steeply from the river proclaimed centuries of golden Benedictine glory. Teenage girls had taken over its seven yellow courtyards and white miles of corridors, and the orangerie was now a restaurant. The monks were out of sight and mind as these new students of music, art and linguistics unlocked its treasures. The girls, exchange students from Switzerland and Italy, were on their last vacation before university, and they inhabited the grand baroque libraries and lookouts with confidence. Giulia knew them from previous trips. There were many embraces and conversations in Italian which I happily joined. In the distance we heard Hermann getting his face slapped. Giulia had steered him to an Italian girl on whom he had practised his new phrases.

When she commented that I was a university lecturer and knew everything about art, I said, before even thinking, 'No. I'm not. I'm just a tourist. Guide me. Please.' They did, their young grace bringing sun into the dark old rooms. A friend calls the habit of letting professional life seep into the rest of your behaviour 'Professional Deformation'. But it was now almost a year since I had retired from the university. I was cured!

'You're lucky,' said the young girls in flower, 'the weather's going to be perfect, and from here the river is at its most beautiful.' They were right. The Danube from this point was as wild and remote as the Congo. Because of the floods, it flowed so high and swift that the Wachau region was the most enchanting in Europe.

We came on deck to watch the mists swirl like clouds around the forested mountains, the ravens, doves and swallows dipping in the flood. Castles and fortresses dotted the towering peaks, and on the narrow shores renaissance towns, washed clean by the rain, displayed pergolas and ripening apricots. At Duernstein we went ashore for a wine-tasting, fatal for everyone except Giulia, who drank only after work. In this case, work extended till ten o'clock at night. Within the walled city 150 metres above the shore, climbing the stairs to the Krensetor and the cellars, we tried green riesling, yellow chardonnay, a spritzige rosé, and some late-picked pinot. Then we tried to get back down the steps. Beverley and several others slipped. Sir Larry sang. Ted commented, 'They move them, the steps, you know, just like Limerick.' When the hungover boat awoke, we were sailing out of the Wienerwald through the marshes to Vienna.

'I'll tell you one thing,' said Sir Larry conspiratorially, 'Have you noticed that every single one of those town clocks we passed told a different time?'

I don't really know anyone in Vienna besides Freud, Mozart, Schubert, Beethoven and Peter Konlechner. Peter K. is out at the Filmarchiv, where in 1987 he showed me the precious original footage of Pasolini's documentary on *San'A* in Yemen. Schubert is unreliable, so I rotate visits to the other three. Freud is dependable. The advantage of his being dead is that you never need an appointment at the Berggasse and he is often careless about leaving his books and antiquities around. One day some wicked borderline case is going to pinch that statue of Horus.

Beethoven moves around so much that it's always safest to hop on the red U-bahn and go straight to Heiligenstadt. They've now got earphones and CD players installed in the walls; you can sit looking into the little garden with its apple tree and sob quietly at the C minor sonata. A Japanese girl was already sniffling. I offered her a table napkin from the *Erzsébet*.

Ludwig is almost completely deaf. Besides being bad tempered with the servants, he keeps on wrapping the butter in the *Kyrie* and accusing his brothers of stealing it. But his pleas for forgiveness are heartbreaking. 'O you men who think that I am malevolent, stubborn or misanthropic, how greatly you wrong me, you do not know the secret causes of my seeming! O what a humiliation when one stood beside me and heard a flute in the distance and I heard nothing!'

Mozart is all over the place. If *The Magic Flute* hasn't just opened at the Theater an der Wien they'll be doing *Figaro* in the gardens at Schoenbrunn. Oh, and on the way back to the Danube I often meet Harry Lime in the Prater, and we take a car together on the Ferris Wheel. Sandra, who was my first flesh and blood companion in Vienna, still waves from the attic window in the hotel on the Ringstrasse, and occasionally we feed the swans in winter. But she knows better than to accompany me to Freud's in summer, because he is so neurotic about time.

Each time I came back to Berggasse 19, he would be moaning how much he hated the city and could hardly wait to get out of it now that it was July. Schnitzler had told him a new joke, and for once he relayed it effectively. 'If you walk down the streets with a woman in this city, they say she's your mistress. With a man — and you're homosexual. By yourself? You're a wanker. There, that's Vienna for you.'

So I took him out for walks, hoping no-one would notice his appalling habit of spitting great gobs of cigar-pulp all over the stairs. He liked seeing the flowers in the Berg Park and sometimes I even got him as far as the Ring to look at a Roman bust. In the Museum I left him to spend an hour with one of my favourite Vermeers. There sat the artist painting blue laurels, light pouring from the same north window onto his maps. Hoping the attendants would understand that I was an iconographer rather than an iconoclast, I opened the Swiss-army knife to find one of its most essential gadgets. Magnifying glasses are indispensable for the traveller. Here they revealed not only the map of the Netherlands but the names of the watery towns you can read on either side. And the yellow of this book. And the blue of love and constancy. His colours. My colours. One day I might just disappear in them.

There was another target. In 1525, the night after Whitsun, Dürer had a terrible nightmare of the Flood. He set the dream down beneath the painting, which was not at all what I'd expected. Over plains as serene as the pastures we'd seen from the boat, the Apocalypse of rain exploded like a nuclear blast. Around it stabbed column-shafts of water. In the grip of visions like this, millions of Europeans left their houses in a wanderlust that led them to rivers where ships of fools consolingly awaited.

I didn't mention the dream to Freud. After five years of analysis he had formed an embarrassing counter-transference, which took the pattern of mistaking me for Robert Fliess, feeling my nose and then fainting. As he did with other favoured patients like the Wolf Man, he allowed us to meet socially. Here again he could be a worry.

That night at the performance of Figaro, I wanted to crawl under the seat when he tunelessly joined the baritone in the aria.

'*Se vuol ballare, Signor Contino,*' he shouted like Sir Laurence. 'I'll play the guitar for you, *stronzone*. That's the way to treat those muck-heap Hapsburgs. Bravo Figaro.'

Several people turned round, but Mozart giggled. (I might add that Mozart and he exchanged stupid poo stories and notes in which they signed their names backwards. 'Liebe Duerf, I let out a real whopper today and Constance kicked me out of bed and made me air the eiderdown. Your spiritual son – Trazom!')

Then it was back to the apartment. He had never met Jules, Nick or Shane, and shook his head when I talked about them. 'Sandra, that girl you lived with in Florence, she was the best for you,' he said, lighting up another cigar, 'even though she did wear those dreadful fishnet stockings. So ... what have you been up to today?' I described how I had leapt into the U-bahn at Vorgartenstrasse with my map and popped up like a mole all over Vienna, emerging at every stop from the Karlsplatz to parks where sunbathers were stretched like Rubens nudes beside the canals.

'Yes, you must have a map,' he nodded.

'The funniest thing was seeing all the singers round the Oper, scratching their powdered wigs and taking off their shirts and blouses in the heat in order to relax with a cigarette. Nice tits, all of them.'

'Ach, you'd like that. I suppose you wanted to fuse with them as usual.'

Who was he to talk about fusing? Every time I came back, I sensed the presence of that Third Man lurking beside us, bent on stealing the Horus, the big Middle Kingdom one, the solar god, the Unifier.

Freud would leave the room to fetch a volume of Schliemann, Evans or Howard Carter, only to remember they'd been sent to London, and I'd end up again having to describe the Palace of Knossos in detail, because he had only seen pictures. As I left, a little ushabti on the edge of his desk nearly fell into my pocket. I straightened it up, though I knew he really wanted me to have it.

216

'Well, do you know where are you now?'

'Vienna. But not for long. I've got to get back to the Stephansplatz for an organ recital. Did you know they've found a saint while they were digging the S-bahn line? He's on display in a glass tomb.'

'I bet he'll liquefy,' grumped Freud.

'Don't be so anti-Catholic. Think of it as archaeology. Where are you, incidentally?'

'Athens. What time does your boat go?' he enquired, thumbing through a timetable dated 1910.

'At dawn tomorrow.'

'Then you better hurry. You'll be in Slovakia before noon. I do wish you'd stop your regressive fantasies about me. They're even worse than your hysterical dissociations.'

'Then I'd never be able to meet you. And you ought to talk. At least I don't go all silly on the Acropolis and wonder if it's really there.'

As we rode the summit of the wheel and could see Vienna as far as the woods, I told the Third Man himself about Freud's curious behaviour. The Wheel played the Harry Lime theme on a gigantic zither.

'For the love of God, dear boy, just take his little idol. Do you really care a damn about all this honesty and reality and brotherly love business? They're just dots, old man, dots. Look at them down there. The Viennese are like the Swiss – all they care about are cuckoo clocks and chocolate. Oh, that reminds me. Next time you're there, could you see if he's got any spare syringes and out-of-date penicillin?'

Orson employed his famous cynical smile.

'Oh, come off it, and stop acting. You know, I once asked Pasolini what it was like working with you.'

His mouth curled wryly.

'Ah, *La Ricotta*. Bogdanovich had the nerve to call it arty. I told him he wouldn't know art from Judge Shit in the Range. So what did PPP say?'

'He said "Welles? Welles dances." '

'You made that up.'

When I skipped back to the boat, Joan was on to me.

'Who is She?' was her purposeful question.

'You mean Michiko? I met her at Beethoven's. She was crying at opus 111 and we had lunch in the fields. But the others were all men, and you wouldn't believe me if I told you who they were.'

Larry insisted that he could hear bells chiming from the shore. When I cocked an ear in doubt, he held up his watch. 'Listen. One ring. Two. Tick, tick, clop, and then, by God, it's like Saint Paul's.'

Watching other people's faces and savouring the flavours of their speech is for me almost an erotic act. When languages mingle and return to Babel, Jahwah's curse unravels like a skein of knotted wool. The Patatares were a source of nourishment throughout the voyage. The others were equally beguiling, and if I make their behaviour sound crazy, I include myself in the laughter.

I could never determine, for example, whether Ted was as mad as Larry, or merely mischievous. Beverley was looking out on the shores with grave disquiet, as if they had not passed a proper resolution about forming themselves into banks. We approached a ruined monastery which Giulia described as the work of an eleventh century hermit.

'Do you think the saint built this himself?' I asked Ted.

'Arr ... I wouldn't know about that. I was too young at the time.'

NIGER II
The Magic Egg of Mali

How wonderful it was to be met at the airport with a smile. Moussa Traore was literally ready to take me to Timbuktu. But first we drove across the Niger, still youthful from its birth in Guinea, to a hotel room directly on its banks. The 'Great River', as it is known in the languages of all the countries it cuts through with its enormous arc, spends much of its 4,180 kilometres in Mali. If you ever have the urge to hop in a taxi and whistle 'Timbuktu, please', make sure it's a driver like Moussa, because he will have to ford streams, drive along sandy river-beds, grind his way up dunes, straddle causeways across marshes, and ferry the Niger at its most complicated deltas. The Niger and its life dominate the country and the city. Even in Hotel L'Amitié, by night-time there were millions of frogs croaking, a sound which always makes me sleep like the logs they're supposed to sit on in nursery rhymes. But first came the introductions to Madame Kindo and the film and theatre officials who had prepared itineraries, linked up boat and plane departures and arranged appointments. The first one was in an hour.

The rest of the day and most of the night was spent with Oumar Sissoko and Souleymane Cissè, Mali's greatest film-makers. They made VHS copies of *Yeelen,* the film which won

Cissè the Jury Prize at Cannes, and several of Sissoko's. Technicians and actors crowded in to talk. They were confident of subverting government censorship or interference by poetry and allegory. Cinema was useless if it didn't provoke social change, they argued. In a country like Mali the filmic image and its capacity for making moral points through an oral tradition of ballads and anecdotes was immense. A renaissance!

After spending the next week in the central Niger delta round Mopti and Djenne, I could better understand the use of landscapes and of tribal and caste divisions. The inspiration from the Dogon animists with their elaborate rituals and proverbs was prodigious. *Yeelen* (light) was as luminous as its title. Images burned my imagination: a son's confrontation with his sorcerer father; his mother emerging from the Niger like a goddess; rival magicians hurling their powers across the sahel; majestic frescoes of a woman, a child, most vividly a white egg sinking in the yellow sand. The shapes and colours of Italy at its most vibrant, the aesthetics of exquisite Japan will always run through me like an electric current. But I have never been bathed in such beauty of faces and fabrics as I was in Mali.

Next morning Moussa sped along the highway to Ségou and rejoined the broad Niger. We branched off to its tributary the Bani and carefully traversed the wetlands and the mighty causeway to Djenne. Our base was to be Mopti, from which all trips north and east could be done with speed and comfort. At San, we lunched on chicken and rice. The great baobab tree in the courtyard of the campement was in leaf. Bluebirds flew around it, and the only unusual feature of the courtyard was the number of large, stark naked women sitting there. They wore their hair close-cut and shaved in intricate patterns. Some had lit their nipples with brilliant white and blue. Naturally, I asked what they were doing. I received an obvious reply. As for the bluebirds, they were really *étourneaux*. I had to look the word up in a dictionary: starlings. Like the women, they simply knew how to present themselves at their best. I was reminded of something.

'What do you think Cissé meant by the picture of the egg buried in the hot sand at the end?'

'I don't know. Ask Souleymane when we get back. What do eggs generally do?'

Yes, I thought. Zaire is struggling to be born. Nigeria is exploding in its youth. But in Mali there is genuine rebirth. The eggshell may be fragile; but the new life is insistent to hatch.

DANUBE III
Stalin's Return to Visegrad

If you come along the Danube from the west, Estergom is the first of Hungary's glories. Marcus Aurelius liked its porphry and limestone rocks so much that he wrote his *Meditations* there. Just like Egypt – Juvenal scribbling away at Aswan. Or, as Larry remarked, Ovid in exile on the Danube. Romans everywhere.

Twenty of us had booked a bus-tour that would take us through Estergom's royal palace and on to Visegrad, an even greater precipice from which the loops of the Danube Knee can be seen bending east and west, north and south, Hapsburg and Ottoman. Our guide was Mrs Berkenyi. She greeted us breathlessly at the foot of the town hall, from which the road ascends to the cathedral. She was polyglot, but established nervously that her best language was French. After Estergom, she suggested, perhaps the anglophones would prefer to go off with another guide. She would take a smaller group by van, and bring us back to the mooring. Despite her agitation, she was apple-faced and, as we learned, a survivor.

The cathedral of Estergom is a neo-classic monster that has achieved eminence by its eminent cadaver. Cardinal Mindszenty lies buried in a crypt of Egyptian proportions. Among the icy Karnak capitals, topped by absurd mosaics,

Beverley cried. She learnt on my arm, 'All that terrible suffering,' she sniffed. 'Can't you feel it?'

As decently as possible, I shot off to Visegrad with the francophones, Giulia, the three Elwoods and Antoii Pööwö, who had made the wise decision that understanding no available language gave one the flexibility of all. With Sir Larry and his wife we made up a party that out-numbered the native French. Elspeth's daughter had been discretely discouraged, and left in her cabin with a good bone. Mrs Berkenyi chattered along the half-hour ride. Her husband Walter had been killed during the Uprising.

A Magyar-Turkish tower dominates the landing place of Visegrad, creating with the fifteenth century church a small square below the road that bursts upwards to the fortress. As we boarded the bus we noticed a monumentally shrouded shape on a plinth that rivalled the height of the twin-spired church. When we asked what it was, Mrs Berkenyi looked only slightly more agitated than before.

'I've no idea. It must be new. I haven't been here for a fortnight. All this was flooded, you know. They're always doing something new.'

We ascended over 300 metres to the citadel. The views extended from Bratislava practically to Budapest. I left the group to wander on my own. There was a waxworks museum at the top, as crude and disgusting as those of St Petersburg and Phnom Penh. It showed peasants being tortured by brutal landowners, and stalls illustrating proper domestic life and animal husbandry. On the way down I met Mrs Berkenyi and the Severins in a panoramic courtyard. She twisted the strings on her bag. 'Please keep together. I don't know where the others are. The van is waiting. I commute here from Szentendre. I must get home.' I assured her we would meet in the square. The group arrived before me. What we saw was hallucinatory.

The statue had been unveiled. A thirty-foot Stalin marched stiffly in late Pharaonic style towards one of his many destinations in Eastern Europe. Someone had invited the Commendatore to supper, and he had come. Communist Youth in kerchiefs waved enthusiastically. A mob of villagers brandished vines and scythes and gave voice to collective celebration. Mrs Berkenyi was lying on the cobblestones.

Neither the Communist Youth nor Sir Larry's rendition of *La Marseillaise* could awaken her. A camera crew appeared around the corner, an irate director yelling the universal Last Judgement, 'Cut!' The extras dispersed and a props woman waved a bottle under the prostrate figure's nose. They should have continued shooting, because Mrs Berkenyi looked as natural as Magnani in *Rome Open City*, her skirt hitched up, and her purse spread like a dead lizard.

It was Antoii who finally revived her. He knelt, stroked her forehead, and murmured words in whatever limbo between Finnish and Hungarian remains. Her eyelids flickered; she took one look at his bald head and sunburnt face, half sat up and cried, 'Walter!' Then she fainted again. Amid wrangling and contradictory advice in ten languages, she rose dizzily to her feet, Pööwö continuing to support her. As soon as she saw the crane and its lounging technicians, she began to apologize. Her nervous laugh became a series of stertorously drawn breaths.

'A film. Of course. How could he come back? Do you know the thing is, he was no colossus really. He was almost a dwarf.'

The Danube split into little rivulets between beech trees, swirling the byways of the flood. 'The power plant project – you must have seen the barrages at Gabcikovo outside Bratislava, yes? Well it nearly ruined the marshlands. We were building part of it at Nagymaros, but thank God there were so many protests we stopped. Over there in Slovakia they're still continuing, so God knows what will happen.'

Larry, Elspeth and Antoii sat beside her, holding her hands and murmuring in canon 'There's a good chap,' 'Quite right too,' and 'Nagy. Nagy.' Piqued by her lapse into frailty and English, the Severins retired to the bus.

'First there were Serbs, and then the Nazis and they were hitting people on the hands to make them drop their luggage. And Walter was a musician. You know the Russians were still here six years ago, and now in Szentendre there's a place called the Dixie Chicken!'

Giulia was relying on Venetian poise to stay cool as she collated the groups, tried to load them into the bus and deal with the still distraught Mrs Berkenyi. Everyone gabbled their version and had their questions. It was explained that the film was about a famous poet.

'Well, if that's poetry, I'm Publius Ovidius Naso,' declared Larry, 'and I'll go and freeze my goolies off at the bottom of the Danube just like him, poor bugger.' Giulia lost her patience.

'Larry, would you mind not talking while I'm trying to explain things?'

He jutted an amiable face three inches towards her nose. 'Would you prefer me to sing?'

'No. I'd prefer you to sit down and be quiet.'

'Well, that's not cricket you know, doing that to the poor woman. Tell you what. We'll get her a drink.' He turned to the driver, speaking with aplomb the variety of German in which I was also fluent. 'Français? Deutsch? Ya, Deutsch! I would like a white wine, bitch, and the Virgin will have a Rottweiler.'

MEKONG IV
Golden Triangles

At the peak of the famously warring but slippery borders called the Golden Triangle, the Mekong is like an ocean. Its sandbars casually divide three (and now four) countries into highways of water that flow past the Buddhist pagoda on which I am standing. On the left bank in the distance I can see nude Laotian women bathing, and others cooking. The Burmese mountains are blue, silent with poppy fields. The Mekong continues its journey from China to the sea. But further down its tributary at the edge of Mae Sai, the dark Shan and the Karan people, with a medley of beggars in rags humping babies on their backs, are streaming into Thailand. Perhaps it's the gems that help, crunching across the bridge in these floursacks of human mules, and displayed in the windows of new shops down the embankment. Shining Meo girls stationed past the last police proffer jade and rubies and gleefully take the money from tourists. Among all this tribal dissent, the only certainty is the river.

Unable to get an individual visa for Laos, I have come up through Thailand to the port of Chiang Kong, and taken a sturdy boat which fought its way against the current to the crowded quay and boardwalks of Chiang Saen. There I persuaded a fisherman to take me as far as Ban Sop. The hills grew steeper and the launch chugged against the heavy waters. As the river opened its gorge I pressed him to take me further.

'No, no. Forbidden. No boat allowed.'

Scooting past us were speedboats so laden with refrigerators, television sets and motor cycles that they threatened to burst their tarpaulins. When I pointed at them he cried back against the noise.

'Smugglers! Too dangerous for foreigners. Many kidnappers!'

At Ban Sop I was allowed to stand at the bridge without crossing it. I knew what was coming across in the sacks and the little boats which plied the confluence of the Mekong with the Sai in Burma: seventy per cent of the world's supply of heroin. The gems which the police inspected were just a glittering disguise.

I am obsessed with this river, and this is the way I've seen it – a film running backwards: delta in Vietnam, confluence at Phnom Penh, and now its might at the top of the Golden Triangle. It has supported human life for millennia. Its flood plains are as visible from the air as a historical slide-show. In the Sixties, stoned out of my brain on Khmer black or Laotian red, I would have written poems about it. Or if I'd grown up under the Nixon doctrine, I'd have chopped above it dropping cutely named bombs.

Back in Thailand its delta forms a more extensive triangle, this one also golden, and silver. At the Vietnamese feast of Lunar Tet the dark new moon brings in the New Year. Year of the Citizen. Year of the Snake. The moon is barely hit by the sun, but its silver arc is faintly there again, bringing back everything that is impassive, inhuman, predictable. Because of my great disappointment at not being able to get a visa and cross the river into Laos, I had been allowed the final treat of being driven in a government car down-river, to the sea and the wharves where the boats leave up the Mekong for Bentre. The docks are crowded with commerce and festivity. Stocky little ferries set off through the clustered sampans up to Vinh Cong and further. I had to be content with going across the Mekong a little upstream. But just being near this damaged river made me as happy as travelling its prohibited length. Because there were frogs again; it seemed an orgy of frogs, thousands of them.

Lizards slither. The trees offer themselves to the heat, to the last fierce rays of the sunset. I'm subject to change, like the moon. Again I recall Resnais. At the end of his film on Dachau, *Night and Fog,* after every denial ('I am not responsible. I am not responsible!'), an insistent voice asks: 'Then who is responsible?' Travellers voyage for the sake of deranging themselves, of finding the unfamiliar, the unhomely. But this is simply bush and city. It's human. It's home.

NIGER III
The Twins of Dogon

I felt even more the approach of home as Moussa and I set up base in the Niger's Inner Delta. Djenne and Mopti are island cities, reached by dykes over marshes themselves dotted with lilies and reeds. Like Aswan they give the sense of harbour. In the afternoon light the winding Niger and its banks glow as if lit from within. Cranes, herons and ibis wade. Bright iridian and scarlet finches flick past the car as you approach these cities, where cow-horns above the doorways ward off evil, and weaver birds pick up every dropped straw or piece of rope. I climbed the egg-domed tower of the Great Mosque with its myriad columns, and looked out over the bay's bustle of trade in incense, Fulani blankets and spices, the market people taking their ease under the tents and acacias. The Hotel Relais sat right on the river. It had a pretty and deliciously cool courtyard with a fountain and scented bushes of flowers. In the evening it was filled with people chatting and drinking Pernod. The drivers and servants observed a rigid class distinction and squatted in the grassy courtyard in front.

These are cities where the cool dark rooms are full of smiths, dyers and woodcarvers; where on the riverbank baby goats cry *'Mère, mère!'* in perfect colonial French as they are hoisted into pirogues. Here live judges, learned doctors, travel writers. The warm mud and jutting beams of Djenne's mosque make it dynamic, kinetic. The vivid flash of hands and shadows suggests at nightfall a city that might have been ruined, because the yellow houses sink back into their surroundings and the earth. But the flashes become cooking-fires aromatic with fish. Glittering slabs of rocksalt piled on oilcloth make the banks gleam, and the evening too begins to glow with kerosene lanterns keeping alight an ancient centre of culture that is richly growing and alive.

From here I would go as far east along the great Bandiagara escarpment of the Dogon people as possible. Moussa put the car on the ferry across the Bani, and then jingled along to the music of a group on the radio called Les Ambassadeurs. He was a fan of the balaton xylophone, and we were soon slapping our hands in counter-rhythm on the sides of the car. At Sangha the rocks became so rough we had to get out. A figure waited in the distance. Moussa handed me over to the boy, who was about sixteen and carried his head with the dignity and assurance of an adult. His name was Amatigue.

'The walk takes about six hours if you want to see the villages on the other side of the escarpment. If you're not back by 6.30, I'll send a search-party,' joked Moussa.

'That is not necessary,' replied the boy aloofly. 'We have been waiting for you, and I have all the permissions and keys. There will be plenty of time.'

His eyes were strangely fixed and white. The descent was easy but long. Stone steps had been cut in the rock, and the path zigzagged so that every corner revealed a new aspect of the luxuriant valley far below. The contrast was almost unbelievable. From the hot, dusty plain, as we descended we entered a world of caves and outcrops, ferns and moss that ended in the approaches to a village. It consisted of lime-washed white huts with thatched conical roofs. The little buildings were perfectly round. These were granaries. Their order and cleanliness were matched by the swept plazas which surrounded them, and the longer, more rectangular buildings with wooden doors and frames which appeared to be lustrously oiled and polished. Ancestral snakes twined about the posts. Standing figures with arms akimbo spread on either side. Pebbles shaped like eggs lay beside them: thunderstones.

Amatigue greeted some elderly people preparing food at the entrance to their huts, and alternatively tolerated and shooed away groups of children who followed us. But when he met a boy of his own age rising from a group of stools occupied by other men, who were carving and turning lengths of wood, he clasped his hand.

'This is my friend Ogotemmeli, a famous name. This is his village, brother of my village. If it doesn't annoy you, he will accompany us.'

The other boy held his friend's hand. Only when he bumped into a corrale did I understand. Amatigue was blind. The white eye meant oncho, river blindness transmitted by a parasitic flybite.

I already knew something of Dogon culture. Sheltered by their cliffs and the homogeneity of their small population, they had made the earliest surviving woodcarvings and textiles on the continent. Formidable metaphysicians, they had resisted Islam because they knew the sun was white-hot and surrounded by satellites. The stars had been scattered in the process of creation; like the Egyptians they studied Sirius. Long before Freud they concluded that humans were basically bisexual. And they grew the best onions in the world.

Their intellectual system attracted me, and during the next five hours I was given a course on it. The boys unlocked the intricately carved doors. There were more vividly etched frames within. Statues stood with arms interlocked, or raised above their heads. Despite the rigidity of the design, their bent knees gave the impression that they might leap into life.

'These are about seven centuries old,' said Amatigue. 'The dry air in the caves preserves them.' Another room held masks like medieval European headpieces with tall peaks of doubled crosses and antlers, like the costumes of the crusaders in Eisenstein's film, *Alexander Nevsky*.

'We may not go in there,' said Ogotemmeli, 'because we are young. That is how death began.'

The next village, built on a slope, had more irregular houses with ochre walls and turrets, nestled among great rocks and trees like a Tuscan town awaiting the Renaissance. People were pounding millet and maize. One of them was Amatigue's mother. She greeted us courteously, spoke calmly to Ogotemmeli in Dogon, offered me a gourd of hot millet beer, and resumed grinding the millet. Amatigue and Ogotemmeli walked through the village hand in hand. They explained the motifs in every door, tracing the forms in the air with their fingers, without touching. The twins were everywhere: man and woman, man and man, woman and woman, hermaphrodites. 'Two by two. And two by two by two. And seven by two. Four seeds for women, three for men. That is how everything is formed, even houses.'

One room contained a cache of animal masks and ceremonial fibre skirts. When I asked if I could buy a mask and a particularly striking sculpture of the twins, Amatigue shook his head. 'In the markets at Mopti or Bamako. But these are not for sale.' Could I touch them? The boys hesitated, then brought them out. Ogotemmeli applied an antelope mask over his face. Amatigue felt around and gave me an exquisite crocodile head. I put it over my head, clowned, and asked them to take a photograph.

'These are perfect. Are they made by master-carvers?'

'Anyone who can carve, carves. I carve.'

'You have a teacher?'

'No. It is always coherent.'

I kept turning to catch sight of a cataract I could hear and partially glimpse, because I was sure I would not see such a sight again.

'You are trying to see the waterfall, aren't you. Water is the semen of the creator.'

I could well believe it. And it produced twins who were the same but always slightly different, always multiplying.

As we left this village, we rounded the escarpment and

reached the floor of the valley. I have seldom seen a more enchanting sight. Perfectly enclosed by the cliffs, it was defined at one end by the lofty waterfall, which fell in a fluent, immaculate line to the valley. Palms, acacia and greater trees like oaks gave dense shade over the grassland and the thin river, ornamented by red hibiscus and soft green fields of grain.

'Does the waterfall have a rainbow about it?'

'Every colour'

'That is where heaven scattered down its seeds. The whole world is its granary.'

The boys unlocked even more secret cave houses built into the hillside. Their exposition of the iconography and mythology of every location and artefact was as clear and accurate as a Cambridge lecture. I had to remind myself that I didn't need a Cambridge lecture. I was here, and reluctant to leave. I lingered for a long time looking over the valley.

'You are like the twins,' I told Amatigue and Ogotemmeli.

'We will become the twins,' said Ogotemmeli. 'Soon we will marry. On the same day.' He shook hands, and headed back down the valley. This was Paradise, the vision I'd carried from Hollywood confections of secret African kingdoms. Amatigue felt the raised hands of his watch. We had two hours to ascend the cliff. I tarried, caught half-way up by a vision of an endless plain to the east, already darkening as the sun fell behind our cliff-face.

'That's the place of the Peul and the Mozai,' he said, 'and beyond it all the way to Ougadougou. But this is the place of the Dogon.'

When we reached the top I was exhausted but in a state of rapture. I kept looking towards the east, where the opposition of the sun was picking out its last shadows of green and yellow. Moussa was waiting.

'Half an hour late,' he remonstrated. 'They were going to put on a dance for you.'

'I don't need a dance. That was fabulous, marvellous. And this man is a little genius.'

Amatigue mumbled his thanks, and his hope that the elders

wouldn't be annoyed because we had been so long. I congratulated him on his excellent French and perfect knowledge. For the first time the self-contained boy shuffled.

'The dance is only for tourists. The people who perform it are top-dwellers, not from the villages. They'll do it tomorrow. There is a bus coming from Mopti. Islamic people as well as Christians like you.'

'I'm not particularly Christian. And I'm sure you're not particularly Islamic.'

He held up his head. 'I am Dogon.'

'You are very intelligent. I thank you with all my heart ...' I fumbled. I hoped to God his blindness could be cured. 'Does one give you a tip, or is that included?'

'If you are pleased.'

I gave him a good tip. He solemnly shook my hand.

'Thank you. I will go to university. And people like you will teach me.'

'On the contrary; you will teach them. Thank you.'

As we staggered over the rocks a mile to the car, Moussa was mellow. 'You enjoyed that?' He was happily drunk from the campement and whatever dalliance he had enjoyed with the glorious naked women there.

'I loved it.'

'We revere the Dogon. They're magicians. Never mind about the dancers. That's *touristique*. Oh, Jesus and Mohammed both, I'm so hungry. I hope they've kept us some food at the Relais. Otherwise, we'll have to hit a donkey and eat it at once by the roadside, like European savages making *le pique-nique*.'

'*Merde!*' I exclaimed. 'I forgot to taste the best onions in the world.'

DANUBE IV
Baths of Buda

Sharp and clear was the astounding city. I looked up from breakfast and gasped. The wedding cake gothic of the parliament, so like an echo of Westminster, filled the boat's windows. And it was a world away from London's sober brown. It was white, dazzling white like a mosque. The palaces of Pest slid beside in every contour of mansard roofs and rotundas. And on the further bank, the last slopes of mountains towered above the Danube against the Buda hills. There were excursions planned to the horse plains of the puszta. And there was a final night on board. But my bags were packed, and the city was intoxicating. As soon as we were moored, just as in Vienna, I leapt off. Easily navigating with the map, I had the underground stops marked in blue, walked to the nearest one in the Sajo út square, changed money, and was off.

The only address I had in Budapest was the one my fellow passenger Lázló had given me a year before on the Mekong. I checked the phone directory. There were so many Ezterházys that I couldn't find it under his initial. There was a G. Esterházy in Andrassy út, however, and that was the same street as his address. I rang. A woman's voice responded: *'Szia?'* I asked if she spoke English, and when she continued in Hungarian, practised the first of many mangled pronunciations of 'Nem ertem', I don't understand. She tried German. In only slightly less contorted phrases I babbled what I called myself, that I searched a man called Lázló who had been in Cambodia with me, and who had given me her next address. I meant 'near', but she suddenly cried 'Ach ja. Der Papa.' And with many rustles and background voices, Lázló came to the phone.

'Noel the tour guide?' he asked incredulously in English.

'Ja Ja,' I affirmed.

'Don't speak that horrible language. Are you in Pest? How did you reach me. I've moved.'

I recited his address. He laughed.

'This is amazing. It's nowhere near the address I gave you. I'm living with my son and daughter-in-law. Where are you now?'

'In Roosevelt Square.'

'Then take the metro to Hosök Tér. Yellow line.'

'When it's convenient. I mean, I don't want to ...' When he let out a grumble that was almost a howl, I knew his voice at once. We settled on lunch tomorrow, with many instructions about street-numbers and the bells.

'That's no problem. I have my 1910 Baedeker and a metro map.'

'I bet you do. At one then?'

The apartment was a palace, not of Renaissance proportions, but as I was led up the *scala grande* I remarked that he must surely be a descendant prince.

'I'm afraid not. Maybe distant cousins. That's why I've given up my flat. We're as poor as everyone else now, though there is interminable arbitration. But we're lucky to regain this. At least it's a whole floor. It actually belongs to Judit, Livia's mother, but she's living at a spa. You'll like Livia. She's an actress. She had a part in a film by Jancsó. I almost didn't recognize you. You look younger.' Before I could reply he held up an arm. 'No. Don't tell me I do. Give age at least the dignity of its experience. I've gained at least seventy new wrinkles.'

'I've shaved my beard. And I've left the university.'

'Ah, perhaps that's it. And how's your wife?'

'Fine. Except we don't live together any more. But she's fine.'

'And your friend? Nicholas was his name, I think.'

'He's fine too. But we don't live together either. It's Shane who's looking after my house.'

László raised his eyebrows. 'What an interesting life you must lead.'

'Um … not really. Just complicated.'

I had brought a bunch of flowers. 'Oh, these will be for Livia. She loves sweet-peas.'

Without exception, every piece of dark Biedermeir furniture lining the extensive walls was decorated with semi-circular shawls of lace. The fussiness extended to the grand piano and the table on which lunch was served. I met his son Gábor and Livia, the woman I'd spoken such terrible German to on the phone. We were joined at table by two tow-headed young men and a little girl. 'My grandchildren,' he said proudly. 'Peter, Tábor and Marta.'

The elder boy Peter spoke good English, and interrogated me insatiably about Cambodia. Was it all so dangerous, the picture his grandfather had given? Was communism so bad there as well, and was it true I had been a hero? László tapped his spoon on the china dish steaming with dumplings, and led an animated discussion in Hungarian.

'They're saying that I was a communist too, which I still am in a sort of way, and they think you must have been some kind of double agent.'

'I didn't say that at all,' replied the boy with spirit. 'I said it all sounded excellent and asked whether we could invite you to come down to Lake Balaton. Because you've been everywhere in the world.'

'I haven't really.'

'Where haven't you been?'

'Lots of places. I've never been to Alaska or Greenland or Saudi Arabia or Iraq or lots of countries. Even this year I went to places in Portugal and Galicia I'd never seen. I lived in England for ten years but there's still more to discover. And I like Germany and the US much better each time I see them. Remember, for example, this is only the second time I've been in Hungary.'

'All the more reason to come to Balaton.'

'Manners, Peter, manners. You'll have to excuse him. He works in the computer shop in the Cybercafe, and I did mythologize you so much that he wants to grab you and put you either on a sailboat or the Internet.'

When I explained that I wanted to go further down the Danube, and was happy at the Atrium, they frowned. Lázló told me that I'd never find a boat and that even if I did it would be horrible. Livia changed the subject by summoning her daughter and presenting another huge platter of perch with orange beans and mushrooms. There was a beautiful church on top of the town at Tihany, she said, from which you could see both sides of lake and river, and all around. And she was coming down after the weekend to do an outdoor performance of Goldoni. Gábor had to work, so there was plenty of room. In German and English they asked what more I wanted to see of Budapest. I told them about the museums and theatres and my arrangement with the hotel to visit the monuments of Statue Park, at which they all burst out laughing.

'Go and have a look at the park here instead. They're just taking off the last bits of Lenin.'

When I told them about Mrs Berkenyi, they mopped their eyes.

'Livia says that Hungarians are much staider than you think. Everyone expects us to be dancing czardas with violins tucked under our arms. But shoot a film on location and they think it's the arrival of Mephistopheles.'

As they let me out the great wooden door, Peter yelled, 'The cottage is full of sunflowers, and we have a yacht!'

Lázló sighed. 'When you've finished your experiments in graveyard art, I'll ring you at the hotel tomorrow.'

Behind the house was a lake where noisy vacationers

splashed in canoes and self-consciously rode tall in pedal-boats. When I remarked on the hidden waters of the city, Lázló smiled. 'Budapest is bubbling with ponds and baths, more than a hundred. Sometimes it seems as if we're a carefully placed crust on an ocean of steam. I'll show you – tomorrow if you're free.'

I did wander in the park. The crane showed where the activity was. I joined the small crowd of people in bathing costumes. Lenin had long ago been reduced to his legs, vast legs certainly, but now as trunkless as Ozymandias. There was a cheer as the bronze creases were plucked clear of the plinth, swung in the air and dumped in a truck. I had seen this before too, in Eisenstein. That time it was the Czar.

The Fine Arts Museum stretched along the arcades. This collection alone could rebuild a decent-sized Egyptian city. The granite statue of Horus was particularly large and splendid. I wondered what he would look like dangling in the air. By the time I got back to the Atrium, it was late. The driver waiting to take me to the statues at Bidafok had almost given up.

'We're getting into rush hour, and it's fifty kilometres away on the main road further down the Danube. The park closes at sunset. You want to risk it?'

See in one corrale all those bastards who had tried to chuck ninety tonne wheatsheaves, flags, giant youthesses and hammers on me everywhere from Warsaw to Beijing? You betcha!

The river reflected the excursion and the dying day by looking polluted and depressed. Industrial complexes smoked above its greasy waters; even when we opened into marshland the ducks and geese huddled in cover. There were ravens overhead. We reached the park.

How were the mighty fallen. They were jumbled round walls of brick and wire. Jack-booted soldiers holding flags apparently made of iron strode in arrested paralysis. From the Heroes' Cemetery the Great Collaborators of the regime had been ripped still lying on their slabs, and set up vertically like moustachioed outlaws in a Western barbershop. The Atrium driver pointed them out: the racist Istvan Czurka; Janós Kadar; the proto-Nazi Miklós Horthy; Stalin's henchthing Mátyás Rákosi.

The iconography of Socialist Realism owes much to the imperial predecessors it pretends to despise. There is always a central figure, a Leader who wears an overcoat and gestures with his cap. Groups of Worker-People, encouraged by his direction, often imitate it and surge forward in the direction of imaginary revolution. The only difference to the otherwise uniform style is the jagged inheritance from constructivism. It must have been particularly fierce in fifties Hungary, abetted by the local artists' love of placing sheets of plate metal together and banging them till they were squashed . Broken bayonets and sickles bristle, and the figures themselves are blockishly out of proportion. Bugle-blowing children are swept along by gashed grey spectres and confronted by mighty labourers about to attack with a shovel, not the spectator, because these monsters were never made for the spectator, but the air, the environment. One particularly desperate group in violent motion seemed to be running after a tram. There was a small group of Americans also taking photos in the gathering dusk. I climbed up onto the plinth of the tram people, struck a fist-clenched diving pose with the rest, and asked the nearest tourist to snap it. As I came down he shook his head.

'I bet you're a perfectly sensible person in ordinary life; probably a university professor or something.'

From the subway at Batthyány, Lázló led me along the banks of the river to a structure half-hidden by trees and immersed in the great hill of Buda above it. The round dome and curved pilasters announced Islam.

'It's Turkish, sixteenth century. A bit shabby, if that's the right word, like the rest of Hungary, but still intact. Today is men's day only.'

The corridors and lockers where we stripped were tiled like a nineteenth century lavatory; the interior plan of frigidarium and calidarium might have been Roman. The architecture and the sense of divided but communal society was overwhelmingly Islamic.

The dome was dotted with holes through which the light came as from a million faraway stars, with more light streaming from the high arabesque windows. It struggled with the steam rising from the circular bath, making everything inside flicker like Eadweard Muybridge's 1901 studies of the nude human body in moments of movement, sometimes revealing a rhythm of natural motion, sometimes cutting whole frames so the scene appeared to jump. The space of the pantheon was filled with figures. Groups of them clustered in the distance, sat on stone benches in the niches, broke the warm water with a dive that sent droplets shooting upwards and mixing with the light to form mist.

They were all naked. Every variety of man conversed, splashed or shook themselves like setters, making the water spray the atmosphere till they became blurred or invisible. There were old men with grey hairs plastered to their chests, their genitals shrunken and hiding in grey triangles; men like Mongolian bulls whose balls swung when they walked and whose eyes were drawn to asiatic slits; huddled men who closed their bodies like tortoises, and proud young athletes who displayed themselves glistening. The parade extended from glorious statues that Praxiteles would have polished, to skeletons who looked as if they had been half-finished by Egon Schiele. The ordinary fact of maleness inhabited the room like the languorous self-possessed women Lady Montagu described on her visit to the bagnio of Sophia.

These men lolled and strolled and took tea from attendants. Fierce Magyar warriors with moustaches lent on their elbows and talked with clerks who must have come straight from the office wearing their glasses, Clark Kents with the body of Superman. Through the fog came tiny perfect gypsies, great dewlapped men whose chins and paunches had long ruled out acquaintance with their cocks, pretty youths and anthropophagi whose heads grew welded through their shoulders. With a tread that shook the stones the Elephant Man passed by, his magnificent proboscis almost meeting the one between his thighs in folds of pachydermic flesh.

In the niches in the small cool baths that circled the main heated one, as planets do the sun, some men had gathered round pairs of others, bobbing gently in the water as the central couples, their bodies shuddering, pulled close. They were visible only from the waist up, but the trembling of the waters gave a hint of what was happening below. Soon they were clasped together, men you might see on a subway or at a bus-stop, ordinary men rendered suddenly beautiful by their heads thrown back in ecstasy. Their eyes closed, their foreheads fur-rowed, their mouths opened and savagely bit at each other as they writhed in pleasure. An attractive bath-attendant trotted amusedly on his rounds, flicking an eye at the performances and handing out towels. He caught my gawping gaze and winked.

Lázló beckoned me into the main pool. I held my breath and took a dive into their midst. Not, I think, through any great beauty of my own, but because I was so obviously a stranger, I was immediately encircled. Where was I from? Were there baths like this in Australia? Where had I met Lázló? They penned me under the spout of steaming fresh water to which I playfully extended my hands. They were pleasant, compli-mentary. I showed off my Australian swimming talents and was immediately joined by a person with the eyes of a snake and wandering toes. With that intuition that cats and dogs have for humans who are allergic to them, and therefore leap hairily into their laps, he began to caress my legs. I stared resolutely ahead and thought of Bognor, then finally turned to him and moved away. He followed.

'Vat's de matter? You aren't gay? You ghave such beaudiful eyes.'

'Thanks very much. I am extremely flattered. Now I must go and talk with my host.'

The excuse didn't fool him, since Lázló had gone off to have a massage. When I spun around the circumference, he was there again. His name was obviously Vlad. After more explorations with his toes I heaved myself out of the pool and headed for the showers. There he was, Nosferatu the vampire transported. The towel attendant smiled sympathetically as he handed me soap and sponges, which I put to immediate use as barricades. They were about as effective as an unblessed crucifix on a member of the Islamic Undead.

I fled to the steam-room, rows of pine benches in which the temperature was high enough to cook goulash. I was thinking how handsome the towel attendant was, and what good shoulders and breasts he had developed when a tall thin shadow opened the door. For the next three minutes Vlad and I negotiated a series of contracts. Would I mind if he sat on the bench in front of me? Of course not, depending on the distance. Then could he sit behind me? Not if he kept on doing those things with his prehensile feet. So could he sit beside me?

'I glurve you.'

The steam and my voice rose together. There never was a ruder pest. The sounds of argument were possibly what brought the towel attendant back. Steam sucked towards him as he opened the door. He was all but invisible, yet his smile shone into the room. He came deliberately forwards with his hand holding something; and when I reached out in the swirl of smoke, it wasn't a towel that I touched.

'I thought you might enjoy it,' said Lázló, walking me towards the giant lions crouching on the bridge. 'You seem to have made quite a hit.'

'You mean with Vlad the Impaler?'

'The one who kept chasing you? He's perfectly harmless. He's a restaurateur; he just liked you. Come on. I mean your success with Attila. We all love him but he's very choosy. And talkative. Ah, you're blushing.'

'Oh God, now it's the Hun. I don't usually go to baths like that, you know.'

'Of course not. You were just interested in the architecture. Don't look so embarrassed. You're perfectly safe with me. I'm so ancient I just go there to gossip.'

'Does your family know about all this?'

He put his arm on my shoulder. 'Naturally. I loved my wife. I love my grand-children. What's wrong with loving men?'

We stood in the middle of the Chain Bridge and watched a little kayaker scudding beneath, the size of a pencil.

'Are you happy, Lázló?'

'Happy? I think life is a comedy. Not that it's screamingly funny. But isn't that the way the Italians use the word? You may go through hell, but you come out of it able to laugh.'

We were still talking when we were interrupted by a familiar stammer.

'One d-d-day I'll be headed towards the North Pole and I'll ... be d-d ... damned if I don't find you coming back with a family of Eskimos.'

Surprised and delighted to see Ted again, I invited him to coffee with me and Lázló.

'Where's Beverley?'

His voice became soft and furred, which it always was when he controlled his stammer.

'The most curious thing happened. You know it's an hour forward here? Well, Bev wouldn't believe it, particularly when it was Larry who told her. She made us all go up that tower, and just as we got to the belfry these bloody great bells started ringing out noon. It was deafening. Bev nearly had a heart attack, and Elspeth spat her teeth on a baby's head. Larry pulled out his watch with that blissful smile he has and said, "See, I told you it was working!" Bev's having a lie-down.'

Ted had remembered the name of the pilgrimage church with the steps and produced his notebook.

'It's c-c-c ... called Bom Jesus do Monte. Right at the top of a kind of staircase. What you said about baroque and the theatre reminded me, because it's a stage. The statues are gesturing like actors, and the gardens full of trees, even gum trees, I think. And the view is amazing. You can see both sides, and all around the smell of flowers. I've made a little map. It's just outside Braga. So next time you're on one of your South American rivers, you should go there.'

'I will, Ted. Thanks. I will.' As long as there are travellers as perceptive and generous as you. He had echoed Livia's phrase exactly. *You can see both sides. And all around …*

After he left, we were joined at Florian's by Peter. It was his lunch-hour and he had brought his sleek-haired girlfriend Lili. Incongruously, or so I thought, the stylish old café was having a fashion parade. Clarinets curdled and techno-music beat as the gilded youth of Pest sashayed insolently down the catwalk, paused, pouted and flounced back. They wore baggy culottes with chain accessories of the kind favoured by their ancestors at Visegrad, Wall Street powerware and skin-tight magenta vinyls.

'Would you wear that?' I asked the girl.

She coolly ashed her cigarette.

'Sure. Better than Farmers.'

'Jeans,' explained Peter. 'Granpa, give him the present.' He passed Lázló a little rectangle wrapped in stars. 'And don't go to Romania. They're awful. And Serbia's worse.'

Having seen the towers of Belgrade in happier times, I didn't want to return to a ripped-up map. Lázló's invitation sounded a much happier way to finish the Danube. I accept-ed. You could enjoy wonderful food and wine at Balatonfüred, which used to be an artists' colony, said Peter, and we could sail right to the caves at the south end of the lake.

I took the Metro to Keleti to book a sleeper for Prague in four days time. From there an express would take me to Frankfurt, where I had an appointment with Vermeer, like the other only-begetters of vision, Masaccio and Piero, a luxuriant painter of calm and stillness in the vortex of motion. The area round the station was squalid. The buildings looked as if they had never recovered from the dust of centuries of war. Even the trees gave the appearance of needing a wash. Travellers swarmed, then dispersed into emptiness. Tribes of backpackers had found places to settle down for the night. In the locker halls, thieves ready to prey on the unwary leant against the tiles and smoked, turning away if you stared at them but not both-ering to move.

The usual grumpy old 'aunties' sat outside urinals with their saucers of coins. Fifty forints is worth about thirty Australian cents, but it's still irritating to be shrieked at unless you fiddle with your pocket. A neon-lit bar escribing Pepsi in red and blue rectangles was the focus for a group of dark-skinned immigrants, prostitutes of both sexes, and a family of gypsies. In between the train announcements, they played heart-ripping music on a ghetto-blaster and danced in sinuous twos and threes. Keleti's station dome is immense. One great arch opens onto the sky like a set for Scheherazade by Bakst The expanse of darkening blue held a bold crescent moon and the first stars.

Next morning I awoke to find a dream escaping over the corner of the bed. As I tried to catch it, I had two complete-ly contradictory ideas: either to float with it across the river, or somehow let the river flow through me. Bells chimed. No wonder Larry could hear them. Had we but world enough and time. I looked in the mirror and thought, 'God, how old I'm getting. It's lucky anyone still finds me attractive at all.' And yet it seemed only last night that my parents had given me the globe and crawled round growling like tigers.

I opened the curtains on a wonderful day and that classic view of Buda with the hill cascading down the Belvedere from the palace to the funicular. Adjoining the hotel was a Secessionist building whose cornices were supported by volup-tuously moulded women, their hair and arms intertwined with leaves. From the street you could hardly see them, but here they were at eye-level, and they seemed to swim around the cunningly designed hexagonal facade. The river was still so high that it too swam in baby waves beyond their jutting breasts. I threw the curtains wide onto the blue and the green of the freshly nourished park. There were churches and gal-leries I hadn't seen. On the other hand, Saints Katherine and Matthias would probably not fall down heartbroken if I didn't visit them. Very likely Copernicus was perfectly safe at Frombork, and knew his theories about the revolution of the planets rather better than I did. Nobody would be surprised if

I didn't turn up at the university to deliver a lecture on their connection with the art of Gustav Klimt in Nicolas Roeg's *Bad Timing*. And the Danube, whatever interruptions it might suffer from my prose or the commissars of Slovakia, had demonstrated that it would continue to flow wherever it liked.

It sparkled and reflected the light of an immaculate sky. Reassuringly it affirmed a magnificent city. I ordered breakfast and decided to go back to bed. Lázló, Peter and Lili would call for me tomorrow at eight to take the train to Fonyod. I opened Lázló's gift. It was a book in English by Géza Csáth, an author I'd never heard of. It was called *The Magician's Garden*. The illustrations curved like the frieze of women. Awaiting coffee, croissants and jam with saffron and sunflower seeds, and every now and then checking the river from the corner of my eye, I settled back in the pillows and began to read ...

'I must be in Egypt, and walking on the shores of that wide river the Nile. I still had to find what period I was in. I thought about that as I strolled along the shore.'

NIGER IV
Timbuktu

A city so fabulous is still best approached by the conduit traced for centuries by merchants and explorers, by road and river along the marshes of that great river, the Niger. Herodotus and Pliny surmised that, just as the Danube cut through Europe, its relative must divide the continent of Africa. Moussa was more specific. He drove me to the Mopti landing, and found a market-boat ready to leave downstream for Konna.

The boat was called a pinasse. It resembled a brightly painted launch with abstract black and orange designs, but it was really no more than a motorized double pirogue with a superstructure of palings and rush, a market boat wobbling and laden with produce. Children clambered everywhere upsetting baskets until their parents firmly told them to sit down. One fat little tub sat beside me and prattled about his father, a blanket-weaver. As we passed a mile-long sandbank in mid-river, people on its banks made signs to stop. The steersmen reluctantly pulled in to allow two ragged women aboard. Around them scampered naked children, and in the distance nude men cast nets like parachutes.

'They are slaves,' said the tub from Mopti contemptuously. Slaves? Yes, they worked for the town when they were needed. When I asked Moussa later he said, 'Oh yes it's true. They were probably Peul. The Bambara and the merchants keep them as slaves.' The noise of the motors was deafening and I moved forward to the tiny forecastle. The passengers were lively and good-humoured.

Savanna unrolled, dunes sliding down unexpectedly. Like all African rivers the Niger has its special features. Like the Nile it fertilizes; like the Congo it is a lifeline for produce. At the Bight I had seen its maritime delta, jagged teeth dotted with tanks and oil wells. Here the air of commerce was dynamic but clean. Salt, gold, cloth, rugs, vegetables passed along a chain of hands. The water was studded with reeds and white water lilies. Women spread washing along its banks, or pounded grain in pairs round large mortars. The water was high, full of September rain. The rice shoots beyond the dykes were nearly drowned, and some of the dykes themselves were underwater. Boso fishermen waded onto them and rhythmically lassoed their nets. A heavy northern breeze against the current encouraged me back to the stern where I sat surrounded by more inquisitive passengers. Had that been my car at the dock? And my chauffeur? Were all people rich in Australia? How many children did I have? Did I want a carpet? As we neared Konna, cattle-egrets announced the pastures. There was no dock. The boat slid onto mud and sand and the steersmen carried me ashore. I was wary. Somewhere around here Ibn Battuta, the greatest traveller of all time, had his own Incident at Edfu in 1382, an extra rush of adrenalin provided by a nearby crocodile.

The mahogany forests vanish. Here begins a truly marvellous part of the earth – the Niger's inland estuary. Red clay gives way to sand. The Niger turns into a paisley scarf of mauves and greys and greens hundreds of miles wide, winding and twisting, a palette on which a divine artist has swirled all possible colours of water and gouache. The sunset that night was a bar of red stretched perfectly across a circle of green that swiftly became black.

On the turn-off to Timbuktu you pass glittering sheets of

salt where a few cattle lick; then, jutting from the white sand, the rusty chassis and half-buried tyres of the jeeps that didn't make it. Or you might be driving through a particle of the dust of Gordon Laing. In 1825 this first European to reach Timbuktu lived and wrote here. I have a photo of myself outside the plaque on his white-limed house. When he started back in 1826, once outside the city he was murdered. His papers drifted across the desert and were lost.

Every city in the world except Nuku'alofa and Timbuktu is bigger than you expected. Timbuktu has shrunk within its ancient boundaries. The mosques are dark and narrow. Their guardians are austere, wrapped in veils to keep away the sand and the djinns, and wary of disrespect to the Prophet. There is a ghostly silence, emptiness. The streets too are empty, like a De Chirico with a monument of mud in far perspective. Stark black shadows cut off diagonal whites. But each of those streets witnessed the birth of a university, the residence or death of a mad explorer, the quiet women potting hibiscus and sweet-smelling pelargonium in the courtyards. And in those court-yards, masons with wooden ladders and buckets are continual-ly, as at Kano, pulling the city up again out of the sand and mud. Its treasures hide inside. The sun will not fade them. In the stores and stalls they glitter and invite the touch of yet another generation of hands. The corridors of the narrow afternoon streets create a breeze.

Timbuktu's market is no tent. It is an ancient building lit from tall slats around the roof. Next to me at a tray of magpie-gathered objects, a white woman in a striped dress was also examining the glass beads with a gleam in her eye.

'These could be Egyptian.'

She was cool, elegant and at home. I was wearing my kepi, and sifted fingers through the treasures.

'You look like a resident, but I haven't seen you.'

We introduced ourselves. Her name was Betty. I told her I'd just arrived and that I'd travelled in North Africa but never reached here, the Sahara's far side where exasperated friends had often told me to go. She laughed a soft chuckle and joined me in handling and dripping the beads.

'Isn't it wonderful to think of them thousands of years ago sprinkling their way across the desert? You collect North African antiquities?'

'I've got a small cabinet. To be honest, about things like this I really haven't a clue.'

'Then you must meet my husband. He can check these pots for us. I'd say Moroccan, maybe eighteenth century. But the beads are definitely Ptolemaic. There are rock paintings not far from here that show chariots. That would suggest either Roman or Egyptian.'

We fell back on our wares until her husband arrived. That's how I came to have dinner with the Governor of Timbuktu.

Her husband Robert turned out to be the American Ambassador to Mali, making a farewell visit to his favourite city before being posted to Toronto. They gave me a lift in their air-conditioned car back to the hotel, where we had drinks with some Peace Corps Americans whom the Robinsons already knew. The hotel staff were not pleased by my announcement that I had an invitation to dinner, because they had prepared a special meal and tourists weren't supposed to be wandering around after dark. But when I told them Moussa would be happy to eat in my place, and that the dinner was to be with the governor, they brightened. Moussa got them to give me a turban and cloak, which proved to be prescient and provident. They were also impressed when the Landrover of white-gloved soldiers arrived to pick me up.

By the time we set off for the governor's palace, curfew had fallen. The breeze had turned into a wind. A swirling sand-storm obliterated the town. As the governor's guests, we were the only people abroad. His palace, of which we could see lights peeping through the sheet of sand, was several stories high, with a pillared terrace, massive doors that shut out the storm, a courtyard, reception room, and a long dining hall with divans and low tables. An elaborate protocol governed our arrival, from the moment we ran sheltered by parasols from the cars into the howling yellow storm and onto the windswept verandah. Mrs Robinson was shaking the sand from her cloak and hair. She gave me a rapid instruction in etiquette.

'We will each be presented to the governor with a brief description of our qualities. Don't worry if they're wrong. We've known him for years, and the major-domo always invents absolute nonsense. At dinner never begin a conversation until the governor has introduced the topic, and don't talk too much to those lower than you on the divan. If you praise the food or the palace, the governor will deprecate it. You do not, of course, agree.'

Chains of silent white-shrouded menservants shook out our cloaks and jackets and guided us through rooms and halls lit by pin-pricked lanterns to the inner precinct, where, in careful composition, sat the governor, flanked by his major-domo, his secretary, his aide and his intimate servants.

The Robinsons were honoured by a formal exchange of gifts on the marble dais. The rest of us were settled in ordained places on cushions round the long low table, careful to tuck our feet away from our host; and the dinner began. The governor was both courtly and frolicsome. He excused the sandstorm on the grounds that we had brought with us the coming of rain. He added that his very handsome twin brother had a passion for irrigation and would construct channels for the tears of hope which he himself would otherwise let flow. The long room itself flowed with servants. Grand Mechoui, an entire sheep of it roasted, sheep's testicles, spinach, rice, dates, caramelized pudding, silver pitchers of cool water, brass ewers of fragrant water for washing were silently laid on the mahogany and the signal for eating was given by an oboe and a single beat on a handheld drum. Water was poured. The food was delicious. The first course was of unleavened bread with lamb, cummin (and sand), then a basil-like herb bashed into a pesto with lamb's broth over rice – and sand – followed by a dessert of caramelized goat's milk junket with cinnamon. And sand. Despite the closed shutters and the soft pluckings and blowings of the court musicians, it bit at the lacework windows and whined like violins beneath the floor.

As an academic I ranked below Monsieur and Madame the Ambassador at the top of the table, and sat opposite the engineer of roads and chief agronomist, heading a line of peace workers and missionaries that trickled down the red couches to a solitary Baptist who had lived in Timbuktu for twelve years in the vain hope of converting some heretic who was faithless to both Christ or Mohammed and simply wanted a bath. 'I think he's running out of water,' whispered the agronomist. 'For a Baptist, that must really be the end.'

For the governor, water was his raison d'être. Water had unreasonably ebbed from Timbuktu. But the Niger was only five miles away. It should be persuaded to return, to lie beside its mosques and universities and water the delicate roses in their courtyard pots. With the aid of engineers and a video camera it would. Tirelessly the governor had surveyed the plains south and west of his ancient city. He had decided that a channel might be dug upstream at Kibara. Between courses his secretary read a list of his projects while the governor nodded solemnly at his brass plate and made gestures to the ambassador, returned with demure nods by the Robinsons. I looked at them for guidance. Betty simply repeated the sideways nod to me with an almost imperceptible shake. It was a diplomatic movement that must have evolved through thousands of years of courteous exchange. It meant shut up and speak when you are spoken to.

Heralding some immense revelation halfway through dinner, the dishes were whisked away. The governor instructed one of his aides to unfold the Victorian cabinet at the end of the hall, and show us a video. With considerable shaking and doubling of the image, it displayed the joyful ruler supervising the construction of a new causeway and canal to Timbuktu; soldier-encircled, talking gracious French, marred only by the dreadful reproduction which striped everything with a rainbow zigzag. The American ambassador and his wife complimented the manifestation with perfect aplomb. Then they turned meaningfully to look at me. The problem was obvious:

either the video was stuffed, or it was simply a tracking error on the machine so elegantly embedded in its nineteenth century cabinet.

Unable to remember the word for 'tracking' in French, (you try it after a couple of sheep's balls), and uncertain whether the major-domo's balls might follow the sheep's if I intervened, I hesitated. But when the ambassador insisted that I was researching West African film and was an intimate of Malian directors and television producers, the major-domo bent and whispered, and the governor's ringed right hand beckoned. I got up and prayed Inshallah that there would be an identifiable knob somewhere beneath the carved wooden Victorian fruitwork, and practised my expertise with the buttons on the unfamiliar Secam system. My guide was the adolescent sexual principle that you twiddle everything until parts of it move. They did. Everything happily came into focus on a steady close-up of the governor's face. His aide politely clapped. The governor was pleased and offered me more sheep-genitals.

To the ambassador's praise, he replied that I was undoubtedly a magician, and that the image we now saw must be that of his more handsome brother, and not himself. Everyone clapped again, and servants passed with silver ewers, so that without excessive exhaustion we could wash our applauding hands. When asked what I thought of the video I ventured that the governor was performing a most remarkable and historical act. Oh, no, he insisted. I had merely seen an image of his brother, a man of infinitely greater power who might one day accomplish, with the aid of the United States, all that he dreamed of. The Niger would once again reach Timbuktu's centre. He would ask his major-domo to tell his brother, and to relay our compliments on his superior beauty of appearance. I flicked a glance at the Robinsons. They were applauding, and Betty nodded at me with the same approving smile. The Baptist choked on whatever portion of the ram he had reached, and coughed.

We took our leave on the terrace, following the ambassador's lead. In an identical protocol of adjutant, academic, engineer and missionary, we bowed and shook hands in a fury of sand that bent us double as we ran to the convoy of cars. I travelled with the peace-workers, preceded by the glove-driven Landrover which was dispatched to guide us. While we bounced along, the headlights projected swirling yellow circles on the deserted streets, and the sand screamed against the windshield. It was of the rage of such a sandstorm that Sallust wrote: 'It is necessary to halt the journey.' One of the peace workers said, 'Boy, I bet we're the only people in thousands of miles out in this Mother. Storms like this rage from here to Mauretania.'

'It must be because of the governor of Timbuktu and his invisible brother. May the waters return!' The sand sang and wiped out everything except our feeling of being among the most special people in the world.

Next day the sun dawned as white and dazzling as ever. The rains hadn't come, of course. Beyond the hotel's geraniums, the desert dunes rolled. I rode a camel out to the Tuareg camp, to visit the last habitations before the Sahara. Beyond these desert nomads, human life becomes a few black dots in an ocean of yellow. The camel was an unusually graceful and co-operative animal which neither groaned nor rolled its eyes horribly as camels do when they would like to bite you. As it trotted through the dunes the city disappeared. The Tuareg tents were stretched low under a few equally flat thorn trees. They were being repaired after the storm. Some children banged on a tam-tam until their father told them irritably to stop. Their mothers sat inside, their skins stained with indigo and heavy rectangular amulets charmed over their necks.

The black-swathed Tuaregs offered to sell or trade the sorts of objects which airline passengers definitely do not need: silver and ebony daggers, ivory-mounted rifles, ceremonial swords. Nearby a few donkeys and a zebra pulled at the bushes. Back on the camel I rode another kilometre. The camp disappeared. The last tree. The last bush. Then nothing. Not a smudge, not a shadow; white sand and sky stretching in every direction. It was in the horror of trackless places such as this that Leo Africanus recorded the Tuareg custom of slitting open their camel's stomachs with silver daggers and drinking the water. I imagined Ouarzazate, its first oasis beckoning on the other side of the Sahara. A breeze lifted the sand like waves. It stung. To the south even three years ago, says Moussa, was a canal from the Niger, on which pirogues could bring goods right to the market. Now it's untraceable and dry as dust. Ghosts of camel trains from Morocco and Kano were easy to conjure. I squinted across in the direction of the Jbel Sanhro directly north.

The last scrub had been eaten by goats, and even this camel, whose belly was safe from my Swiss knife, snorted at the idea of going further into the wilderness. Across a townless expanse on the Michelin map lay Ouarzazate, Pasolini's Thebes. I recalled twenty years ago my brilliant idea of hitchhiking from the dunes of Ouarzazate across the Atlas mountains to Marrakesh. Now on its southern outpost, I gazed into the emptiness of the Sahara, the gap between here and there that is always waiting to be filled. How wilful I had been when young, how determined to overrule everyone and see everything, how drugged with the power of spinning rather than the realisation of being spun. Curiously, inquisitively, love had lasted. Not just an ordinary love, but the love which moves the sun and the other stars. It made the globe around me quiver with life. Soon I would be in Venice, ready to rest and set out again. The immense desert filled me with a surge of exuberance.

The camel is crouched waiting, the same gentle beast with red tassels that knows the desires of the traveller's feet crossed on its neck. Deserts ineffably insist upon hallucinations; the optical trick of the binoculars exaggerated the globe's curve where it waved in the haze. I could see across the void a little figure from the sixties. Others began to join him. Multitudes rounded the ridge, laughing, crying, singing: Pasolini, Mustafa, Paing–Paing, Palla, Giulia, Kelim, Kele, Larry, Mrs Berkenyi, little Buddhist nuns, Ro and Spike; those devoured by rivers and those denied their waters; writhing Africans caught in the waves of a wonderful dance. One group stretched out their bound hands, the terrible line of youths and girls I had seen pulled one by one like dominoes into the river. Perhaps some of them had reached the shore.

ACKNOWLEDGMENTS

All the persons and events in this book are real. Nick, Ro, Julie and Shane will find themselves represented as they were during these voyages. Other companions will recognize themselves instantly, even though I have changed their names. Particularly in cases where they might be in danger, such as the Congo, Cambodia, Burma, Vietnam and Nigeria, I have renamed hotels, missions, and any other agency by which they might be unwillingly identified. In several cases they have been condensed into composite characters; in others, events which occurred outside their experience have been assigned them. They are, in any case, heroic voyagers on their own behalf, and I have tried to be faithful to their words and actions.

First thanks go to my family and friends, childhood mariners Shirley and Dorothy, writers, brother Anthony the Snake Charmer, and nieces Nadina and Cybele, the latter already in print at age thirteen. May flagons stay Christopher Pearson, who comforted me with more than apples and allowed the publication of passages on Cambodia and Myanmar first printed in *The Adelaide Review*. Billy Mutta of the Kenyan Institute of Mass Communications, Zachary Mohammed of the Nigerian Television Authority. Madame Michele Nardi of the Côte d'Ivoire Centre Culturel and Madame Kindo Fatum Kouyate of Bamako made two sections of these voyages possible; the Al'Shara'a clinic of Kano and the Polyclinique Ste Anne of Abidjan kept me alive enough to complete them. To film-makers and writers Timité Bassori, Gnoan M'Bala, Oumar Sissoko and Souleymane Cissé my debt is immense. Chika Anyanwu and Martin Mhando continued the experience by helping found the African cinema course at Flinders University.

Experts the world over have lent their special touches. In Vienna Peter Konlechner; in London and New York, Norman MacAfee, Susan Sontag, William Weaver, Geoffrey Nowell-Smith, Tony Rayns and the late Derek Jarman generously shared their knowledge of Pasolini. Ted and Sarah Braun provided Tuscan hospitality of the warmest kind; and Moussa Traore drove where no car has floated before. Throughout the period of writing, Meryl Tankard inspired me with the universality of movement and dance, and Michael Duffy gave a counterpoint with his incisive and intuitive editing. To John Baines, delighted thanks for keeping me informed about the hieroglyphic nature of Kentish license-plates; and to master-navigators Bill Maidment and Robert Gillen my heartfelt admiration.